GIVE
FATHER'S BO

Kenn Harper is an Iqaluit businessman. He first heard of Minik
when he was visiting his wife's community in Qaanaaq in northern
Greenland. He interviewed surviving Eskimos who had known
Minik, and trawled through the archives of Arctic exploration in
order to piece together Minik's story.

GIVE ME MY FATHER'S BODY

THE LIFE OF MINIK
THE NEW YORK ESKIMO

Kenn Harper

Foreword by Kevin Spacey

PROFILE BOOKS

First published in Great Britain in 2000 by
Profile Books Ltd
58A Hatton Garden
London ECIN 8LX
www.profilebooks.co.uk

Reprinted 2000

First published in the United States by Steerforth Press in 2000

Printed and bound in Great Britain by Biddles
www.biddles.co.uk

The moral right of the author has been asserted.

A CIP catalogue record for this book is available from the British Library.

ISBN 1 86197 252 0

To my daughters, Aviaq and Mikisoq
And in memory of their brother, my son,
Mamarut
May 25, 1975–August 6, 1995

To many a good person the thought at once arises: "Poor things (the Polar Eskimos); ... why wouldn't it be a good plan to take them away from their awful home to a pleasanter region?" ... I answer at once, "God willing, never ... "

ROBERT PEARY, Arctic explorer

Our tales are narratives of human experience, and therefore they do not always tell of beautiful things. But one cannot both embellish a tale to please the hearer and at the same time keep to the truth. The tongue should be the echo of that which must be told, and it cannot be adapted according to the moods and the tastes of man.

OSARQAQ, a Polar Eskimo

This Minik seems gradually to have become a legendary figure to the Polar Eskimos who have many anecdotes to tell of him and his doings.

ERIK HOLTVED, ethnologist

CONTENTS

FOREWORD

ANYBODY WHO MAKES his living in the acting business is always on the prowl for a good story, and a few years ago, in Canada, I stumbled across a great one. An article in a Toronto paper outlined the life of Minik Wallace, the youngest of a group of polar Eskimos brought to New York City in 1897 by the famed Arctic explorer Robert Peary. Four of the group, including Minik's father, soon died, and in time Minik himself was gradually set adrift — by officials of the American Museum of Natural History, whose department of anthropology apparently had encouraged Peary to bring them an Eskimo "specimen" to study; by Peary, who was preoccupied with his efforts to reach the North Pole; and by William Wallace, who took in Minik and gave him a name but whose life was eventually swallowed up by financial troubles and personal tragedy. Within a few years of his arrival in New York, Minik had forgotten his native language, his education had come to a halt, his health was shaken by recurrent bouts of pneumonia, and he was left without family to fend for himself.

When I managed to find a copy of the book — *this* book, originally published by the author, Kenn Harper, a dozen years ago, and sold mainly from a general store on Baffin Island in what is now the new Arctic territory of Nunavut — I found a story that grabbed hold of me and wouldn't let go. In *Give Me My Father's Body* the saga of Arctic exploration is told for the first time through the eyes of Eskimos, whose rugged endurance and knowledge of the Arctic were largely what made Peary's epic journeys possible in the first place. The wealth and power of New York City on the cusp of the twentieth century of course dazzled the child newly arrived from the world's northernmost human community. But America's excited curiosity in the Eskimos quickly faded, and Minik soon encountered another side of America — one of pride and arrogance, and of a cold indifference that seemed to be explained by the boy's dark skin.

The reader watches this tale unfold much as Minik did — slowly, through small events and casual remarks. The world-famous Peary, a kind of demigod when he's first introduced, is gradually revealed to be a careless, self-absorbed man, who for years refused to return Minik to his home in Greenland. The scientists who "studied" Minik and put the skeleton of the boy's father on display were subject to crackpot theories of racial difference. Their refusal to return the body or even give a reason why it was kept at the museum helps to explain the recent passage of laws compelling museums and other cultural institutions to return to native communities sacred objects and human remains long treated as museum property.

But shining at the heart of this often dark tale, told with such care and restraint, is the spirit of Minik himself — cut off from his people, his language, and his sense of belonging in the world, he never surrendered his hope of going "home," his demand for the return of his father's body for a proper burial, or his belief that people would understand and come to his aid if only he succeeded in explaining himself. Eventually as a young man in his teens, Minik finally shamed a group of Peary's backers into providing him with passage back to Greenland.

Once there he relearned his native language, became a skilled hunter, and hired himself out as a guide and interpreter to later explorers, but Minik found himself caught between two worlds. He longed to speak English, could communicate some of what he felt only to white men, and found that a part of him preferred the bright lights of Broadway to the Northern Lights. Inevitably, Minik began to dream of another trip "home" — this time back to New York City.

And there you have it — Minik had no home. Plucked from his own world, never wholly welcomed by another, he was condemned to look forever for what he had lost. The entire story is captured in the gaze of the child Minik in one of the photographs in this book — a small boy in spiffy cap and coat, holding a bicycle too big for him, looking directly into the heart and soul of whoever's behind the camera for something warmer than curiosity.

This too short, too sad life, unfolding at the end of the great age of Arctic exploration, was pieced together in an amazing effort of research and writing by Kenn Harper, who has lived over thirty years among Inuit (as the descendants of history's Eskimos prefer to be called today). Unlike most white men in today's Arctic, he speaks Inuktitut, the language of the Inuit, and heard of Minik first-hand from Greenland Inuit in the mid-1970s. The tale had a mythic quality — the boy swept off to a magical land where fantastic adventures awaited him and a benefactor promised great wealth, his sudden return years later. But after Minik left Greenland the second time the polar Eskimos heard no more; none could tell Harper what happened to him, where he died or when. There was no end to his tale. Over a period of eight years Harper searched out the answers for himself in Greenland, in New York City, and in Denmark.

The story of Minik has the simplicity and resonance of myth. But Harper's telling of it sketches in a whole age and world, bringing to life the bustling city of New York, the infant science of anthropology, America's astonished discovery of the polar Eskimos, the American racism that treated people of color as "specimens," the huckstering public entertainers who added Eskimos and other exotic peoples to their menagerie — there is not a page in this book without its horrors and its wonders.

When you get to the end of a great story there comes a moment of silence. The lights in the theater come up or you turn the last page in a book as good as this one, and you sit stunned. There is nothing to say. And then in the next heartbeat you think of a million things to say.

But I'll stop here.

KEVIN SPACEY

INTRODUCTION

N O ESKIMOS HAVE BEEN more studied than the small group of Polar Eskimos of northwestern Greenland, the most northern native inhabitants of the world. They have been described by explorers, examined by anthropologists, idealized by novelists, and, since their displacement from their favored ford in 1953 by the American military, lionized by journalists. Their stories have been told, analyzed, and retold by numerous adventurers and academics whose international reputations received initial boosts from their work among the Polar Eskimos.

This book tells the story that they have all missed — Freuchen, Rasmussen, Malaurie, and all the others who have written about them in so much detail. Freuchen devoted a few pages to it, Malaurie a few lines. Rasmussen did not mention it at all.

This is the story of Minik Wallace, the New York Eskimo, a young man whose sad and adventurous life became legend to his fellow Eskimos. The legend stretches one's credibility, but the truth behind that legend is stranger still.

I first heard of Minik in Qaanaaq, in northern Greenland, from the Eskimos themselves. But uncovering the real life of Minik led me far from Qaanaaq — to the Royal Library in Copenhagen; the United

States National Archives in Washington; the American Museum of Natural History, the New York Historical Society, the New York Public Library, and the Explorers Club, all in New York; and the library of the American Philosophical Society in Philadelphia. It took me also to the small towns of Cobleskill and Lawyersville in upstate New York and to Pittsburg in the mountains of northern New Hampshire.

This is not a book about Robert Peary and Frederick Cook, although both men play parts in the story, Peary a more prominent one than Cook. It is not a book about the North Pole controversy, a vicious debate over who was the first to reach the North Pole. Cook claimed to have reached the prize in 1908, Peary in 1909, but both claims were announced to the world within a few days of each other in September 1909. The resulting dispute was fought in the press for months, and has been fodder for numerous books since. Although the controversy is mentioned, I have avoided taking sides in it.

While cognizant of the fact that today some Eskimos prefer to be known as Inuit, I have nonetheless used the term Eskimo throughout the book, and this is consistent with the usage in the historical sources used and quoted.

I have regularized the spelling of Eskimo personal names in this book. In popular American sources Minik's name has generally been spelled "Mene," although in scientific journals it was consistently "Minik." All Greenlandic and Danish sources use "Minik" and this is consistent with the spelling of the official Greenlandic orthography. I have used that orthography for the name Minik, as for all other Eskimo names in the text. For consistency I have modified the spellings of Eskimo names in direct quotations. An appendix lists the Eskimo words and names used in the book and compares them with the variant spellings of the same names that readers will find in the books of Peary, MacMillan, and others.

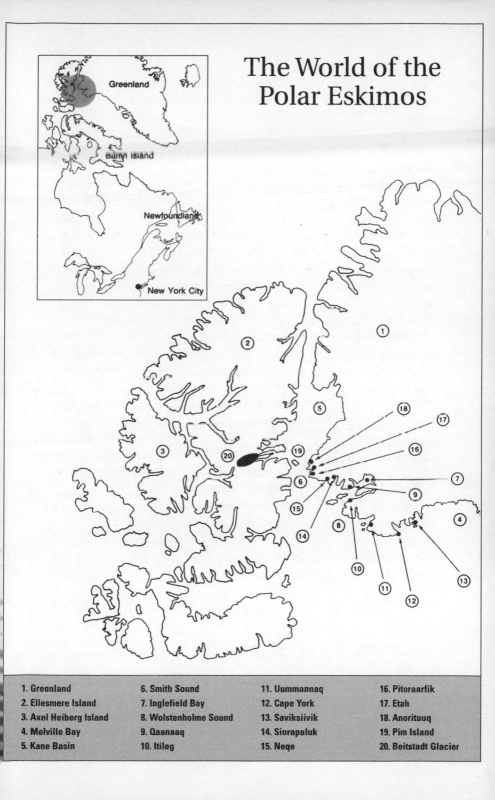

The World of the Polar Eskimos

1. Greenland
2. Ellesmere Island
3. Axel Heiberg Island
4. Melville Bay
5. Kane Basin
6. Smith Sound
7. Inglefield Bay
8. Wolstenholme Sound
9. Qaanaaq
10. Itileg
11. Uummannaq
12. Cape York
13. Saviksiivik
14. Siorapaluk
15. Neqe
16. Pitoraarfik
17. Etah
18. Anorituuq
19. Pim Island
20. Beitstadt Glacier

PEARY'S PEOPLE

QISUK AND NUKTAQ WERE at Cape York already when the vessel hove into view. They recognized her from a distance — it was the *Hope* again, the same chartered Newfoundland sealer that had come the year before. They waited as Captain John Bartlett worked her carefully through the last few miles of drift ice and anchored at this favorite rendezvous of whalers, explorers, and Eskimos on the northern shores of Melville Bay. Then the familiar cry rang out. *"Tikeqihunga,"* shouted an imposing figure from the deck. "I have arrived!" The man they knew as "Piuli" had returned once again.

It was August of 1897. This was Robert Peary's fourth expedition to northwestern Greenland, the home of the Polar Eskimos. This visit would be a short one, like last year's had been. The explorer had but one purpose on this summer excursion — to secure a large meteorite that lay on an island thirty-five miles to the east of Cape York and haul it off to New York.

In 1891 Peary had arrived for the first time in the district and established his headquarters in McCormick Bay. He had had grandiose plans for that expedition, among them to determine the northern limit of Greenland, to make ethnological studies of the Eskimos, and to discover a practical route to the North Pole, the elusive prize of centuries.

On that expedition Robert Peary met for the first time the fabled Polar Eskimos. These were people quite unlike the Greenlanders he had met five years earlier in Disco Bay, who had had over one hundred years of contact with the Danish colonial government and had become accustomed to the ways of the white man. The people of Disco Bay had told fabulous tales of these wild Eskimos to the north, who still lived in much the same way as their own forefathers had done throughout the Arctic. Peary finally saw these untamed natives in 1891. He liked what he saw. For the next eighteen years, they would be "his" Eskimos.

The Polar Eskimos had seen white men before, of course, but never one like Robert Peary. Physically he was most impressive. At six feet tall, he dwarfed most of them. Although lean, his superbly muscled body was conditioned to the precision of a finely tuned instrument. He was immensely powerful. He had that austere handsomeness that so befits the career adventurer. His hair was reddish blond, and his long, bushy mustache gave him a look of studied arrogance. But it was his eyes that one noticed first. Steely gray-blue in color, they gave the impression of seeing through a person, rather than looking at him. They betrayed his quick and ready smile, which was not really a smile at all but a public-relations gesture; the mouth smiled, but the eyes were devoid of emotion.

The Eskimos learned early that he was excitable. He was easy to anger and could harbor a grudge for a long time. He set difficult objectives for himself and would tolerate no obstacles in the way of their achievement. Members of his expeditions, be they white men brought along from the south or Eskimos recruited in the north, were nothing more to him than tools to be used in the accomplishment of his goals. Even his most laudatory biographer acknowledged that "many in Peary's command used to return hating him in a way that murder couldn't gratify." For the Polar Eskimos, he was the most determined and the most difficult white man they had yet encountered. But they served him, as they served all those who came among them, for he carried trade goods with him on his ship and rewarded well those who did his bidding.

The first white man to visit the Polar Eskimos was the British explorer John Ross. Some time before his arrival, a woman of the tribe had prophesied that "a big boat with tall poles would come into view from the ocean." Sure enough, one day in the early summer of 1818 a ship arrived and lay to by the ice edge. The Eskimos thought it a marvel of ingenuity and described it as "a whole island of wood which moved along the sea on wings, and in its depths had many houses and rooms full of noisy people. Little boats hung along the rail, and these, filled with men, were lowered on the water, and as they surrounded the ship it looked as if the monster gave birth to living young."

The ship remained long enough for Ross to make contact with the Eskimos. Fortunately, he had along a West Greenlander who could interpret, after a fashion, for him — though his dialect was very different from that of the Polar Eskimos. Then, as unexpectedly as it had arrived, the ship "turned towards the sea with the sun shining on its white wings and disappeared into the horizon."

Ross was surprised to find people living this far north. And the Arctic Highlanders, as he called them, were equally surprised to meet Ross, for in their isolation they had thought that they were the only human beings in the world.

It was a small enough world that they inhabited, a narrow strip of coastline bounded on three sides by glaciers and on the fourth by the sea. The broad expanse of Melville Bay and the glaciers that descend to it separated them from the West Greenlanders to the south. The Humboldt Glacier in Kane Basin bounded their area on the north. To the east, the great expanse of the inland ice was everywhere only a few miles distant. This immense icecap and its tributary glaciers had always limited the extent of Polar Eskimo habitation and travel. When Elisha Kent Kane, the American explorer, met the Polar Eskimos in April of 1854 at Rensselaer Harbor, he noted, "If you point to the east, inland, where the herds of caribou run over the barren hills . . . they will cry 'Sermeq,' 'glacier'; and, question them as you may about the range of their nation to the north and south, the answer is still the same, with a shake of the head, 'Sermeq, sermersuaq,' 'the great ice-wall': there is no more beyond."

3

In Ross's and Kane's time, theirs was a self-supporting society of about two hundred people relying on hunting and collecting for their food. They lived in small camps, usually of a few families each, and within the confines of their ice-enclosed strip of coastline they were nomadic. A long and oppressively dark winter dominated their lives. The sea ice usually did not break up until late July or early August. Even then, summer brought warmth but not freedom, for the Eskimos were landbound during the scant two-month ice-free season — they had lost knowledge of both the kayak and the larger umiaq, the women's boat. Their loss confined the population to shore, where they lived the summer on caches of food put up during the long and glorious spring. With summer movement so restricted they chose their summer camping grounds in areas where they could supplement their diet with the meat and eggs of the little auk. This godsend came by the millions each spring to nest on the fabled bird cliffs; it was such easy prey that everyone — men, women, children, and the aged — were able to take part in the catch. The birds provided not just food but also skins for the inner coats of both men and women.

If the immobility of summer was limiting, winter was not much better, for the midwinter darkness restricted movement almost as effectively as did the open water of summer. Four months separated the autumn setting of the sun from its reappearance in February and the height of the dark season was a time of laxity and occasional depression. When Kane wintered for the first time, seventy miles to the north of Etah, he had with him a young Greenlandic Eskimo man, the first of those from more southerly parts of Greenland to come among the Polar Eskimos. Suersaq (white men called him Hans Hendrik) had been born below the Arctic Circle, where the sun never permanently disappears, and he described his experience of that first winter:

"Then it really grew winter and dreadfully cold, and the sky speedily darkened. Never had I seen the dark season like this, to be sure it was awful. I thought we should have no daylight any more. I was seized with fright, and fell a-weeping. I never in my life saw such darkness at noon time. As the darkness continued for three months, I really believed we should have no daylight more."

When the ice formed in October, the Eskimos were finally able to leave the bird cliffs and move to the settlements where they would pass the winter living in stone houses. Before the dark was upon them, they hunted marine mammals at the floe edge — ringed seal, bearded seal, walrus, and narwhal — and sealed on the smooth ice at the heads of the fjords. Polar bears, indispensable for clothing, were also hunted in the fall and winter. As food had been cached in spring for the immobility of summer, so it was cached in the fall for the dark period ahead. Often it was insufficient, and starvation was common in late January and February. At times like these hunters gathered at Neqe — the very name means "meat" — where open water was close by throughout the winter. There they hunted walrus until the more favorable conditions of spring allowed more travel and sealing on the ice.

Despite the hardships, this was home to two hundred people who lived for the magnificent months of sunshine that are the High Arctic spring. The sun made its reappearance in mid-February and, from then until mid-June, rose progressively higher in the sky each day. By early April the darkness of the few previous months had been supplanted by twenty-four hours of daylight. The sea still formed a smooth surface for travel. Families packed, traveled, visited with friends and kin, and moved on. Sea mammals were plentiful in the waters at the floe edge and seals basked on the ice surface. Indeed, life was glorious.

In their isolation, the Polar Eskimos had lost not only the knowledge of seagoing vessels, but also the use of bird spears, fish leisters, and the bow and arrow. Incredibly, the last loss meant that they were not able to exploit the local caribou. A fortuitous immigration of Canadian Eskimos from Baffin Island in the 1860s reintroduced the kayak, the bow and arrow, and the leister. By the time Peary came among them, the Polar Eskimos were, as a result, better supplied than they had been when Ross paid them his brief visit seventy-three years earlier.

When Kane lived in the northern part of the district, he noted tersely, "They have no wood." Driftwood rarely found its way to their shores, and the Polar Eskimos often used bone as a substitute, Narwhal tusks or bear and walrus bones fitted together were used as weapon shafts, and whale bones as sled runners. Wood, when it could be secured, was a priceless treasure.

5

GIVE ME MY FATHER'S BODY

It was the desire for wood, above all else, that made the arrival of ships such a welcome event, though they showed up infrequently. In the wake of John Ross two distinct types of white men began to frequent Melville Bay. One group, men like Ross himself, came to ask peculiar questions and pursue elusive goals. It was hard to understand their motivation, but it mattered little as long as they traded or paid for the services of the Eskimo men with wood, guns, and the other commodities they carried.

The Polar Eskimos could make more sense of the ways of the other newcomers, for they were skillful hunters who came, when the ice of Melville Bay was passable, in sailing ships in the late spring in search of the largest treasure of the northern sea, the bowhead whale. The Polar Eskimos had dubbed them *upernaallit,* "those who arrive in spring." They too carried trade goods. They also expressed more than a passing interest in the women of the Eskimos, and many were especially generous with gifts of wood, knives, and needles to the men who would let their wives visit the ships. The greatest bonanza of all was a shipwreck — a tragedy for the crews involved, but it could never happen often enough as far as the Eskimos were concerned.

Peary had approached the Eskimos with some wariness in 1891, influenced by reports of earlier explorers about the natives' treachery and thieving nature. Their behavior aboard ship had amazed Kane, who called them "incorrigible scamps" and wrote, "When they were first allowed to come aboard, they were very rude and difficult to manage. They spoke three or four at a time, to each other, and to us, laughing heartily at our ignorance in not understanding them. They were incessantly in motion, going everywhere, trying doors and squeezing through dark passages, round casks and into the light again, anxious to touch and handle everything they saw, and asking for or endeavoring to steal everything they touched." Before long they were busily running back and forth from the ship to their sleds, carrying off their loot.

After studying the narratives of Arctic exploration, Peary had concluded that the travel methods endorsed by earlier explorers had led to unnecessary hardship and death. British explorers in particular had disdained the use of dogs for hauling sleds — they claimed the dogs ate too much — and used man-hauled sleds instead. As a result many expeditions that went north had stayed in the north — their remains lay dead on the tundra and the beaches. Peary shunned their "orthodox" methods. Instead, he would go among the natives, live in proximity to them, and use their travel methods. What could make more sense, he thought, than to use the Eskimos' dogs as the means of traction, and the Eskimos themselves to hunt for fresh meat for dogs and men alike? They would be paid cheaply with trade goods brought from the United States, so all sides would benefit. And so the 1891 overwintering had been in a sense an experiment to see if Peary's "radical" ideas about living in large part off the land and off the fruits of the Eskimos' hunting endeavors were practical. He was pleased to discover that they were.

In 1893 Peary was back again, and this time he would overwinter for two years. His announced goals for the expedition were to continue the mapping and surveying of northern Greenland, complete the ethnographical studies of the Polar Eskimos, and, if conditions allowed, attempt to reach the North Pole. After the favorable experiences of his previous expedition, he felt confident in relying more on the Eskimos, and he developed closer ties with some of them this time. Two of them were Qisuk and Nuktaq, who had both worked for him in 1891 and were happy to do so again. They were impressed with Peary's tenacity and personal toughness. Here was a man who at least had enough common sense to use the native dogs to haul the sleds, although they were perplexed and amused by the donkeys he brought along to haul supplies from the beach to his housesite. He brought his wife along, an act that had convinced many of his critics in the south that the man was indeed crazy, for Mrs. Peary was obviously pregnant with her first child when the ship left for the north. The baby was born in December and named Marie Ahnighito; she was nicknamed "The Snow Baby."

A Peary biographer summarized succinctly the explorer's adaptation to his northern environment: "He learned to drive and care for dogs in native fashion. . . . He learned to dress like an Eskimo. . . . He learned the technique of building a snow-igloo. . . . He learned the value of laying in a supply of fresh meat during the proper hunting seasons. . . . He learned where game was most plentiful by listening to native teaching, and what methods of search were most success- ful. He discovered the psychology of the native, and so was able to organize the tribe almost with the efficacy he would have used with a large band of trained white helpers. . . ."

But although Peary lived among the Eskimos, he clearly did not feel them to be his equals. They and Matthew Henson, his black ser- vant and dog driver whom he once berated for not calling him "Sir" often enough, were in Peary's estimation members of inferior races. Strong, knowledgeable, and reliable providers, they were somehow not as good as a white man. They, even more than his white col- leagues, were the means to an end. He once had the effrontery to write, "I have often been asked: 'Of what use are Eskimos to the world?' They are too far removed to be of any value for commercial enterprises; and, furthermore, they lack ambition. They have no lit- erature; nor, properly speaking, any art. They value life only as does a fox, or a bear, purely by instinct. But let us not forget that these people, trustworthy and hardy, will yet prove their value to mankind. With their help, the world shall discover the Pole."

Peary's attitude toward the Eskimos, on whom he depended, often for his very life, tarnished the work he might have accom- plished. He was intimately associated with the Polar Eskimos for al- most two decades, yet, in the opinion of a noted anthropologist, he "did not produce a single good ethnograhic or archaeological study." He was unable to speak the Eskimo language well, even after eight- een years of association with them, and he misunderstood many as- pects of Eskimo culture.

The Eskimos knew him as Piuli — the best they could do at pro- nouncing his name — or "Piulerriaq." He was, they realized, a man of tenacity and drive. Uutaaq, who accompanied him on his final poleward dash in 1909, called him "a great leader," but to others he was an enigma. Knud Rasmussen, the Danish adventurer, put it the most charitably when he said that "their respect for the man was greater than their love." An anthropologist who heard the Eskimos talk about Peary almost half a century after he had left the district characterized him as a man who accomplished his aims "by threats, coercion, and the power of his authority." He appropriated the entire band of Polar Eskimos. They were "his," just as surely as were his sled, his Arctic gear, and anything else he needed in the fanatical pursuit of his goals. They could work only for him. Their dogs, he insisted, were to be available to him alone for barter. It was the same with their furs and the ivory tusks of walrus and narwhal, which he acquired in exchange for cheap trade goods from the United States and sold for a handsome profit. In his writings, the Eskimos were "my faithful, trusty Eskimo allies, dusky children of the Pole" and "effective instruments for Arctic work." At the end of his Arctic career, after an association of almost twenty years, he had the arrogance to write that "these people are much like children, and should be treated as such."

His ego was enormous. He felt that "their feeling for me is one of gratitude and confidence," and he concluded that "it would be misleading to infer that almost any man who went to the Eskimos with gifts could obtain from them the kind of service they have given me; for it must be remembered that they have known me personally for nearly twenty years. . . . I have saved whole villages from starvation, and the children are taught by their parents that if they grow up and become good hunters or good seamstresses, as the case may be, 'Piulerriaq' will reward them sometime in the not too distant future."

To be sure, some Eskimos genuinely liked the man. The influential Uutaaq was among them. But many others retain a quite different memory of him. In 1967 an elderly man in tiny Siorapaluk, the district's most northerly village, reminisced about Peary, the man he referred to as "the great tormentor":

"People were afraid of him . . . really afraid. . . . His big ship . . . it made a big impression on us. He was a great leader. You always had the feeling that if you didn't do what he wanted, he would condemn you to death. . . . I was very young, but I will never forget how he treated the Inuit. . . . His big ship arrives in the bay. He is hardly visible from the shore, but he shouts: 'Kiiha Tikeqihunga! — I'm arriving, for a fact!' The Inuit go aboard. Peary has a barrel of biscuits brought up on deck. The two or three hunters who have gone out to the ship in their kayaks bend over the barrel and begin to eat with both hands. Later, the barrel is taken ashore, and the contents thrown on the beach. Men, women and children hurl themselves on the biscuits like dogs, which amuses Peary a lot. My heart still turns cold to think of it. That scene tells very well how he considered this people — my people — who were, for all of that, devoted to him."

2

THE IRON MOUNTAIN

WHEN JOHN ROSS FIRST encountered the Polar Eskimos, he observed with surprise that they used metal tools. They alone, of all Eskimos, had discovered a local source of iron — three meteorites at the northern extremity of Melville Bay, about thirty-five miles to the east of Cape York. A legend had grown up around these meteorites — that they were a woman, her dog, and her tent, hurled from the sky by a supernatural power. The Eskimos tried to explain to Ross how they obtained their metal tools, but he understood them imperfectly. When he reported the event he inadvertently created another northern myth, that of an Iron Mountain on the shores of Melville Bay.

Since Ross's time, many expeditions had gone in search of the mythical mountain. Most were sent out for exploration or whaling, and finding the iron was a secondary objective. The searchers never found the iron mountain, but over the years they learned that the iron was meteoric in origin. In 1883 Baron Nordenskjold's expedition tried to make Cape York with the sole purpose of discovering and bringing home the meteorites, but the ice of Melville Bay proved impassable that year. Until 1894, no white man had ever laid eyes on the treasure.

Robert Peary heard about the meteorites in 1892 from the Eskimo Qisuk, one of his regular hunters and dog drivers. When he returned the following year, it was with the announced intention of searching for the so-called iron mountain, which he too was convinced must be meteoric iron. The Eskimos were hesitant to take him there. After all, wasn't this their source of iron? What would he do with it if he found it? Would he be content merely to look at it? One could not imagine a man wanting to undergo a lengthy journey just to gaze at three large stones! Perhaps he would carry them away, as he was carrying off so many other things from their land. It was true that they used the stones less now than had their forefathers; they traded for knives and other metal implements with the "upernaallit" who stopped by from time to time, and now from the great Peary himself, but one could never be certain that these voyages would continue. Perhaps there would come a time when they would need again the woman, her dog, and her tent.

If Peary planned to carry the stones away, the Eskimos wanted no part of it. Only bad luck could ensue from any such attempt, and it would surely follow those who helped in it. Many years before, a group from the northernmost part of the district had tired of the exhausting trip to Saviksiivik — literally "the place where one finds metal" — and they laboriously detached the head from the woman to cart it off to their wintering district. They lashed the head to a sled and started for home, but it was late spring and the ice was rotten; when they were well out from shore, it gave way under the tremendous weight of their cargo. The sled, the dogs, and the woman's head all disappeared beneath the water. There could be no misunderstanding such an event — it was a punishment exacted by the spirit of the iron woman on the hunters for trying to remove the stones. Since that time it had been considered bad luck to take more of the iron than was needed. The iron lady had never begrudged them the small fragments they had chipped from her scarred body over the centuries, but one must not be greedy.

At last Peary found a guide who agreed to take him to the place. After a long and difficult sled journey from his headquarters in Inglefield Bay, they reached the site in May of 1894, dug away the snow, and found a large brown mass. His guide, Aleqatsiaq, identified it as the headless woman. It would take some stretch of imagination, Peary thought, to see this as a woman. He spent the following afternoon measuring, sketching, and photographing the treasure, then claimed it as his own: "I scratched a rough 'P' on the surface of the metal, as an indisputable proof of my having found the meteorite. . . ." Aleqatsiaq also showed him the site of the largest of the meteorites, the tent, on Bushnan Island, a few miles offshore.

When Peary returned to his headquarters at Anniversary Lodge, he told his wife, "This means that if the ship comes I can put one or two of the meteorites aboard her. By their sale or exhibition your brother . . . can raise enough to send a ship next year." The ship, the Falcon, did come, but she was unable to reach the site; the ice of Melville Bay was once again protecting the meteorites from intruders. Peary remained in the Arctic for a second wintering. The following summer, in the relief steamer, Kite, he was more fortunate. He reached the site in August and, with the help of a crew of Eskimos, got the three-ton woman and her thousand-pound dog aboard and departed for America.

Peary was accustomed to being in total charge when he was in the North. Back in America, it pained him to have to realize once again that he was a mere lieutenant in the Navy. Moreover, he had powerful critics in high places who resented his being perpetually on leave on Navy salary. He was fortunate to have secured the meteorites, for at least he had something tangible to show for his two-year absence. However, he failed to accomplish most of his other aims and the scientific results of the expedition were meager. He had not even made an attempt on the North Pole. Before departing from Greenland in August of 1895, he penned a simple entry in his diary: "I have failed." By the time he arrived in the United States, he was despondent. "I shall never see the North Pole," he told a reporter, "unless someone brings it here. I am done with it. In my judgment such work requires a far, far younger man than I."

But with Peary, whom a biographer characterized as "the man who refused to fail," such despair never lasted long. The Navy assigned him to a post in Brooklyn, and while there he began to make plans to return north the following summer to bring the largest meteorite, the tent, to the United States. He requested leave for a summer voyage in

13

1896. There was strong opposition to it, but through the influence of powerful friends, his request was granted.

The *Hope* took Peary north in the summer of 1896, but bad weather prevented him from bringing home the meteorite. His empty-handed return made him an easy target for his critics and he was derided in the Navy and the press for his fruitless obsession with Greenland. He knew that this was the time when the future of his career as an Arctic explorer was most in jeopardy. Yet even before leaving Cape York, he had instructed Qisuk and Nuktaq to be at the cape awaiting his arrival the following summer. He would return, he promised. "The summer's voyage and the Arctic atmosphere," he wrote, "had brushed away the last vestige of the previous year's exhaustion and morbidness. I felt once more my old-time elan and sanguineness."

He began to make plans for a major expedition to reach the one geographical prize that remained in northern exploration, the North Pole. On January 12, 1897, the American Geographical Society awarded him its first Cullom Gold Medal for establishing the insularity of Greenland and for his explorations about Inglefield Gulf. On that occasion, Peary announced his plan for reaching the top of the world. He described what came to be known as the "American Route" to the North Pole. He would acquire a strong ship and force her through the passages separating northern Greenland from Ellesmere Island, the ice-choked waters of Smith Sound, Kane Basin, and Kennedy and Robeson Channels, right to the Arctic Ocean. There he would establish the northernmost land base possible, on the northern shore of Ellesmere Island or Greenland, and from this base he would "assault" the Pole.

As with the Eskimos whom he had appropriated for his own ends, so with the American Route to the Pole. Peary came to look on all of northwestern Greenland and Ellesmere Island as his private domain. Any other explorer who ventured there was a trespasser, an interloper, or a poacher. He claimed that "the knowledge an explorer has acquired of the particular route which he is . . . developing and by which he hopes, by repeated efforts, to reach the Pole, is as much a part of his capital as the gold and silver in the vault of a bank, and until he abandons that route, no one else, without his consent, has any more right to take and use it, than a stranger has to enter the vaults of the bank and take its treasure."

But his critics were busy again. On April 12, 1897, while he was still planning his expedition, he received orders to transfer to the West Coast for a new position with the Navy. He realized what was afoot. On the West Coast he would be far removed from the influence of his friends in New York and Washington. If he transferred west, he was finished. He countered with a most audacious proposal — a request for five years' leave — and once again, through the influence of prominent people, his request was granted. "Never was a man more fortunate in his friends than I," wrote Peary a year later. It was true, but more than sheer luck was involved. The friends had been carefully cultivated over the years for the influence they could bring to bear in his favor.

Although the five-year leave was granted, there was insufficient time to prepare for an expedition of the scope he envisioned in the few short months remaining before summer. But there was still the matter of the remaining meteorite. If he could secure it, it would increase his prestige in America even more. So in 1897 Peary left again on the *Hope* for Melville Bay. He reached Cape York on August 12. Ice conditions were favorable and Peary decided to try for the meteorite immediately. He embarked Qisuk and Nuktaq and all the other able-bodied men at Cape York and headed for Bushnan Island. By August 12 the meteorite had been brought on board. It was a monumental task, for the tent weighed 37.5 tons (a far cry, though, from Peary's estimate of 90 to 100 tons). The *Hope* left the island the same day and steamed six hours to Cape York. There, Peary wrote, "I sent my faithful Eskimos ashore, accompanied by several barrels of biscuit, and loaded with guns, knives, ammunition, and numerous other articles which I had brought to reward them for their faithful service."

All the Eskimos did not leave the ship at Cape York, though. Qisuk, Nuktaq, and their families were still aboard. They were Peary's people, and like the meteorite in the hold, they were bound for America.

Nuktaq was the older of the two men, a swarthy fellow with a straight black mustache and a small beard. He was in his forties. A stocky man, he measured one inch over five feet and was incredibly strong. His wife, Atangana, said to be a powerful shaman, was perhaps five years older. She was only four feet, ten inches tall; this, combined with her plumpness, gave her a particularly well-fed look. Peary had a special interest in the couple, for in 1894 when his wife Josephine had returned to America, she had taken with her their little daughter, Eqariusaq. The girl had passed the winter with Mrs. Peary and the Snow Baby and returned to her northern home the following summer.

Nuktaq was somewhat used to the strange ways of white men in the north. He had heard stories of their erratic behavior from his father, the famous Qulutana, who in 1854 had befriended a desperate party of eight white men, led by Dr. Isaac Hayes, who were deserting from the expedition under Kane. Qulutana and his fellow hunters had generously supplied Hayes and his deserters with food, though it was in scarce supply. But the Americans, for some imagined reason, came to distrust their benefactors and convinced themselves that the Eskimos were about to murder them. One evening while Qulutana and two hunters were visiting, having brought the Americans bear and walrus meat, Hayes drugged the soup he offered them. While the Eskimos were asleep, the Americans stole their clothing, sleds, and dogs, leaving them naked in the tent. When the Eskimos awoke they quickly fashioned makeshift ponchos from blankets and boots from strips of cloth and set out in pursuit of Hayes and his party. Hayes had been unable to handle the dogs, and the dogs and empty sled had returned to the tent. With this team the Eskimos overtook Hayes and his party, who turned their guns threateningly on them. Hayes made the Eskimos understand that if they would drive his group back to Kane's ship at Rensselaer Bay — for he had reconsidered his desertion and decided to return — he would not harm them. Otherwise he would shoot them immediately. Qulutana realized that these white men were like children out of their element and must be humored. He agreed — what choice did he have? — but, ever the pragmatist and eager to make the most of a bad situation, he first fashioned a snowhouse and took Hayes and his perplexed party in for a feast and a much-deserved rest. After Qulutana had delivered the recalcitrant deserters to the ship, Kane and he became fast friends; Kane described him as "a man of fine instincts, and I think, of heart."

Nuktaq had heard his father tell this story, and he grew up wary of the unpredictable white man. But Peary tried to recruit the best hunters of the tribe, and Nuktaq was certainly one of them. The items with which the American paid were the items a man with a family needed, and so Nuktaq worked and hunted for Peary. Moreover, he liked the explorer, for they had many qualities in common; Nuktaq respected him for his independence and toughness. Peary referred to the Eskimo as his "faithful hunter and dog driver."

In the winter of 1894, Nuktaq and his family had lived in a small house attached to Anniversary Lodge in Inglefield Bay. When Peary left in 1895, he told Nuktaq that he and his family could have the entire lodge as soon as his ship had disappeared from view. The impatient family entered the house almost immediately after the ship left and began to inspect every nook and cranny. Atangana, in her curiosity, dropped a torch and the lodge burned to the ground before the ship was even out of sight.

The other man was Qisuk, a younger man in his late thirties with shoulder-length hair. A good three inches taller than Nuktaq, he too was very strong and said to be one of the best hunters in the district. He was known for his good nature and Peary had nicknamed him "The Smiler." He inherited his easygoing manner from his father, Arrutarsuaq, whom Peary had dubbed "Horace Greeley"; Peary wrote that "the old man is aging . . . though still sturdy. . . . He is just as affable and unassuming as ever." Unassuming he may have been, but he was also a powerful shaman. Once, at the floe edge at Anorituuq, a rope had broken and a bear he harpooned had escaped; his harpoon sank into the water. Calling upon his helping spirits to aid him, he went into a trancelike state and dove to the bottom of the sea to retrieve it. His hunting partner would long recall the sound of his chanting deep under the water. He had come up with the harpoon.

Qisuk had been working off and on for Peary since the latter's arrival in 1891. When Peary first met him, he had been living at Itilleq on the southern coast of Inglefield Bay with his wife, Mannik, and their young son, Minik, who had been born in 1890 or 1891. Mannik

had worked for Peary too, as a seamstress, preparing the skin clothing that Peary insisted the members of his expeditions wear. In late
1894 they were living at another of the small camps in the bay, for
Peary noted, "Panippak . . . tells me that . . . he saw Majaq on his way
from Natsilivik up the gulf to Quinisut, to exchange wives with Qisuk.
This shows that the sound is frozen over as far out as Natsilivik, and
that Majaq has a soul above monotony." But in 1897 Qisuk was wifeless, for Mannik had died in an epidemic that killed thirty-one members of the tribe a year earlier. His son, Minik, about seven years of
age, was motherless.

Nuktaq and Qisuk helped Peary with the difficult task of getting
the huge meteorite aboard the ship that summer. While that operation was in progress, a scientist traveling on the ship had promised a
jackknife to the first child who could deliver him an Arctic owl. Peary
wrote in a children's book he published some years later that "little
Minik had meanwhile heard of the promised knife, and started up
the cliff to see if he could capture a real uppissuaq. He had climbed
some distance when he saw far above him a gerfalcon, which he
knew was waiting for his prey. Minik had with him his little bow and
arrows, which he could use with much skill. Climbing still nearer,
and moving cautiously so as not to frighten the bird, he drew his bow
and sent the arrow flying to the mark and killed the falcon, which
tumbled almost at his feet. . . . He then found the owl's nest, and hid-
ing himself, awaited the coming of the owl. After a long wait he saw
her flying towards him with a bird in her claws, and it was not long
before she reached the nest and received the arrow that was sent
from Minik's bow. Minik came down the cliff with the two birds. He
received a knife and a piece of board as his reward." Qisuk was proud
of his young son, a hunter already!

With the meteorite safely on board, Peary invited Nuktaq and
Qisuk to travel south with him. Nuktaq would be accompanied by
his wife and their adopted daughter, Aviaq, a pleasant girl of about
twelve with straight blue-black hair falling to her shoulders. Qisuk, of
course, would take Minik along with him.

Many years later Minik recalled the beginning of his southern
odyssey. In his brief account he telescoped several years of Peary's
activities in the district:

"I can remember very well when the big ship came far up there where I lived with my father and my people. I was a little boy then, and I had never seen a ship before. I had never seen anything bigger than my father's kayak. The big ship brought to our little village more white men than we had ever seen.

"I lived in a little igloo with my father. My mother was dead and I had no brothers or sisters. And so I loved my dear father very much and he loved me. He promised me that just as soon as I was big enough he would make a little kayak for myself, and when the traders came again he would buy me a knife.

"He and the rest of the men saw the big ship when it was far out in the water and they went out in kayaks to meet it. I stayed on shore and watched. Soon Lieut. Peary and the white men came ashore and tried to make us understand. We knew what white men do, so our men hid all the furs and ivory to keep them from being stolen. Soon we understood that they were going to stay there and build a house. We helped them and the men got knives and pieces of board as pay. A piece of board is one of the most valuable things we can get.

"After a while the white men went away, but they came back again. Then Lieut. Peary asked if some of us wouldn't like to go back with him where there were great buildings and railway trains and lights and many people, and where the sun shone every day in winter and where people didn't have to wear heavy furs to keep warm.

"He coaxed my father and the brave man, Nuktaq, who were the strongest and the wisest heads of our tribe, to go with him to America.

"They promised us nice warm homes in the sunshine land, and guns and knives and needles and many other things. So one day we all sailed away for New York."

This was a convincing invitation, coming from the man of whom the Eskimos would later tell Knud Rasmussen, "He asked with so strong a will to gain his wish, that it was impossible to say no." Of course the Eskimos were eager to please this man who now, it was apparent, controlled the supply of trade goods in the district. And anyway, hadn't Nuktaq's daughter, Eqariusaq, come back well fed and unharmed from America a few years earlier? How could they refuse? Minik continued:

"Our people were afraid to let them go, but Peary promised them that they should have Nuktaq and my father back within a year, and that with them would come a great stock of guns and ammunition, and wood and metal and presents for the women and children. So that my father believed that for so much good and comfort for his people they should let him and Nuktaq make the trip. Nuktaq could not part from Atangana, his wife, and his little girl, Aviaq, so he took them with him. My mother was dead, and my father would not go without me, so the five of us said a last farewell to home and went on Peary's ship."

From Cape York the *Hope* steamed north as far as Cape Sabine, stopping at various Eskimo camps along the way. Peary wanted to meet certain Eskimos whom he had come to know and give them instructions for the winter for laying in supplies of meat that he could utilize when he returned the following year to begin his attempt on the Pole.

At one of these camps he met a young man, Uisaakassak, who petitioned him for permission to go to America as well. His reason was simple: It had been decided that twelve-year-old Aviaq should someday become his wife and he did not want to part from her. A brief entry in Peary's journal for August 26, 1897, reports, "Uisaakassak wants to go to America & I take him."

3

ARRIVAL IN AMERICA

ON THE LAST DAY OF September the *Hope* reached New York. By midafternoon, she was moored at the foot of Dock Street in Brooklyn. As the ship was being made fast to Excursion Wharf a large crowd gathered, for her arrival had been anticipated — a week earlier she had put in at Sydney, Nova Scotia, for coal, and from there Peary had cabled New York the news of his imminent arrival with the Cape York meteorite and six Eskimos.

On the following day, twenty thousand people visited the vessel to see the long-sought meteorite and to get a glimpse of the Eskimos. The authorities were prepared for the crowds — admission was by ticket only. Early on the morning of October 3, tugs towed the ship to the Brooklyn Navy Yard, where more crowds — ten thousand on that day alone — visited the docks to see the meteorite brought on land. A newspaper reported, "The crowd afterward boarded the vessel to see the Eskimos, who had attired themselves in their native costumes for inspection. Aviaq and Minik, the children, attracted considerable attention, and were plentifully supplied with candy and peanuts which they seemed to enjoy immensely."

One of the ship's officers remarked, "The children are sick from the quantity of sweet things given them. We feed them with raw meat, and the candy has had a bad effect on them."

To the little group of Eskimos, the curiosity of these crowds of New Yorkers was overwhelming. Thirty thousand visitors in two days alone! Peary had told them that many, many people lived in America. And it was true that each time a ship arrived in northern Greenland, there were new and strange faces among the familiar few crew members who seemed to return time and time again. But no amount of forewarning could have prepared them — whose tribe, indeed whose whole world, numbered only 234 people — for such incredible numbers of human beings, in all shapes, sizes, and colors. Peary had promised them they would be safe. And now that they were seeing, for the first time, the skyline and human masses of New York, they knew that they were indeed at the mercy of Peary and those who did his bidding.

What were Peary's reasons for bringing these six Eskimos to New York? Was it selfless charity, a kind gesture to reward those who had served him well, as he would later maintain? Or was there something in this for Peary, a hidden reward for a seemingly generous act?

Peary prided himself on being a man of science. In his books and speeches he often described his search for the North Pole as a scientific quest. He brought back scientific specimens from each of his northern expeditions and many of them made their way, often by circuitous routes, to the American Museum of Natural History. Perhaps these six Eskimos were just specimens, much like the skulls and skeletons he had collected earlier, but more interesting because blood still coursed their veins. He felt a certain affinity for them — the men had, after all, been in his employ for some time — but he had also felt a morbid affinity for the bodies of other Eskimos he knew by name, which he had exhumed the year before from their fresh graves and carted off south to grace the halls of the museum. He had written in his diary on August 22 of that year, "The ship's men brought off the cask containing Qujaukitsoq and his wife and the little girl together with the accessories of his grave. . . ." The American

Museum of Natural History purchased those skeletons from him on his return.

More to the point, Peary had found a patron, a wealthy man to be humored, coddled, and flattered, for Peary was well aware that the Navy would not forever tolerate his prolonged absences from its service. Sooner or later, he would be forced to rely on private sponsorship if he were to continue his northern explorations.

The patron was Morris Ketchum Jesup, a man who had made his fortune in railroad supplies and banking. In 1884 he had retired from business to devote the rest of his life to his many philanthropic interests. A deeply religious man, he had been one of the founders of the Young Men's Christian Association and had been its president in 1872. He made substantial gifts to the Union Theological Seminary in New York, to Yale, Harvard, and Princeton Universities, and to the Woman's Hospital in New York. But he reserved his greatest love and his greatest gifts for the American Museum of Natural History; he had been one of its incorporators in 1868 and assumed its presidency in 1881. Like Peary, Jesup was not a scientist. Unlike Peary, though, he never pretended to be one. But he was a lover of science and, through his wealth, had dedicated himself to bringing science to the common man. Indeed, it was his presidency, which lasted until his death, that largely shaped the museum as an instrument of popular education and research.

It was sheer chance that brought Peary into the circle of Morris Jesup — chance and the tenacity of Josephine Peary. When she left her husband in Greenland in the summer of 1894, the Pearys doubted that they would have enough money to send a relief ship up the following year to bring Robert Peary home. He had decided that, if a ship did not come, he would sled down the western Greenland coast and take a regular Danish supply vessel to Copenhagen. During the winter Mrs. Peary had had second thoughts about the chanciness of that arrangement. She knew that, somehow, she had to send a ship. But the cheapest ship she could charter would cost at least $10,000 for the summer. Having no funds of her own, she had canvassed scientific institutions and secured pledges amounting to $5,000. She then approached an old family friend, Judge Charles P. Daly, president of the American Geographical Society. Daly put her in touch with Morris

Jesup but warned her that he could bring no influence to bear on Jesup and that she must present her own case strongly.

Jesup, after hearing her out, insisted that she state her appeal at a meeting of the museum's Board of Directors. She impressed the board, but Jesup had the final say, as he always did, and his reply humiliated her deeply. For Jesup, though he could be extremely generous, did not want to be seen as a soft touch. Moreover, he wanted to make sure he was appreciated. "You go ahead," he told her. "Do all you can: solicit, and lecture; and then whatever you still need I shall see is made up." The interpretation the proud Mrs. Peary put on these words was that "when she failed, she was to come in and drag her failure in for the alms of charity." But, humiliating though the experience had been, the Pearys had gained a powerful and wealthy ally. He had told Mrs. Peary, "You must understand that, while I am interested in the scientific aspect of your expedition, my chief interest is that I want you to get your husband back."

From that day on Jesup was an ardent supporter of Peary. In 1898 he and a group of wealthy friends would form the Peary Arctic Club, and he would later become its president. The goals of the club were "to reach the farthest northern point on the Western Hemisphere; to Promote and Maintain exploration of the Polar Regions." Jesup never lost faith in Peary, though his faith was tried sorely on several occasions. He was to remain president of the Peary Arctic Club until his death.

Peary undoubtedly felt that the scientific benefit to be derived from an anthropological study of these Eskimos would be a major credit to the museum and, through it, to the vanity of Morris Jesup, who that very year had endowed a major archaeological research foray into the north, The Jesup North Pacific Expedition. Yet Peary made the decision to bring the Eskimos to the United States without Jesup's knowledge. Morris Jesup had never asked him to bring back living specimens for research and was surprised when he learned that he had. Others at the museum were not surprised, however; at least one of the scientists had suggested to Peary that he bring a single Eskimo back to New York for a year, and a later memo in Jesup's hand says, "I understand Peary brought this party here at the suggestion of the Department of Anthropology."

In fact, although Jesup did not realize it, it was Dr. Franz Boas, a member of the museum's staff, who had given Peary the idea. As a young geographer Boas had spent a year living among the remote Eskimos of Cumberland Sound on the east coast of Baffin Island in northern Canada, a year that shifted his interest away from geography to the young science of ethnology. With the publication of some papers on his year of Arctic research, the scientific world had become interested in his work. He had emigrated to America from his native Germany and the Smithsonian Institution had published his large monograph, "The Central Eskimos," in 1888. It was the first detailed ethnological study of any Canadian Eskimos and Boas used the acclaim he received for it as his springboard to a distinguished career in American anthropology.

Boas never returned to the Arctic, but he maintained a deep interest in it and its people. From 1892 through 1894, he served first as chief assistant in anthropology at the World's Columbian Exposition in Chicago and then as curator of the museum established there to house its permanent collections. Eskimos were brought to Chicago from Labrador for "exhibit" at that exposition. In 1895, Boas joined the staff of the American Museum of Natural History and became assistant curator there in 1896. In that year, he asked Peary to bring back from his summer's cruise one Eskimo who could stay in New York for a year or so. Such a thing had previously been done, he claimed, without the individual suffering from it. Peary liked the idea but had not been able to bring anyone back with him that summer.

The following year, as Peary was making plans for his voyage north, Boas again contacted him, writing, "I beg to suggest to you that if you are certain of revisiting North Greenland next summer, it would be of the very greatest value if you should be able to bring a middle-aged Eskimo to stay here over winter. This would enable us to obtain leisurely certain information which will be of the greatest scientific importance." Boas, then, had been hoping for the arrival of one Eskimo in New York. He was probably as shocked as Morris Jesup at the arrival of a group of six. But he commented on the purposes for which the Eskimos were brought to the United States in a manner that leaves no doubt that they were taken there in the interests of the museum. "It was believed," he wrote, "that much valuable information of an ethnological character could be obtained from them, and that their presence here would be very instructive to scientists interested in the study of the Northern races."

Peary had expanded on Boas's idea of bringing one Eskimo to the United States for study. If the presence of one Eskimo would enhance his reputation with the institution controlled by his benefactor, he reasoned, might not a larger group earn him even more prestige? He would later deny that he was involved at all in the decision to bring the Eskimos to New York, claiming that he was acting only on the Eskimos' own suggestion! This was a silly and irresponsible denial. There is no doubt that he brought them to secure publicity, official notice, and the goodwill of the officials of the American Museum of Natural History. This fact is admitted by one of Peary's most ardent admirers, who wrote that "it was his idea that they would provide an interesting ethnological and anthropological study."

He intended, too, to carry on the Arctic explorer's tradition of exhibiting Eskimos before audiences as a means of securing funds for the continuation of his explorations. Even while the *Hope* was at Excursion Wharf, an admission fee had been charged to allow the curious to view the attractions, human and otherwise, that Peary had brought from the Arctic. But one person whom these New York crowds did not see was Peary himself, for he had left the *Hope* at Sydney and proceeded by train to Washington to report to his superiors at the Navy. At every stop, he was met by reporters, and he told them, "We have on board six Eskimos, namely, three men, one woman, a boy, and a girl. . . . They will remain with me here this Winter, to arrange the ethnological specimens, and will return with me next summer." He had already laid plans for the next summer's voyage, and he claimed, ". . . When I leave again . . . it will be to remain up there until I reach the pole, or lose my life in the attempt."

Although Jesup was not aware of it, Peary expected all along that the Eskimos would go to the American Museum of Natural History. And so, on October 1, the day after their arrival at the docks, the newspapers reported, "A collection of the implements, tents, sleds and clothing of the 'Greenland Highlanders' . . . was brought back.

These will be placed in the American Museum of Natural History. Six Eskimos were carried on the steamer . . . and will help Lieut. Peary arrange the materials he brought home." And two days later a paper reported, "All of the Eskimos will leave the ship to-day and go to the Museum of Natural History, where they will arrange the exhibit of their implements. . . ."

While Peary assumed that the American Museum of Natural History would be happy to have the Eskimos, neither he nor Boas had made any arrangements for their reception there. A museum memo states, "It was felt that it would be unwise to place the Eskimos in an asylum or in a hospital because the artificial, and to them, unnatural confinement of such places would prove unfavorable. Mr. Morris K. Jesup . . . was appealed to and . . . rooms were provided for the temporary occupancy of the Eskimos, who were placed in the custody of Mr. Wallace, in whom he had every confidence. . . . These rooms were clean, and . . . the Eskimos received kind and considerate attention."

Years later, Minik, the youngest of the party, recalled that arrival in New York: "Oh, I can remember it very well, that day when we first saw the big houses and saw so many people and heard the bells on the cars. It was like a land that we thought must be heaven."

But he added another observation, one of consternation and disapproval over part of the cargo that Peary landed:

"When they took us ashore, they brought five big barrels — they held the bones of our people who had died, and I had seen them digging them up out of their graves to bring here.

"When we asked them why, they told us that they were bringing them here to put in nice boxes, where they would be kept safe forever. But I don't know where they are now. Our land is cold and stony, but I guess they would have been better off there if they had been left in the stone graves my people made for them."

The Eskimos were housed at first in the museum's basement, but even here they were not free from the eyes of the curious. Newspapers refer to "the several scores of visitors, who received permission from Superintendent Wallace of the museum to inspect the newcomers."

But there were many others who were denied admission: "The

unusual crowd that thronged the museum was disappointed when told that the Eskimos were not on exhibition. Some of the visitors understood that they could have access to the temporary abode of the strangers, and came there for that purpose, but they had to content themselves with a glimpse through a grating above the basement, and many lay prone, peering through the spaces in the hope of catching a glimpse of the Eskimos."

The Eskimos were not sure which was more oppressive, the heat or the crowds. Nonetheless they tried to bear the former and be polite to the latter. They had looked forward to this trip to America, with all the wonders that Peary had described to them, and to all the treasures they would take back home. Peary was surely a great leader and everyone in northern Greenland had come to realize that it was wise and, indeed, profitable to do his bidding. If these hordes of white-faced strangers were Peary's people too, then it would be well to treat them kindly. All the visitors were treated to a round of handshaking with every member of the little party. Matthew Henson, Peary's black servant, whom they had come to know and trust on Peary's earlier expeditions, was on hand to provide interpretation. He was the only one of all those who ever accompanied Peary north who learned to speak the language of the Eskimos in anything but a halting fashion.

The newspapers made light of the appearance of the Eskimos: "For the first time since their arrival in this city, they laid aside their fur garments, and yesterday wore a combination of American and Eskimo costume, which, while by no means picturesque, presented a striking appearance.

"Qisuk, the head of the party, and ranking chief, by grace of one of the attendants got hold of a light overcoat, and, though several sizes too large for him, he wrapped it around his body and seemed proud of it. His nether garments consisted of a pair of golf stockings of rather loud pattern and somewhat too comfortable a fit."

The men of the party expressed a tremendous interest in American girls and "insisted upon their rights to propose an exchange of wives." Until their arrival in St. John's and New York, they had seen only two white women in their lives. The first was Josephine Peary, who had wintered twice in northern Greenland. They recalled with amusement how Equ, an Eskimo hunter, had met her in 1891. Equ had heard that the chief of the recently arrived white men had brought his wife with him, and he made a trip to the camp to see this spectacle. Upon his arrival he presented himself outside the house and asked to see the white woman. Robert Peary and his wife both stepped outside. It was the first time Equ had seen either. After looking them up and down carefully for a few moments, he asked, "Which one is the woman?" Upon learning the answer, he promptly proposed an exchange of wives with Peary.

Peary hadn't liked that, they remembered, though they all thought a man should be flattered by such an offer. But perhaps it was worth a try here in this large city. They knew that after Mrs. Peary had gone south, Peary had developed a fondness for Aleqasina, one of the most beautiful of the Eskimo women, and often borrowed her from her husband, Piugaattoq, rewarding him much more liberally than the other hunters under the guise of paying him for his services as a hunter and driver.

The happy-go-lucky Qisuk was wifeless and could do with a partner to help him with his son, Minik. And Uisaakassak was impressed by these women he saw here — they excited him much more than the flat-chested Aviaq! Perhaps a few of the many women they saw here could be induced to go north and share their polar nights. The newspaper reported that "when . . . some ten or fifteen young women were introduced to them they at once began instituting inquiries as to the willingness of their new acquaintances to enter into matrimonial agreements. Through the interpreter they gave an account of their possessions and what consideration they were willing to allow for the acquisition of a good-looking wife. They had no special preference, but would take any one who would present herself for acceptance. When their rather verbose offerings were declined with thanks they showed keen disappointment."

The same newspaper report is the first to mention how little Minik first took to America. "Qisuk's little son," it stated, "was happy in the possession of a knickerbocker suit and blue flannel waist, which he took great delight in exhibiting to the callers, his chubby, greasy, little face beaming with delight at his civilized appearance. For the first time in his life, probably, he had a real bath yesterday, and, though it took some coaxing to get him to enter the tub of water, after the performance was over, he was so pleased that he has been anxiously inquiring through Matthew Henson, the coloured interpreter, when the next bath was forthcoming."

William Wallace, building superintendent at the museum, took Minik for a ride through Central Park and reported that "the little fellow could hardly be torn away from the menagerie, where he saw some polar bears, and the site of a bicycle made him howl with glee. He would not let riders pass without hailing them, and was amazed at the size of the 'big dogs,' as he called the horses he saw in the driveways."

By this time, though, the Eskimos were sick. They had all caught cold. It was fall in the city, and while to the New Yorker the weather was splendid, the Eskimos found the heat oppressive and their colds quickly developed into pneumonia. They knew they were ill. The newspapermen did not realize the gravity of what they saw in the basement of the American Museum of Natural History one early October day, and in their insensitivity they reported, "One of the most amusing forms of entertainment consisted in an illustration of the manner in which the Eskimos attempt to conjure away illness. This in their opinion can only be accomplished by rubbing the sides of the body and singing a weird sort of a lullaby that with all its peculiarities is not absolutely discordant."

It was not, however, a mere exhibition. It was an attempt, perhaps by old Atangana, the shaman, to invoke the helping spirits to ward off illness. It didn't work. The helping spirits — the *toorngat* — did not respond and the Eskimos would later claim that "in the United States . . . the angakkoq [shaman] has no power, because there are no toorngat."

By November 1, the entire group of six was in Bellevue Hospital. All were ill with pneumonia, Atangana the most critically, and it was thought for a time that she would die. For some time they all remained at Bellevue, although later some of them returned to the museum, where drier and more comfortable quarters had been prepared for them in an apartment on the sixth floor previously reserved for the museum's caretaker. They returned often to Bellevue for checkups.

Minik and Aviaq, the children, were the favorites of the staff at

Bellevue. The attendants became "much attached to the children. Minik . . . became as great a pet in his ward as the little girl Aviaq was in hers. The nurses amused themselves by teaching the children English words."

Boas, who observed the group closely, commented that Minik "had begun to pick up a few English words as soon as he reached this city" and counted him the brightest of the group.

4

AN ESKIMO ORPHAN IN NEW YORK

O N FEBRUARY 17, 1898, Dr. Boas received a letter from Bellevue Hospital — Qisuk was dying and the other Eskimos, who were all in the hospital again, should be removed from the institution and placed in a private house. Then, suddenly, Qisuk died that very day, before the move could be made. Minik was an orphan far from home.

From Minik's own hand we have an account of his father's death in those last heartrending days in Bellevue:

"He was dearer to me than anything else in the world — especially when we were brought to New York, strangers in a strange land.

"You can imagine how closely that brought us together; how our disease and suffering and lack of understanding of all the strange things around us . . . made us sit tremblingly waiting our turn to go — more and more lonesome and alone, hopelessly far from home, we grew to depend on one another, and to love each other as no father and son under ordinary conditions could possibly love. Every morning he would come and sit beside me until I wakened, almost crazy to know how I felt, and yet too tender to arouse me from my rest. How he would smile if I was a little better, and how he would sob, with big tears in his eyes, when I was suffering.

"Aside from hopeless loneliness do you know what it is to be sad — to feel a terrible longing to go home, and to know that you are absolutely without hope? Ah, you cannot know. And then add to this the horror of knowing that death was waiting near by for us, and that one must go first and leave the other all alone — awfully alone; no one who even understands your language — no one except grief! Aside from these tortures my poor father was suffering frightfully from disease. His neck was swollen from tuberculosis, and his chest ached so badly that he could not rest. And yet, in spite of all this, his whole thought was constantly of me. He watched over me night and day, denying himself sleep and even food, and when anything was brought for me to eat he insisted on giving it to me himself — coaxing me and praising the food — and if I seemed to like it, big tears would come in his eyes and he would laugh — half laugh and half cry — and pat me on the cheeks.

"He wanted to do everything for me with his own hands and watched every one who came near me. His greatest suffering was when he grew so weak that he was obliged to remain still in bed and could not come to me. And I cried all the time, and could no longer eat for fear my father would die. Then I grew better . . . because I was so anxious to be with him, and soon I was allowed to go to him and lie near him. He did not notice any of the doctors' torture after that.

"One day a doctor accidentally or carelessly burnt my arm with an iron. My father saw the sore, and when I told him that it was a burn, he got out of bed, enraged, as weak and sick as he was, and I am sure he would have killed the doctor. I was terribly frightened, and for the first time I lied to my father; I told him that I had burned my arm on a gaslight. Then he took me in his arms and kissed me and said in Eskimo, 'Minik must be careful for his father's sake.' The next morning my father was dead. The strain had been too great for him and he nearly suffocated during the night, and cried out for his home, his family, his friends and me. I put my head under a pillow, crying hard. They tried to take me from the room, and my father saw them and realized what it was. He called to me and I ran into his arms. He knew that he must leave me, and his grief was terrible. 'Father's spirit will stay with Minik always,' he said in Eskimo, choking hard. Father was

34

dying then I know, but I think his poor heart broke and that is what killed him.

"I thought my heart was broken, too! That sad, long, lonesome day!"

To follow the hospital's suggestion that the other Eskimos should be moved to a private house, Jesup again relied on William Wallace. His home was in the Highbridge area of New York, and he had a small cottage on his property. The Eskimos were moved to this cottage and a housekeeper hired to look after them. By good fortune Wallace was able to find in the vast city of New York a woman of part-Eskimo blood from Labrador, whom he engaged as maid for the party. She was able to talk with the Greenland Eskimos, though with considerable difficulty, for the dialect of Labrador differs markedly from that of the Polar Eskimos. Nonetheless she brought to three the number of New Yorkers who were able to speak with the Eskimos in their native tongue, though all used different dialects. Matthew Henson was the one they could understand the best, for he spoke their language with ease. The other was Franz Boas, who spoke a Baffin Island dialect and continued to take an interest in them.

It was indeed a boring life they led in the Wallace cottage. A reporter asked Boas, "What do the Eskimos do all day?"

"Oh, we try to give them little things to keep them busy," answered the doctor. "Their work doesn't amount to much, but they have made some carvings, and occupied themselves either indoors or around the place with any employment that suggested itself to them. They do not seem discontented."

On March 16, less than a month after the Eskimos had moved to the cottage at Highbridge, tragedy struck the small group again. Atangana, the wife of Nuktaq, died that day. She had been the first to become seriously ill in the early winter and had never fully recovered from her illness.

One of the scientists who studied the hapless group of Eskimos in New York was an American-born ethnologist of German descent, Alfred Kroeber. In 1897, when he first met the Smith Sound natives, he was only twenty-one years old, about the same age as Uisaakassak, and perhaps he empathized with the unfortunate young man.

He studied the Eskimos, under the direction of Franz Boas, during the winter and through the period of the deaths of Qisuk and Atangana. Of all the scientists involved with the Eskimos, he was in human terms the warmest. A liberal both politically and socially, throughout his life Kroeber maintained an enormous interest in, and sympathy with, common people.

In his pioneer study of the Eskimos of Smith Sound, Kroeber published a detailed account of the behavior of the Eskimos, particularly Nuktaq, upon the death of Atangana. He was sensitive enough not to intrude on their privacy at this time; rather, the account was secured from "an attendant (speaking Eskimo)," probably the Labrador-born woman Wallace had recruited to nurse the party, though it is possible that it may have been Matthew Henson. The report is pathetic in its detail of how Nuktaq attempted to follow traditional Polar Eskimo custom in mourning his wife, despite her death in a foreign place. Kroeber believed strongly that an individual's culture could not be comprehended without an understanding of his environment, and he commented, with understatement, that "perhaps the customs are somewhat modified by the unusual surroundings."

"When informed that his wife was dying," Kroeber wrote, "Nuktaq picked her up and carried her out of the house into the barn. . . . When informed she was dead, he asked whether she was still breathing, or quite dead. When sure of the latter, he prepared to see her. He put on fresh underclothes, dressed fully, putting on coat, hat, and gloves, and asked for a cord, which he tied below his hips, outside his trousers. He also stuffed his left nostril with paper, and, taking hold of his coat on both sides, walked out to the corpse. He was followed by his adopted daughter, and Uisaakassak, his son-in-law.

"When we entered the room in which the corpse was, Nuktaq began to talk to the body, speaking fast and in a very low voice. . . . After a while he approached her. . . . With one hand he lifted up the blanket covering her, and passed his other over her body from her forehead to her heart. Then he took her by the shoulder, and shook her hard, telling her to remain where she was. He also spat on her forehead three times, telling her to wash herself. . . . He ordered her to stay where she was until he took her away. He reproached her with being an angakkoq and not being able to cure herself, and added, 'I am sure I shall die myself.' He said to her that, if there were anything she desired, she should appear to him at night in his dreams, and he would satisfy her, but that she should not come near him at other times. He ordered her to stay where she was buried, and to trouble no one, nor to follow him when he was kayaking. . . .

"Finally they left the room. The others went out first, and then he followed, going backward until he was outside the door.

"For the next five days, Nuktaq did not leave the house. . . . He wore his hat and coat all the time, and did not move about. For two nights he sat up in bed after the others were asleep, talking. After these two days, when informed that his wife had been buried, he no longer wore his hat, except when he was moving about. . . . During these five days he would not leave his room. He had all his food brought in to him. He demanded his meat rare or raw. . . . He drank no tea or coffee, but only water. . . .

"After these five days, the mourning observances were less strict. Early on the next morning, before sunrise, he left the house with his daughter. . . . He wore the cord he had worn on the day of the death, and as he went out made a scratch on the porch with a short stick, at the place from which he started. Then they walked about the house twice without stopping . . . going in a course opposite to that of the sun. . . .

"The following day he again took a walk exactly like the preceding. . . . A few days later he walked a little farther — as far as the barn — and on returning made three scratches on the ground. . . .

"On the tenth day after the death he was very anxious to see the grave. He said that on the tenth day after the burial the grave was always visited, and again ten days later. He said that this was necessary, and was much troubled at not being able to go. . . .

"Throughout this period the observances were similar to those of the first five days, though less rigorous. Both the men moved about little, and put on their hats whenever they did. Nuktaq went outdoors but rarely, and when he did, wore his gloves. . . . He also refused to have his hair cut. None of the party went outdoors after dark. . . . They all had their own cups, knives, and plates, and were careful to keep them separate. . . . He would do no work, nor make anything, such as kayak or sleigh models. He said that he would not do this until several months had passed. . . .

"Before her death, Atangana had requested that, when she was buried, the stones should not be put too close together, for fear that she might not breathe. She did not want to be buried under the sand, and wanted no coffin. She asked, moreover, that no clothes be put on her, except a shirt . . . and that her face remain uncovered. Nuktaq asked whether this had been done, and requested that she be buried as she would have been at home.

"The dead woman was not mentioned: even an allusion to her . . . excited his disapproval. All her property was either removed or destroyed, at Nuktaq's command. He ordered everything to be thrown away or burnt, and her cup and plate to be broken. By accident a part of her dress remained in the room in which she had been, and her husband never entered that room. . . ."

The scientists at the American Museum of Natural History were embarrassed. It was one thing to bring primitive people from a far-off land to study them for a year. But it was quite another to have members of the group dying there, almost in front of the prying eyes of New York's newspapermen. Eleven days after the death of Atangana, the *New York Tribune* announced in a headline that the Eskimos were "Going Home to Greenland." The accompanying article featured an interview with Franz Boas.

"When you found they were sick so much, didn't you think of sending them North again?" asked a reporter.

"Yes," replied Boas, "but there was no opportunity to send them. There were ships going north as far as Newfoundland and Labrador, but that would not have been anywhere near their home, and we could not land them in a strange country. When Lieutenant Peary starts on his trip this summer he will take them back with him. They are all fond of him, and were delighted at the prospect of coming here last summer."

But where was Peary? From the time the Eskimos had arrived in New York, he had never come to see them. Nor is there any record of him having inquired as to their welfare. Upon hearing of the death of

Qisuk, he sent a brief telegram of condolence to the museum: "Deeply regret Eskimo's death. Confident everything was done. Entire responsibility mine." He made no public statement. This man, who loved the attention of the press so much, was a publicity hound only when that attention was favorable to him. But this fiasco he had created could in no way show him in a good light. He would be called inhuman for having brought this group to a land where unaccustomed illnesses ravaged their vulnerable bodies, which had been so strong and healthy in the starkness of the north. Critics would say he should have known, that he should have realized that the germs of civilization would wreak havoc on the unsuspecting Eskimos. Hadn't there been an epidemic in the Cape York district in the winter of 1895–96, a sickness that spread rapidly among the tribesmen, racking their bodies with chills, then fever and a constant hacking cough before death mercifully claimed them? Weren't some of the victims the very people whose graves Peary had ransacked in 1896, and whose bones at this very moment were in the museum? Wasn't it true that this sickness had probably been brought in that summer by the members of the Peary relief expedition aboard the *Kite?* And didn't he know that some of the Eskimos had begun to say, with a black kind of humor, that each year now they got ill even at the first sight of a ship?

Peary knew all this and more. It was certainly unfortunate, but this attempt to secure the attention and congratulations of scientists and the public had backfired, and it was just as well for him to step aside and let the American Museum of Natural History bear the brunt of the inevitable criticism. Morris Jesup, of course, must not be seen in a bad light, but Peary was confident that he would not. The man had not become a multimillionaire by being foolish! Let Boas make the public statements and put off the probing questions of the press. Peary would wash his hands of the entire business. Besides, he was busy. He was involved now in something far bigger than anything he had ever attempted before. In the spring of 1897 the Navy had grudgingly granted him a five-year leave of absence, arranged through President McKinley himself, to launch a major expedition to the North Pole. He was busy now planning for it, and its success could not be jeopardized by six — then five, then four — mere Eskimos.

On March 31, 1898, William Wallace wrote to Morris Jesup to tell him that he had suggested to Boas that the remaining four Eskimos should be taken to the country. Wallace had a place in the country and could arrange for their care for a cost of $12 per week. He added, "I would like very much to be relieved of the personal care of them, and respectfully ask that some arrangements be made whereby I might be relieved of them." Jesup noted on the bottom of Wallace's letter, "This matter is left with Wallace and anything he should decide to do I shall approve."

Wallace had a dairy farm in Lawyersville, in mountainous upstate New York, and it was to this farm that Nuktaq, Aviaq, and Uisaakassak were moved in April. It was hoped that the clear mountain air would help them regain their health. Minik had gotten over his illness and remained behind in New York, living temporarily at the home of Morris Jesup.

Lawyersville is a small village, a country crossroads really, and while there the Eskimos lived in a long, low house across from the local church. It was owned by William Wallace and he recruited a local lady, a Mrs. Snyder, to care for the Eskimos.

The people of Lawyersville were perplexed by what they saw in their midst. They were rural folk and many had not traveled far from home. Yet they were certainly used to strange goings-on at the Wallace place — the previous spring a boa constrictor had escaped from a cage there, disappeared into the forest, and never been found. And they had certainly heard of Eskimos — the local paper just down the road in Cobleskill referred to them occasionally in reporting the travels of Peary and others. By why bring them to Lawyersville? The two adults spoke no English and insisted on wearing their heavy fur garments as they trudged about the park between their house and the church in the growing warmth of an approaching summer. The townsfolk knew that two of their number had already died in New York, and, hearing the coughing of the remainder of the group, they would not be surprised if the rest went the same way.

They did not have long to wait. Nuktaq died on May 14. The Cobleskill paper reported that his adopted daughter, Aviaq, was "very ill of consumption" but that "a lad named Uisaakassak is also at Lawyersville. He is healthy."

40

Within ten days Aviaq was dead too. Minik was still in New York, and Uisaakassak was the only Eskimo remaining in Lawyersville. He moved into an old shed near the church; the paper reported that "he had refused to return to a house in which an adult had died, in keep ing with an Eskimo custom."

On May 25, Wallace wrote again to Jesup, saying, "Only one of the Eskimo now remains in the country; the other two having died. It is very difficult to keep him there contented. I am having him returned, as Mat Henson is looking after the 'Windward' for Lieut. Peary. I shall send the Eskimo to Mat on Friday morning." For the next month Uisaakassak lived with Matthew Henson aboard the *Windward* at her dock in the North River off Canal Street.

When Peary arrived and told Uisaakassak that he was finally about to head for home, Uisaakassak "jumped about the deck and danced with glee, every few minutes stopping, however, to mop the perspiration from his brow with a most disgusting look." He complained to the reporters who were present that "the sun was burning the back of his neck and making him ill, and he hoped he would soon be where there was no sun as cruel as the American." Henson acted as interpreter for the crowd of well-wishers who came aboard the vessel shortly before her departure. One of them pinned a miniature American flag on Uisaakassak's cap and an American shield pin on his coat. Uisaakassak, in sign language, thanked the donor and then through Henson added that "he would always keep it to remember America by, although he did not like this country a bit. It was too warm and there was a great lack of walrus meat. . . ."

The *Windward* departed for Greenland on July 2. Minik remained in America. The Wallaces had taken a liking to the little orphan, and Jesup, with whom the boy had lived for a short time, had decided that they should keep him.

In May of 1898, Robert Peary was putting the finishing touches on two thick volumes describing his Arctic expeditions to date and outlining his plans for the future. He told in detail of the heist of the meteorites and the interest they held for the world of science. But there was not a word about the removal of six Eskimos from Smith

Sound to New York. Nuktaq and Qisuk are mentioned, to be sure, in the context of their faithful service to Peary as dog drivers and hunters in the north. But the book is silent about their coming to America. Instead, at the end of a lengthy appendix on the Smith Sound Eskimos, Peary waxes nostalgic for his beloved north and its people. "As I sit here writing now I can see them," he wrote, ". . . and many a familiar face rises in memory." Then, among those he lists, he mentions "Qisuk, or the 'Smiler,' the walrus killer of Itilleq" and "Nuktaq, my faithful hunter and dog driver." He speaks of them as if they were still alive, living healthily in Greenland, patiently awaiting his return, although Qisuk had died three months earlier in Bellevue Hospital and Nuktaq had passed away that very month.

Conveniently ignoring the human tragedy for which he was responsible, he concludes his wistful piece of deception: "Fortunately for them, with no possessions to excite cupidity, with a land in which no one but themselves could conquer a living, they are likely to be left in peace, to live out the part appointed them by the Creator, undisturbed by efforts to understand the white man's ideas of God, of right, of morality, and uncontaminated by his vices or diseases, till the 'Great Night' ends forever, and the 'Great Ice' dissolves in the convulsions of the last day."

In *Snowland Folk*, a children's book he wrote later, Peary falsified the record even more. He tells about the summer voyage on which he had secured the meteorite; in one brief passage, he writes, "Among the tribe was a good-natured Eskimo, Qisuk, nicknamed the 'smiler,' whose little boy afterwards came to the United States. . . ." Thus Peary acknowledged that Minik, who still lived, came to America, though he fails to mention that it was at Peary's behest, and he does not mention Qisuk's tragic trip at all.

Yes, Peary did not relish criticism. When it came to writing for his fawning public, he had a very selective memory indeed. Peary had washed his hands of the whole sordid affair.

5

MINIK, THE AMERICAN

IN NEW YORK, MINIK LIVED with William and Rhetta Wallace in their comfortable home in the Highbridge area of the city. It was a well-to-do neighborhood and included a popular resort area lined with fine restaurants and hotels. The Wallaces' son, William Jr., nicknamed Willie, was eleven years old and became the Eskimo's constant companion. Rhetta Wallace took a special interest in Minik; he was someone she could care for in place of the little girl, Maretta, she had borne in the summer of 1895, who had lived only a year. Minik had been very ill in the spring of 1898, while the other Eskimos had been dying in New York and Lawyersville, but after a long convalescence he had apparently made a full recovery. A healthy red glowed through the dark skin of his cheeks and he had regained his usual strength.

William Wallace was employed at the American Museum of Natural History, where he was one of the most trusted employees of Morris Jesup, the president of the institution. Wallace had started work there in 1886 as a clerk, thirty-one years of age, ambitious, and eager to please the demanding Jesup. He advanced quickly in the museum and three years later became superintendent of buildings, the position he still held in 1897, when he was one of the first to meet the Eskimos Peary took to New York. At the museum, Jesup turned over the care of the Eskimos completely to Wallace, though he maintained a kindly interest in the party. He had firm confidence in Wallace's ability to handle this situation in the same intelligent way that he had handled many other difficult tasks for Jesup.

When Nuktaq, Aviaq, and Uisaakassak were moved to Lawyersville, Minik had remained behind in New York. After a short stay at the Jesup home, he moved in with the Wallace family. It was thought that the move was temporary and that he would be sent back home when Peary left for the north again that summer. When he first went to the home of the Wallaces, Minik was broken in spirit and in health. He cried most of the time and "lived in mortal fear of having to return to the Museum." The Wallaces very quickly fell in love with this little orphan and decided that they would like to keep him. When the *Windward* departed for Greenland in July, Minik remained behind in New York. He became one of the family and the Wallaces treated him as they did their own son, Willie. He grew particularly attached to Mrs. Wallace and told her one day, in his halting English, "Minik's father is gone, but Aunt Rhetta is here — Minik no cry more ever."

Morris Jesup was instrumental in William Wallace's decision to take Minik into his family. In 1898, Jesup held a consultation with Wallace and his wife and told them that if they would take charge of the boy, he would compensate them for Minik's financial support. In a letter in August of that year, Jesup confirmed the agreement and urged Wallace to "give Minik a name," suggesting that he legally adopt the boy. There is no indication that Wallace ever did legally adopt Minik, but from that time on he was known as Minik Wallace. He took the middle name Peary.

In New York he was from time to time the subject of attention in the newspapers, often on the feature pages of Sunday magazine supplements. This was a time when large numbers of immigrants were coming to the United States and becoming integrated into American life, and the newspapers reflected a vision of America as a land of opportunity. Most of the articles were mildly racist in tone — one bore a section entitled "Taming a Little Savage" — and stressed how lucky Minik was to have been taken away from the "dreary region" that was his "barren Arctic habitat" and how fortunate he was to have an opportunity to grow up in America. One began, "If there is one small boy in this city who . . . has reason to be thankful for a decided change in his circumstances which occurred about a year ago, that boy is Minik. . . ." Another claimed, "Born in a land where life means nothing more than a mere physical existence, he has been brought by accident into an American home to enjoy all that that means. . . ." One went so far as to claim that "he is an American now . . . and President McKinley is hereby notified that he can expand to Greenland if he wants to, on the strength of Minik's residence in Tremont, N.Y." Another noted that "his expression has gained wonderfully in intelligence in the last year." He was, like all immigrants, expected to be thankful for the opportunity to enjoy "the care and comforts of civilization," and a paper was pleased to report that "no boy in all the city shows a higher appreciation of those comforts than little Minik."

One report, more sensitive than most, concluded, "We hope that this little ward of the United States, a guest from the far-away Northland, will grow up to a manhood that will combine the best qualities both of his land and of our own." Another, more chilling in its conclusion, called him "an experiment, and a promising one, in the effects of civilization upon one of the least known aboriginal races."

Minik quickly became aware of the unique interest he held for New Yorkers. Indeed, he had been made aware of it a few days after his arrival in 1897, when the curious had prostrated themselves on the sidewalk to peer through a grate into the basement windows of the American Museum of Natural History to catch a glimpse of the Eskimos. He grew accustomed to seeing articles about himself in the papers and eventually came to regard interviews as "one of the ordinary duties of life."

As his command of English improved, he grew fond of telling the reporters tales of adventure in the north. "Rather guarded and conservative in his statements," he preferred to tell stories of his own choice, rather than answer the questions of the reporters. Perhaps many of his listeners thought the stories to be tall tales, but they are not unusual episodes from the life of an Eskimo boy:

"Once my father had a very good dog. One day it fell into a big — very big — crack in the ice. Then my father say to me that I go down after the dog. My father tie a rope around my shoulders, and then they let me down into the big crack in the ice. I tie the rope around the dog, and the men pull us both up, so we have saved the dog."

"My father let me drive his dogs. . . . I drive ten dogs. One day I drive the dogs, and they see a fox, and they run away, very fast — I could not hold them. Then the sled hit against a big piece of ice — big as this room — and tip over, and I am thrown out. . . . The ice hold the sled, so the dogs could not run anymore, and Nuktaq came and caught them."

"We play hide-and-seek over the snow in the winter. We hide behind the big pieces of ice. But we always have to watch, or the bears might come and catch us. We have always four boys together, so some can call if the bears come; one boy is never alone. The bears are white, like the ice, and we do not see them, and they come softly."

Life in New York was totally different from the life Minik had known as a child in Greenland — many a building in the city housed more people than Minik's entire tribe numbered — but Minik adapted to it well. He made friends easily. He was kindhearted, affectionate, and "never better pleased than when he is able to do a favor for some of his friends."

In the fall of 1898 Minik did not attend school. The Wallaces, overly protective of him, were concerned that his health might fail again and they wanted him fully recovered before he began his formal education. They enrolled him in Sunday school, however, so his introduction to American education was gradual. In January of 1899, when students returned to school after their Christmas break, he finally enrolled in the Mount Hope public school in the Bronx borough of New York and proved to be a good pupil. The Wallaces also engaged a tutor to help him with English after regular school hours. Arithmetic was his favorite school subject. In fact, many years later he would sum up his entire school experience with the sentence, "I learned to read and write and to know grammar and fractions and lots of other things."

Minik hated to get out of bed in the morning. Once up, however, he was happiest outdoors. He loved sports, especially football — one reporter described him as "uncommonly sturdy" — and riding the bicycle William Wallace bought for him. With Willie Wallace as his inseparable companion, he also learned to skate and ride ponies. He excelled at swimming and won third prize in a local swimming race. One of his favorite hobbies was catching snakes.

When a reporter asked him if he did not get cold playing hide-and-seek among the icebergs of northern Greenland, Minik had replied that only his cheeks got cold, but that he often felt very cold in New York. It is a peculiarity of the far north that one does not feel the cold as one does in lower latitudes because of the low humidity in the air. In New York, Minik suffered from the damp cold of the winter and the unaccustomed heat of the southern summer. Mrs. Wallace said, "He doesn't like to be too warm, and sometimes when he gets heated playing out of doors, he just stops and takes off some of his clothes and lays them down by some stone wall, and then he goes on playing. He has lately lost, in that way, some underclothes, his overcoat, and a sweater."

Because William Wallace worked at the American Museum of Natural History, Minik visited the institution often. All the employees knew him and he was greeted with "handshakes, smiles and familiar pats on the back" each time he made his way to Wallace's office on the fifth floor. These visits were part work and part pleasure. The anthropological department, where Franz Boas was in charge, was interested in the boy. He had, after all, been brought south in the interests of science. The department's artist made a tinted clay portrait head of him, and Boas and a few others who were interested in the Eskimo language made a point of talking with the boy often, in an effort to learn something of the speech of the Polar Eskimos. But there was no one with whom to speak Eskimo at home, and Minik began to forget his native tongue quickly.

He felt at home with the museum's Eskimo exhibit, much of which was Polar Eskimo material brought south by Peary. A reporter observed that "he can impart information concerning Esquimau folk and their life to Mr. Wallace and others. He can go to the Esquimau exhibit, identify every article that Lieut. Peary brought down with him and tell the name and the history of the stuffed Eskimo dogs." He enjoyed looking through the pages of Peary's book on his Greenland expeditions, a thick, two-volume work published in 1898, and identifying the people and places that illustrated the book.

Minik was eager to please those about him, especially Mr. and Mrs. Wallace, but he occasionally resented some of the attention he was given, especially on those occasions when he was made a living exhibit in the hated basement of the museum. On one visit, when "seated on a bench among the Esquimau exhibits in the basement, Minik was asked by Mrs. Wallace to repeat the story of an adventure on the ice fields in which he had taken an important and perilous part, the embarrassment became painfully evident. A crowd of everyday New York little boys and girls had begun to swarm all around the group, some almost climbing over the back of the bench in their curiosity. It was time to bring the seance to an end. Enough had been done, said and sung to bear out Mrs. Wallace's statement that in the quiet of his own home Minik can tell some very interesting tales of the Arctic Circle."

In spite of this regular involvement with things northern, Minik did not seem to be homesick for his Arctic. Except on one occasion when he told a reporter, "I am going back north and be a chief like my father," he usually said that he did not want to return north. He was, of course, a mere child, but the novelty of life in America had not worn thin and the Wallaces were a kind and doting family to be a part of.

In the summer of 1899, Herbert Bridgman, secretary of the Peary Arctic Club, suggested to Wallace that Bridgman take Minik north with him on a summer supply voyage for Peary, thinking "if Minik still retains his native tongue, he might be of considerable use as an interpreter." Wallace replied that Minik had been ill again for some time and that his health was too delicate for such a trip. When Bridgman went north, he took a package of photographs of Minik to give to the Polar Eskimos.

Although Minik was still under ten years of age, some thought was given to what work he should prepare himself for as an adult. Jesup had agreed to pay for Minik's care and education "with a view to preparing him for northern work." Knowing Jesup's interests, it is likely that he envisaged Minik someday returning to his people as a teacher and missionary. In fact, a newspaper article claimed that Minik was "being educated by Mr. and Mrs. Wallace, with a view of sending him as a missionary to his people." Another story concluded that "with such foster parents as Mr. and Mrs. Wallace and with such kindly and generous men interested in him as Morris K. Jesup he is sure to be assisted in attaining any position which he can reach." As for Minik himself, he decided that he liked New York. "I want to stay here," he said, "and when I get to be a man I want to be a farmer and grow things. All Esquimaux just love to grow things because in our country nothing grows. We think it is fine to see a tree or a bush or a flower."

The house in Highbridge was only one of Minik's homes in those early years in the United States. The other was the Wallace summer place in Lawyersville, near Cobleskill, in the mountains of northwestern New York state.

In 1885, a year before he joined the staff of the American Museum of Natural History, William Wallace had married Rhetta Guffin, who came from an old Lawyersville family. By 1892 he had purchased property in the area and established a large dairy farm and an icehouse for refrigerating milk shipments. By 1896 it was an impressive operation; in that year one shipment alone to Binghamton, New York, was five thousand quarts — it took a whole railroad car and used six tons of ice for refrigeration. The price was 1½ cents per quart. Wallace's dairy farms were not confined to Lawyersville, for he also owned a farm in East Windsor and another in Newburgh, where he also raised Brahma cattle. Business was good, so good that in November of 1897 the Cobleskill paper reported that "Mr. Wallace has more orders for milk than he can supply." The following year he leased another local farm to stock with cattle, and in 1900 he bought one more local property, paying $900 for it. In 1893 Wallace bought a historic house that had once been a popular inn; the price was considerable for the time — $2,000. Wallace used the place as a home when in Lawyersville. By 1898 he had expanded his interests and that fall he began work on a tenant house in Cobleskill.

All this was done while Wallace maintained his employment at the museum in New York. He had built up an impressive business, but he had done it on a part-time basis. He looked forward to the day when he could leave his employment at the museum, live in Lawyersville, and devote all his attention to his expanding business empire. He was confident that that day was not far off, for in April of 1898 — the same month that three of the Eskimos were taken to Lawyersville — he and his wife transferred their church membership from Park Presbyterian Church in New York City to the Reformed Church of Lawyersville.

William Wallace was well known in Lawyersville and in neighboring Cobleskill. The local newspapers generally referred to him as "Superintendent of the American Museum of Natural History," giving the impression that he was an administrator or a scientist, rather than superintendent of buildings. It was a misconception that Wallace did nothing to correct and may have fostered, for he liked the prestige that the title accorded him. The papers regularly noted his comings and goings between Lawyersville and New York. Here was a man who had made good, an outsider to be sure, but one who had married a local girl and done well for himself.

Wallace became known also as a local philanthropist and the newspapers devoted even more attention to this aspect of his activities in and around Cobleskill. He created and supported worthy causes, and his financial largesse was well known. On one occasion he presented, on behalf of the American Museum of Natural History, four large double exhibition cases to the County Historical Society. In May of 1899, he announced his intention to deed a site, part of one of his properties, to the local church for the building of a parsonage. On Children's Day in 1898, he presented to the Reformed Church a beautiful bookcase and over one hundred carefully selected volumes in honor of a boy, one of his wife's relatives, who had recently died; this was to be known as the Dwight Guffin Karker Memorial Library. The newspaper concluded its report of this generosity with the statement, "Mr. Wallace is the children's friend and he is always making them happy with some generous gift."

In June of 1899, Wallace announced the Wallace Prize Debate, to be held as part of the commencement ceremonies at the local school. He offered a $50 prize. The general subject, announced in advance, was "The Extension of our National Domain." But the debate was to be extemporaneous — "Mr. Wallace believes that it does a young man more good to stand squarely upon his feet and express his own thoughts even imperfectly, than it does to copy the thoughts of others and weave them into a polished oration" — so the specific subject was not announced until the night of the debate. Perhaps Wallace had done some soul-searching as a result of the disastrous consequences of Robert Peary bringing six Eskimos to the United States to enhance his own reputation as a benefactor of science and as a Polar explorer: The specific subject that Wallace announced that night was "Resolved. That it is contrary to the true policy of the United States to acquire far distant territory."

Mrs. Wallace and the children passed their summers on the Cold Spring Farm in the quiet mountain hamlet of Lawyersville. These were peaceful times for Minik and young Willie. Mrs. Wallace knew everyone in the area and was related to many of them, so Minik and Willie were never short of places to go and people to visit. Minik became well known in Lawyersville and on the streets of Cobleskill, where he made friends just as easily as he had in New York City. The mountain air was good for Minik. He felt more at home against the backdrop of the Adirondacks than he did in the city; these mountains, though not snow-covered in summer as were those of northern Greenland, were nonetheless not choked with people as were the man-made mountains of skyscrapers and apartment houses in the city. Here he was free, or at least as free as a doting foster mother would allow him to be.

There were still the lessons to attend to, of course, for the Wallaces had engaged a local man, Professor Henry VanWoert, as an English tutor for the boy. From time to time the Wallaces passed extended periods in Lawyersville while school was still in session, and on those occasions Minik attended the local school as well. But he loved to steal away from school down to the local streams, where he could swim. He developed a reputation as quite a fisherman on these trips, for he would catch fish from the streams with his bare hands and eat them raw on the spot. In Lawyersville he and Willie were also able to indulge one of their favorite pastimes, catching snakes. The locals looked on Willie's passion for snakes with disfavor — the boa constrictor that had escaped from the Wallace farm in the spring of 1897 had never been found.

Minik also attended Sunday school at the Reformed Church. On his return home after his first visit to the Sunday school, Wallace asked him, "Well, Minik, what did they do with you in Sunday-school?" Minik replied gravely but without hesitation, "They took my five cents." He was taught to kneel beside his bed each night and, with head bowed, repeat the familiar children's prayer, "Now I lay me down to sleep." One evening he tried to get out of performing this nightly devotion with the excuse that he was too tired. His maid insisted, however, and the prayer was said. The next night he showed a little ingenuity, for "when he started for bed he was heard murmuring softly to himself all the way upstairs and even after he began undressing. Finally he ceased, looking much relieved, and, glancing up roguishly at the maid who was superintending the process of retiring, he remarked sententiously: 'See Lizzie, pray said!'" Later, when exhausted after a hard day of play, he would sometimes say, "Tired to-night. Not too much pray to-night!"

Even in the small village of Lawyersville, the Wallaces could not resist the occasional temptation to show off their little Eskimo charge. Thus on Children's Day in early July of 1898, he was present at Sunday school and "sang in his native language a song usually sung at the death of an Esquimo." And at the annual Cobleskill fair for that year, the fair's president "introduced the Eskimo who lives on the Wallace place, in native costume from the exhibition stand. . . ."

For William Wallace, now in his early forties, life was going well. He had a good position at the American Museum of Natural History and an impressive home in an auspicious area of New York City. In Lawyersville he had a growing business empire and the respect of the local community, both for his shrewd business acumen and for his philanthropy. A stable family and good church connections rounded out the life of this successful man who seemed the embodiment of the Protestant work ethic so much admired by Morris Jesup, his superior at the museum, and by the good Dutch farmers of Schoharie County. This was, indeed, the good life.

For Minik, too, life was like a dream. He shared the Wallace home as their son, unofficially adopted, and was treated just as was Willie, the Wallace's own boy. He had many friends in New York and in the mountains. His command of the English language was progressing nicely and he was able to make himself understood wherever he went. The scientists at the museum maintained a kindly interest in him, and if that interest was self-serving, he was not aware of it. He loved the summers in the high country of Lawyersville, where he could be wild and free, roaming the hills and valleys of the Wallace farm at will. Life, indeed, was idyllic.

But the idyll was not to last.

6

THE WALLACE AFFAIR

O N NOVEMBER 20, 1900, the *New York Times* carried a short item in the small print of its section on legal decisions made in the city court. Three separate judgments had been filed involving William Wallace. All resulted from charges filed by Booth Brothers and their business, the Hurricane Isle Granite Company. Two were filed jointly against William Wallace and a Mr. George A. Twele in the amounts of $1,122 and $958, the third against William Wallace alone in the amount of $395.

Someone noticed the item and left a copy of the newspaper, with the small article marked, on the desk of Professor Albert Bickmore at the museum. Bickmore clipped the section and took it immediately to Professor Henry Osborn, a museum official, who handed it to Morris Jesup. Jesup was concerned. He asked Bickmore to get together with Wallace and find out whether the reports were correct.

A few days later, Wallace visited Bickmore at his house, where the professor showed him the newspaper excerpt and asked if the report were true. The meeting was a cordial one between two colleagues. Wallace and Bickmore had worked together at the museum for over a dozen years. Wallace acknowledged that he had incurred this indebtedness because of his farm at Lawyersville.

The dairy had not been successful of late and he had borrowed money from Booth Brothers to continue the operation. He added that he had recently paid off $600 of the debt from his salary and would shortly pay off the balance by taking a loan on a life insurance policy. Soon, he assured Bickmore, he would be entirely free from his financial difficulties. Bickmore asked if he owed money to any other parties; Wallace replied that he did not.

Bickmore, however, was not entirely satisfied; he felt, as he put it, "somewhat anxious" about Wallace's financial affairs. Remembering that he had often seen Wallace and a contractor named Cockerell in conversation at the museum, Bickmore arranged a meeting with Cockerell to see if he knew any more details about the *Times* report. The two met on December 3. When Bickmore read to Cockerell the *Times* report of judgments against Wallace totaling $2,475, Cockerell replied that "he feared that all of Mr. Wallace's debts would amount to nearer $25,000." Bickmore was astonished. Cockerell added that he had heard that Wallace owed a great deal to the estate of a Mr. J. B. Smith, another contractor. When Bickmore asked if Wallace owed Cockerell personally any money, Cockerell was evasive. Any transaction that might have taken place between them, he said, had occurred some time ago and he now regarded it as settled.

A few days later, Cockerell called on Bickmore. He had more information to add to his previous report. Some months ago, he told Bickmore, George Chesley, one of the museum's carpentry contractors, had completed part of a contract and needed some money. Cockerell had given Wallace a check for $3,850 to pass on to Chesley. Some time later Chesley had to initiate legal action against Wallace. Cockerell then gave Chesley directly a second check in the amount of $3,850, but Wallace had never reimbursed him the amount of the original check. But Cockerell had more to tell; he said that "there was usually a long delay in the transmission of bills from Mr. Wallace's office to the Controller and that not long ago when the city owed him . . . some $30,000 which he needed at once, he had given Mr. Wallace $1,000 to promptly attend to forwarding his bills and they were promptly sent down to the Controller for payment." Cockerell added that he had learned that the amount Wallace owed the estate of J. B. Smith was about $8,000.

If Bickmore had been astonished earlier in the week, he was now speechless. On December 8 he composed a lengthy statement detailing what he had learned about the financial affairs of "our friend Mr. Wallace." Morris Jesup would certainly want to know all about this matter. It was one thing for Wallace to play fast and loose with his own money, but if he had been misappropriating the museum's funds for his own use and accepting kickbacks from contractors to process their bills quickly, then that was another matter entirely.

Jesup, in the meantime, had begun his own investigation and had already learned a little more about Wallace's financial affairs. On November 26, Mr. J. C. Cady, of the architectural firm Cady, Berg, and See, the museum's architects, had written Jesup a brief note, telling him that Wallace had been "engaged extensively in the milk business. A man by the name of Geo. A. Twele became engaged in it with him and at length got him into great trouble through his dishonesty."

Jesup asked Wallace for a complete report of his activities and his handling of museum accounts. When the report was presented, Jesup replied to him, "I have just seen your report. . . . Your statement is not satisfactory and does not cover the requests made in my letter. . . ." He added, "I am deeply grieved at what you have done."

On January 11, 1901, William Wallace resigned from his position at the American Museum of Natural History; his resignation was accepted without question.

His troubles were far from over, however. When George Chesley heard of Wallace's resignation from the museum, he became concerned. He had been engaged by the museum for several years, principally for building display cases. Between 1896 and 1901 Wallace had borrowed $9,965 from Chesley; Chesley claimed that Wallace had borrowed the money "on the pretext that it was to be used to carry on the business and work of the museum."

Wallace had paid back $6,995, Chesley said, but still owed $2,970 at the time of his resignation. Chesley sued for this amount. The court found against Wallace in a default judgment in the total amount of $3,168.79. In March Wallace applied to have the case reopened, denying that he had claimed the money was for the use of the museum and insisting that he had repaid it all. Chesley and he were "old friends," he claimed "and had been accustomed for years to exchange notes and checks. The money lent by Chesley . . . between 1896 and 1901 had been lent in this way. . . ."

The museum's lawyers were guarded in what they would reveal to the press about the Chesley claim, a lawyer stating only, "I can say nothing as to whether Mr. Wallace did or did not borrow money from contractors, but I can say that neither he nor any other employee of the museum had any right to borrow money from any contractor. The work upon the museum is city work and the city pays no bills without the approval of the museum authorities."

The museum, meanwhile, had launched its own full-scale investigation into Wallace's management of museum funds. Allegations were made that some of the bills presented by contractors for work done and material supplied were exorbitant and that a number of contracts had been awarded that were "never contemplated by the officers of the museum."

In addition to investigating contracts let by Wallace in New York for museum work, the museum also sent an investigator to Cobleskill and Lawyersville to look into Wallace's affairs there, to ascertain if museum funds had been used in the conduct of Wallace's business ventures. Wallace claimed that no museum money had been used in his personal enterprises, but the investigation did not bear this out. The carpenter, Chesley, had worked at Cobleskill for four months during the summer of 1900. The museum had paid him for three months but on investigation found that he had been doing museum work for only one month; the remaining three months had been spent in working for Wallace personally. Another museum employee had spent a month at Cobleskill and drawn museum wages for the month, but the investigation concluded that he "did not do a particle of work for the Museum throughout the entire month" and "spent all of the time working on the private property of Mr. Wallace." One admitted to spending six or seven days there, at the museum's expense, bringing in Wallace's hay.

But what had been the interest of the museum in having its employees spend time in Schoharie County at the Wallace farm at all? The answer is a bizarre one, and it is a further indication that Morris Jesup had put his faith in Wallace to perform far more than the normal duties one would expect of a superintendent of buildings.

On the Cold Spring Farm, in rural Lawyersville, there is a steep embankment behind the house where a spring flows year-round. On Wallace's suggestion the museum had established there a facility, variously referred to as the "macerating plant" or the "bone-bleaching plant." Animal specimens were brought there to be cleaned and scraped; the natural flow of spring water allowed the operation to be performed cheaply and cleanly. The museum had purchased a steam pump to be installed at the macerating plant. The whole operation was an official undertaking of the museum, done with the full knowledge of its officials.

It was in this bone-bleaching operation that the museum's employees were assumed to have been working. Instead, they had been spending much of their time working for Wallace's various interests. Museum material had also been misappropriated. A small engine had been taken from the museum for installation at the macerating plant but was found to have been set up instead at Wallace's creamery.

During the operation of the macerating plant in the summer of 1900, Wallace was desperate for money to continue his business enterprises. The people of Lawyersville remember that summer as the one in which he brought a dead elephant to the Cold Spring Farm to be cleaned so that its bones could be mounted as a skeleton for the museum. First a boa constrictor on the loose, then Eskimos — fur-clad and sick — dying in their midst, and now a dead elephant! This Wallace was indeed involved in some strange business, they thought. He claimed that the elephant was a baby that he had purchased in Philadelphia for the museum. Yet even this dead elephant came up in the museum's investigation of Wallace. The elephant, it turned out, was not from Philadelphia, as he had claimed, nor was it a baby. Museum officials interviewed a former employee who had gone to Lawyersville to attend to the beast. The elephant was an old one that had been owned by a circus and been killed in Madison Square Garden! Wallace had put in a healthy bill for the work involved in having it "macerated over time," but the museum found that it had been "turned in as regular work with other material then being cleaned for the Museum." The former employee's attitude to Wallace, the report noted, "would not indicate any obligations for favors."

The museum's cursory investigation indicated serious mismanagement of its financial affairs. Jesup went immediately to the president of the park board, the city comptroller, and the mayor to apprise them of the situation. He also advised the museum's executive committee; to it he described William Wallace, whom he had previously always praised as a dedicated and devoted employee, as "merely superintendent of the Museum building, his position being substantially that of a head janitor." The museum's accountants and lawyers were called in and an exhaustive investigation was conducted. In midsummer of 1901, when that investigation was complete, Morris Jesup wrote a long letter, marked "Private," jointly to Professors Henry Osborn, former Assistant to the President, and Hermon Bumpus, recently appointed Director of the Museum. In it, he described the fiasco as a crisis in the affairs of "a great institution and cause."

He outlined the system of checks and balances on expenditures of the museum's funds. There were three subdivisions of the museum's business: endowment, maintenance, and construction. There could be no fault found with the endowment account. Likewise, with the maintenance funds, investigation had shown that the account had been well maintained. Indeed, the city's park department and comptroller had often praised Jesup on the excellent system that was used. Jesup concluded that "the City has paid no bills for labor, and Maintenance, but what were, I believe correct."

The third subdivision of the museum's business was construction, which included repairs, alterations, and — curiously — the preparation of specimens; this involved the expenditure of money "appropriated by the City under power granted by the State." The museum kept no account of the expenditure of money for construction. Instead, such money was accounted for directly through the city's park board, and payments were made through the city comptroller's office. The architects involved in the museum's renovation and expansion maintained an office in the museum, and Jesup had believed that "everything that went into the building, construction, repairs, etcetera, was under their supervision and direction." Their accounts went directly to the city comptroller for payment. In this system for the payment of expenses identified as for construction, expenses that escaped the scrutiny of the museum's own financial officers, William Wallace had found the loophole that he had taken advantage of so well. Wallace had been using his work order-book slips, "given him for the express purpose of ordering for the Maintenance Account solely and alone," to order materials and commission work for the construction account, and the city had been blindly paying the bills. Indeed, as early as 1895 there had been rumors of scandal in the handling of the construction account when an electrical contractor charged that the city had been overbilled by at least $25,000 on one job alone.

Wallace had had the connivance of the chief architect, a Mr. Berg, in this scheme. Jesup had suspected Berg some time previously of mismanagement. At one point Jesup had interviewed Berg in the presence of Wallace and had "laid down the law" that neither Wallace nor anyone else connected with the museum had any authority to order anything for the construction account. The bylaws of the museum stated clearly that none of its officers or employees should ever create a debt against the institution in excess of $10,000 without the vote of the trustees or the executive committee. Money expended for construction, however, was not governed by this provision because it was paid directly by the city and was not, technically, a debt against the museum. Yet Wallace had been ordering goods and services at inflated values through his use of maintenance account order-book slips for payment by the city from the construction account. The contractors, who had been collecting these "fabulous prices," as Jesup called them, had been paying kickbacks to both Wallace and the architects. Jesup referred to them as "those who have resorted to dishonest means to get orders from a dishonest man, and with the connivance of a dishonest architect."

Jesup personally interviewed one of the contractors, who told him boldly that "he paid for the orders." After the contractor had paid his kickback in advance to Wallace, Wallace had prepared and backdated certain bills; in the meantime the architects had drawn up false specifications, charging a commission for their services. Wallace passed on the backdated bills to the architects, who presented the lot to Jesup for approval, asking him to certify the plans and the bill for payment by the city as quickly as possible because of the contractor's long wait for payment. Jesup, blindly trustful of his employees, now had to admit that he had been in the habit of automatically approving such claims for payment by the city. Certainly he had been guilty of carelessness, and as a result of that carelessness the city's money, though not the museum's, had been misused.

The museum's inquiries turned up some other incredible details of the actions of a desperate Wallace to keep himself financially solvent. One of the investigators met a policeman, an officer named Mahr, who had recently been at the Rulin-Fitzsimmons prizefight at Madison Square Gardens and had met Wallace there. Wallace told Mahr that he had had a private "tip" that Fitzsimmons was to win the fight and had bet all the money he had, two or three thousand dollars, on him. When Rulin won the fight, a distraught Wallace approached Mahr with a suggestion that the commissioner should claim some irregularity and force the bookmakers to turn the money over to the other side.

From Wallace himself there had been no overt indication to the museum's authorities that he was in any kind of financial difficulty. It is true that in June of 1899 he had written Jesup a long letter complaining that his salary was inadequate and outlining all the work he did for the museum on his own time, but this was viewed as a normal request from a hardworking man. The raise he requested was denied, however, and he had written again to Jesup, protesting, "I am called on in all cases of emergency to go about the city for the Museum and I stated to Mr. Strong that your ruling that my salary was to cover all my expenses made it hard on me."

Jesup had placed total trust in Wallace until earlier in that year when Professor Osborn, only recently appointed as Jesup's assistant, voiced suspicions he felt about Wallace. He said that he thought Wallace was "not what he should be" and showed Jesup a letter "from some woman about money not accounted for."

This curious letter, written in April of that year, concerned Thanksgiving turkeys. It was from William Wallace's sister, Anna Minckler, the wife of a farmer in Sullivan County. Six months earlier she and her husband had sold their entire stock of turkeys — 271 pounds — to Wallace to market, as they had done the previous year. But no money had been forthcoming and Wallace had ignored their letters. "We try to make an honest living," she had written in a letter addressed to Jesup, "and . . . it seems rather hard to get cheated out of the money which I really think he means to do." Jesup had asked Osborn to speak with Wallace and then apparently had forgotten the matter. But later John Winser, secretary of the museum, had gone to Jesup with some other matters concerning Wallace. Jesup recalled, "I investigated these, and could get no proof on which to act, but I did take some of my confidence from Mr. Wallace in many ways simply on suspicion."

Now he had to admit that Wallace had been dishonest. It hurt him, a man who thought much of his ability to accurately judge another's character, to have to write, "Wallace, a trusted servant, for twenty years, turns out a dishonest man. I did trust him with entire confidence, and no doubt was cast on his character until about the time Professor came as Assistant; he was always faithful, attentive, loyal to duty, working early and late, he seemed to have the Museum's interest completely at heart, always at his post constantly Winter and Summer, and almost the only one from whom at all times I could get information."

Jesup's first consideration, when faced with immutable proof that he had placed his faith in a dishonest man, was to ensure that the institution he had created was held blameless from any financial liability and from any public scandal. A large number of contractors had presented claims against the museum for work that had been ordered illegally by Wallace. Much of it had not been completed, some of it not even started, and the museum claimed it was not liable for the charges. Some of the contractors were threatening to make the whole affair public, a threat that Jesup suspected they would not carry through because of their complicity in the matter. The newspapers had hinted obliquely at scandal in mid-March, when Wallace had unexpectedly made his application in the Supreme Court to have the default judgment in favor of Chesley set aside, but that was as far as the matter had gone.

The claims against the museum totaled an enormous sum — originally $584,790.94. A few went back ten years! Many were from the years 1897 to 1900. Some, Jesup concluded, were probably fair, representing work that "was done by proper method, and innocent people were misled." But even some of these could not now be paid because, under the law, money that the city appropriated from the state for the support of the museum could not be used for retroactive expenses. Were the city to be sued, the city could make the museum a party to any claim, calling neglect on the museum's part. This was the type of scandal Jesup wanted no part of and he offered to settle these claims personally, provided that they were first examined carefully and their value fairly assessed. By the end of the whole affair, Jesup had personally paid about $71,000 to settle claims that he and his advisors figured were valid. A few contractors dropped their claims, and claims amounting to $322,246.69 were "examined by the municipal authorities, adjusted by a board of appraisers, assumed by the City, and paid by the Comptrollers."

Jesup was concerned, too, for his own personal reputation; the museum, after all, was an institution he had largely created. "The only mistake I have made," he wrote, "is in trusting and placing confidence in a man that I believed was honest, and trustworthy and loyal." But he concluded his anguished letter to Osborn and Bumpus on a frank note: "I am not strong in body or mind just now: this trouble has un-nerved me."

7

SCAM

THE KICKBACKS WALLACE received on the huge amounts of claims that turned up in the museum's investigation must have been substantial. One wonders: Is this how he had been paying for his farms and the rapid expansion of his business interests in Cobleskill? Or had he simply been subsidizing them with kickbacks from contractors after business turned sour in the late 1890s? The answers will probably never be known. But the museum's investigation revealed claims against the institution going back as far as 1890. It is probable that Wallace had been embezzling a little at a time for many years, perhaps even since 1892 when he purchased his first Lawyersville property. Then, desperate for money when he found himself overextended near the turn of the century, he had let the whole affair get out of hand.

Another question remains, though. Why did he think he could get away with it? Moreover, why did the American Museum of Natural History not press charges against Wallace if he had been guilty of a serious breach of trust and of a major misappropriation of museum funds?

The answer is that the American Museum of Natural History did not want a scandal. Morris Jesup always went to great lengths to protect the institution he had created from any public scandal, and it was for that reason that he offered a personal bailout to the museum with $71,000 of his own funds. Were charges to be pressed against Wallace, however, it is likely that a scandal of an even more odious nature would develop. For William Wallace knew of some other unsavory activities that had been going on at the American Museum of Natural History, and Jesup and his advisors knew of them too. They knew of them because they were directly involved in them.

Robert Peary was engaged in a lucrative business dealing in Arctic furs and narwhal and walrus tusks, which he was acquiring in a one-sided trade arrangement with his Eskimos. (Some years later, Joseph G. White, a crew member of the supply ship *Erik* in 1908, swore that "most of the time Peary and Matt Henson . . . were busy trading with Eskimos and making big profits on the fur and ivory, and giving the Eskimos very little . . . coffee, biscuits and candy.") Having appropriated the Cape York meteorites as his own, Peary also provided the Eskimos with metal, knives, and other trade items. The system was one-sided, but the Eskimos did not complain. To them the items Peary brought were a godsend, for there was no trading store in their area and the whalers — the upernaallit — on whom they had come to depend for many items they regarded as necessities were coming less frequently now that the population of bowhead whales had decreased so drastically. Peary benefited from these circumstances. He employed a sales agent in the United States, but the front for getting much of his goods into the country was the American Museum of Natural History and the Peary Arctic Club. Morris K. Jesup was the president of both organizations.

Peary had worked hard to establish a reputation as a benefactor of the museum and as a man of science himself. Much of that effort had been devoted to covering the circuitous route he had devised for getting material, perceived by the public as his gift, into the museum while at the same time, away from the eyes of a public that saw him as a generous donor, being paid handsomely for his gifts.

The evidence necessary to prove this charge against Peary and his cronies is scattered. That some evidence exists at all is remarkable, for Morris K. Jesup, his fellow members of the Peary Arctic Club, and many of his associates at the museum were men with strong legal and financial backgrounds, much averse to putting to paper anything remotely incriminating. They were men who delighted in seeing their achievements documented in print and praised in the newspapers, but their private deals were often oral. But not so with Robert Peary. The man's ego dictated that he would save much material, even of an incriminating nature, simply because his name was on it.

The circuitous trail of Peary's furs and ivory led from Greenland to New York, usually via St. John's, Newfoundland. The shipments were consigned as specimens for the American Museum of Natural History, where, as scientific objects, they would not be subject to import duty. Once they had arrived safely at the museum, often with some fanfare as a generous donation from Peary, much of the material was later released to the Peary Arctic Club, which would give it to Peary's patrons, in return for donations to the Peary cause through the club, or turn it over to Peary's sales agent. The sales agent succeeded in remaining anonymous, though he was a highly placed person, related by marriage to Rear Admiral Colby M. Chester, once commander-in-chief of the Atlantic Squadron and a man who would in 1909 be the leader of a supposedly unbiased three-man subcommittee appointed by the National Geographic Society to determine whether or not Peary had reached the North Pole.

In 1898, at the beginning of his four-year expedition in northern Greenland, Peary sent a note from Cape York to the Peary Arctic Club on the returning supply vessel: "I send the president of the Club . . . two bundles of narwhal horns, seventeen in all." Ten years later, he was still involved in this lucrative trade. In 1908 Peary confiscated Cook's collection of two hundred fox furs, an unspecified amount of walrus ivory, and "two or three bundles of narwhal horn," which he had appropriated from a cache at Neqe owned by Dr. Frederick Cook, by then his rival in polar exploration. Cook later valued the stolen material at approximately $10,000. The furs and ivory were sent to St. John's and on to New York on the *Erik*, the Peary supply vessel on which a number of paying sports hunters were also traveling.

Rudolph Francke, Cook's former assistant who took passage out of the Arctic on that vessel, wrote, "The sportsmen know who received part of the furs and horns and that they went on board the *Erik* to the United States, and it can be possible that the President of the United States will receive some of the horns." The following year, when the Cook-Peary controversy over the discovery of the North Pole broke, the *Brooklyn Daily Eagle* attempted to trace this shipment of fur and ivory but could find no official record of it. It could report only that the officers of the Peary Arctic Club had stated that "a consignment of goods was sent down by Peary, and that it passed through the Custom House. The duty was paid by a Custom House broker regularly employed for the customs business of the club, and the bill for duty and other expenses has been sent to the club."

That the *Eagle* was unable to discover any official trace of this shipment reaching the Peary Arctic Club is not surprising, however, for the club, in its statement, had totally falsified the routing of the shipment. The old ruse of using the American Museum of Natural History as an intermediary had been used again. In the fall of 1908, Hermon Bumpus had written from the museum to Herbert Bridgman, secretary of the Peary Arctic Club, "We shall be very glad to receive the material consigned to the Peary Arctic Club by Commander Peary, at Etah. It will be all right to have the entire consignment sent to the Museum, and after examination, we will forward to Mr. Crane [of the Peary Arctic Club] such material as he may desire."

Cook would later allege that Peary and his friends had made over a million dollars in trading over the course of Peary's Arctic career.

In 1907, Peary had written directly to the ever obliging Bumpus: "Among the material sent up from the 'Roosevelt' some time ago, were a number of walrus tusks of various sizes. . . . These tusks can be of no value as specimens for the Museum, and they will be of distinct value as souvenirs for those interested in the work . . . and I shall be indebted if you will kindly give instructions to have them gathered up and sent over here to the Grand Union Hotel."

Jesup, although he was president of both organizations, expressed some concern over the fact that material that he sometimes would have liked to keep for the museum ended up nonetheless at the Peary Arctic Club, presumably because of the instructions under which Peary had consigned it. In June of 1907, he directed his secretary to write to Bridgman, "He [Jesup] feels that in everything received by the Peary Arctic Club, the Museum of Natural History should have priority of choice."

With material that remained in the museum, Peary benefited not only from the sale of animal specimens, but human as well.

In 1896, he had busied himself picking up the skulls and bodies of Eskimos who had died in the previous winter's epidemic — people he knew by name — from their graves and taking their bodies to New York. The museum's records show that Peary did not donate these specimens to the museum; instead, the museum purchased them from him. Such was also the case over the years with other specimens, both human and artifactual.

Financially, the biggest prize of Peary's Arctic career would be the Cape York meteorites. If the reward for bringing them to the museum was to be substantial, he thought it was worth taking time to lay the groundwork properly. He waited almost too long, but his usual luck held and he collected handsomely for them.

Peary had acquired two of the meteorites in 1895 and the third, the most difficult, two years later. He had decided, as soon as he discovered them, that they belonged in the American Museum of Natural History. In 1898 he wrote, "From the dazzling May morning in 1894, when Aleqatsiaq . . . showed me how his grandfathers had removed fragments of the iron and fashioned their rude knives, I felt that these unique meteorites deserved more than to be simply ranged in order among so many other inert masses of iron in some great collection." He set the stage for their acquisition by taking the artist Albert Operti as his guest on his voyages of 1896 and 1897 to plan a museum setting worthy of the American Museum of Natural History, a setting that would have all the Cape York meteorites displayed with scenes from the lives of the Eskimos. He concluded his two-volume work on his first five northern expeditions with a sentence claiming that these Cape York meteorites were "peerless and unique among all the meteorites of the world."

Once collected, the meteorites were taken to New York and displayed in the American Museum of Natural History. The public perceived this as a generous gift from a man dedicated to the cause of Arctic science. What this fawning public did not know was that the meteorites were merely on long-term loan, pending a sale. That sale, though, was still some time off.

In 1907, Peary was still negotiating with Morris Jesup over the sale of the meteorites, which had reposed at the museum for a decade, Jesup's letter to Peary on the subject is instructive because it illustrates the manner in which the Peary trail to the museum was often covered: "I have offered the three meteorites now at The Museum to a friend, to be offered to another friend, the same for purchase at fifty thousand dollars, to be presented to the Museum." Failing that, he stated that "the Museum of Natural History shall be the resting place of these meteorites, and that [if] no outside person can be found to purchase them at the price you name; that your desire is that I have them at the price that may be agreed upon between us, for presentation to the Museum."

Jesup, indeed, was never easy when being solicited directly for money. He liked people to be in his debt and he liked to be thanked for his favors. He could be a petty man. In 1905 he had a dispute with Franz Boas, then curator of the museum, over the organization of the museum's ethnological exhibits, which he directed should be labeled and arranged clearly enough to "enable a person like myself of ordinary capacity to go through these collections and understand by the study of them what they were supposed to represent and get some idea from the collections, of the life, habits, and customs of the people." In concluding that Boas had failed entirely, he demanded to know the reason. He added a postscript to the letter: "P.S. You must remember the patron I have been to the Museum, the time, thought, and money I have given, and it is for that I ask that at least an attempt may be made to please me." Shortly after Boas left the institution.

He could be petty, but he could be manipulated as well, and Peary had early learned the art of using those who fancied having their names appended to remote headlands in the last unexplored reaches of the Arctic. He humored Jesup, and over the years Jesup, while never being a soft touch, kept Peary's interests to the fore while ensuring that the explorer remained properly grateful.

"A friend of a friend" had been offered a chance, for $50,000, to become a patron of the museum and the money, were it forthcoming, would go straight into Robert Peary's pockets.

To the dismay of both men, the friend of the friend did not take up Jesup's offer. And to the dismay of Robert Peary, Morris Jesup died in

January of 1908, before any deal had been concluded for the sale of the meteorites. With Jesup gone, the sale stood a good chance of never being completed. Shortly after Jesup's death, though, while Robert Peary was busy with the organization of what would be his final expedition, Mrs. Peary took up the challenge of selling the meteorites directly to the museum. In a letter to the museum's new president, Henry F. Osborn, she was uncharacteristically blunt in stressing her financial need: "I think it only fair to state that the meteorites are my property, and that the money obtained for them will not be expended in Arctic Exploration. It is all I have with which to educate my children in the event of anything happening to my husband. Of this Mr. Jesup was cognizant and he approved entirely my keeping the proceeds as a nest egg."

The Pearys had constantly stressed, both to Jesup and to their many other patrons, that they were poor folk, living on the kindness of their benefactors while Peary devoted all his energies toward his polar goal. A year later, however, a few weeks after Peary had claimed the conquest of the Pole, Mrs. Peary received a letter from her bank acknowledging the purchase for her account of $10,000 in U.S. Steel Bonds, a tidy investment for a woman claiming to live on the largesse of her friends. Later that year she sold the meteorites to the American Museum of Natural History for $50,000.

William Wallace knew the details of the early years of this long-time fraud in which the museum, Peary, and the Peary Arctic Club were involved. He had been involved in it too, in a peripheral way, though he had never benefited financially from it. But as the trusted servant of Jesup, performing duties far beyond what his official title at the museum called for, he had been responsible for ensuring that some of the routine matters of the scam worked. He had outfitted the *Kite* for its relief voyage of 1895. He had received the material consigned to the museum by Peary from the Arctic and had rerouted much of it to the Peary Arctic Club. And he knew where much of it had gone from there. All around him at the museum, Wallace had seen a misuse of museum funds and influence. He had watched as Peary continually coddled Jesup and established an unwarranted reputation as a generous benefactor of the museum. While Wallace's position at the museum did not warrant him having "a piece of the action" there, he had nonetheless developed a love of the grand gesture and a desire to share the lifestyle of those with whom he associated in New York. The farming business at Lawyersville and the operation of a boardinghouse there would be his vehicles to a life to match that of those he envied in the city. His philanthropy to the local institutions in Lawyersville paled beside the largesse of Jesup, the man he pathetically, perhaps subconsciously, tried to emulate. Yet it was a start. He could justify, to himself at least, the funds he was appropriating in New York for his own use in Lawyersville. It wasn't museum money, in any case, that he was using; rather, it was kickbacks from the dishonest and overeager contractors, kickbacks that he shared with the museum's equally dishonest architect. Because he was not appropriating the museum's money directly, he had been able to convince himself that he had not betrayed the trust that Morris Jesup placed in him. It was his own scam, less exotic perhaps than that of Robert Peary, which had the blessing and connivance of Jesup, but he hoped nevertheless that it would allow him to eventually leave the museum and live the good life of which he dreamed in the clearer air of Schoharie County.

Unlike Peary, Wallace had been caught. And when he was caught, Jesup, who had not suspected the activities of his trusted servant, was merciless. Wallace had been forced to resign in January of 1901. Four days after his resignation, Jesup had him back in his office for a brief interview; he had heard reports that Wallace had threatened to make certain disclosures that would bring scandal on the museum, and he wanted to ask him directly if that was his intent. Wallace denied it. A month later the museum's lawyer, who had met with Wallace's counsel, remarked in a memorandum to Jesup that "at present Wallace seems to have the idea that we need him."

Wallace always maintained his innocence and denied that he had ever received kickbacks from contractors. And despite the weight of the evidence against him, the same museum lawyer, reflecting on the whole affair nine years later, commented, "I shall have to say . . . that I am far from clear that Wallace was dishonest. The impression upon my mind was of a man of routine and narrow training and gifts finding himself in a place of large unrestrained power with the expenditure of large sums of money, and with the result, owing at least in material part to vanity, that his head was turned and that he enjoyed the idea of exercising this power without regular and precise communication with Mr. Jesup."

Wallace's threat that he might publicly disclose his knowledge of the transactions that had taken place — and continued to take place — between the museum, Peary, and the Peary Arctic Club was a serious one. He had something on the museum and Morris Jesup. But Jesup had something on Wallace as well. The threat did not succeed in letting Wallace keep his job. It did succeed, however, in keeping him out of jail.

8

"DESTINED TO A LIFE OF TEARS"

THE MUSEUM'S INVESTIGATIONS also included an accounting
of "bills paid by the museum in connection with the Greenland
Eskimos." It totaled $1,022, a pittance in comparison with its
other expenses. Of this amount, $418 had gone directly to Wallace for
board of the Eskimos and their nurse, and $202 had been spent on
autopsies, undertakers' expenses, and express fees on the bodies.
The balance, about $400, had been spent on clothing, medicine, and
the salary of the nurse. All expenses were incurred during the period
of February to May, 1898, although many were not paid until some
time later. Wallace appears not to have been reimbursed for some of
the money he put out — or at least claimed he had — on behalf of
the Eskimos, for in 1899 a clothing supplier sued him personally for
$190 for goods Wallace had procured "which we understood were for
the Esquimaus and employees." Once the investigation into Wallace's affairs had commenced, the museum would not agree to pay
any more outstanding bills for the Eskimos' care; a dentist from
Cobleskill sent in a claim for $22 for treatment of the Eskimos in April
and May of 1898, and before Wallace left the museum he personally
gave its secretary the amount in cash, which was forwarded by a museum check to the dentist.

Four of the Eskimos had died, and one had returned to Greenland. If they had not been the responsibility of the museum, in whose interest Peary had brought them to America, then whose financial responsibility had they been? Wallace had personally paid for at least some of their care. But more to the point, whose financial responsibility was the one Eskimo who remained in America? Peary was back in the north again, and had been since the summer of 1898; he could not be appealed to, nor would there have been any point in doing so, even were the man available. He had hardened himself against any connection with the distasteful episode he had caused. According to him, the Eskimos were the museum's responsibility. But from the date when Wallace left the museum, that institution assumed no further financial interest in the Eskimos who had been there or in Minik, the one who remained.

In 1898, Jesup had encouraged William Wallace to take Minik into his family. He agreed to pay Wallace whatever was needed for Minik's financial support, and in a letter written that summer he urged Wallace to "give Minik a name," suggesting that he legally adopt the Eskimo boy. This was an experiment in acculturation in which Jesup had wanted a part.

But Jesup now wanted no part of Wallace. The suggestion was put forward that Minik be taken from the care of the Wallaces and sent to a New England private school, but the Wallaces balked at the idea. The disclosure of the financial affairs of William Wallace had come as a horrible shock to Rhetta Wallace, who had no idea that her husband was involved in such things, but she stuck by him and the family remained together. As far as she was concerned, Minik was an integral part of that family and she would not hear of him being taken away. Morris Jesup, however, refused to pay another cent for the boy's support—not that he had spent much on him in the first place, for Wallace had been supporting the boy himself and, when times were good, had apparently not minded doing so. Only now, when he was strapped for funds, did he appeal to Jesup for money to support the boy. Wallace requested compensation for his previous care of Minik and the continuation of the support that Jesup had promised. He received neither.

In April of 1902, Wallace contacted Jesup by letter with a claim for the support of Minik. Jesup seems to have had a wonderfully selective memory; he was able to remember copious details of those events in which he appeared in a favorable light and nothing at all of events in which he was criticized. He wrote to his secretary, saying, "You probably know something of the relations between Mr. Wallace and this boy, which commenced about February 1900, or possibly before that time," and asked the secretary to inform him of "anything in your mind or memoranda that relates to this boy and Mr. Wallace's custody of him, and how it came about." The secretary, John Winser, replied to Jesup with a terribly garbled chronology of the events surrounding the bringing of the six Eskimos to America, the deaths of most of the party, the return of Uisaakassak to Greenland, and the assumption by the Wallaces of the care of the boy, Minik. He told Jesup that he had "never heard you speak in any way that would indicate that you would be responsible for his maintenance," although the record showed that on one occasion Jesup had sent Wallace $50 for the boy. Wallace had told another museum employee that he had never been able to get anything from Jesup for Minik. He was exaggerating the case, it seems, but any assistance he had received from Jesup had been trivial. Winser reminded Jesup, though, that there had been a great deal of scientific interest in the boy and Wallace was insisting that "you had requested him to care for the boy as Mrs. Jesup wished to see the results of the experiment as to what civilization could do for such a child."

Winser's letter was that of a sycophant to his master. Nonetheless, it was apparent that there was good ground for assuming that Wallace's claim for financial support for the boy was valid, even though the museum's files and memoranda failed to confirm it. There was, in fact, no reason why the museum's records should confirm the arrangement, for the museum was not a repository for living exhibits, especially so since the embarrassing events of 1897. The agreement had been a personal one between Wallace, an individual who happened to be employed by the museum, and Jesup, a man of many interests, the museum being but one.

But Jesup found in Winser's reply what he wanted to hear. He juggled Winser's information around in his mind and convinced himself that he bore no liability for the boy. His mean-spiritedness toward Wallace was justified as far as the museum's affairs were concerned.

But the boy was no longer the museum's affair. With the boy Wallace was doing only as he had been asked to do — he was caring for him and expecting support from Jesup for that care. Jesup would not hear of it. Like Peary, he washed his hands of the whole affair. Minik was on his own with the Wallaces.

Mercifully, word of Wallace's disgrace did not reach Schoharie County. The Wallace family continued to live in New York, but with Wallace no longer busy at the museum, they were able to spend longer periods of time in Lawyersville. Wallace was in deep financial trouble, but he managed to hold his shaky business empire together for a time yet. The Cobleskill newspapers became uncharacteristically silent on his affairs, for there was no longer money left over for the flamboyant philanthropic gestures Wallace had enjoyed making in years past. But if they were silent about the sudden lack of gifts to the local church, school, and historical society, they were silent too on the misfortune that Wallace had brought upon himself in New York City.

For Minik and Willie, the opportunity to spend more time in the mountains was a joy. They were free during the summers to wander the hills and pastures of the Wallace farm. The farm was quieter now, with no museum employees there, and the macerating plant no longer operated, but that only added to their sense of freedom and well-being. Some things didn't change. Willie continued to bring snakes from New York, and they continued to escape from their cages and startle the good people of Lawyersville. Minik continued to indulge his passion for soft drinks and was well known to everyone on the streets of nearby Cobleskill.

His health continued to be a cause of concern for the Wallaces, who loved him. In the spring of 1903, he was taken very ill and spent some time in Fordham Hospital, in New York, where it was feared for a while that he had contracted tuberculosis. This was a chilling thought for the Wallaces, who had seen four of Minik's kinsmen die of the lung ailment. But he recovered and was soon active again, playing baseball and football with the many friends he had made.

There was another member of the Wallace family whose health was also a problem. Rhetta Wallace was never robust, and early in 1904 she became severely ill. The children had not known that her health was so poor. One day Minik came home from school and ran into the house calling for "Aunt Rhetta." William Wallace met him, admonishing, "Hush, Minik — Aunt Rhetta is very sick." Minik's joy disappeared at that moment. Instinctively, this boy who had seen so much death and misery in his short life knew that Rhetta Wallace was soon to die. The old expression of sorrow that had so clouded his face after his father's untimely death returned, and he seldom smiled anymore. When Mrs. Wallace was confined to bed, he refused to go to school and rarely left her bedside. William Wallace observed that this "poor little fellow . . . destined to a life of tears" treated Rhetta Wallace very much like Qisuk had treated him during his own illness.

Rhetta Wallace was indeed dying. When the end was near she "beckoned her family to her and whispered her last message to each of them. Then she turned her head to Minik, and smiling feebly she said, 'Aunt Rhetta's last kiss is for her little Minik.' The next instant she was dead."

While this may smack of sappy journalistic overstatement, nonetheless the obituary of Rhetta Wallace — "a woman of kind heart and cheerful personality" — in the newspaper of her beloved Cobleskill states simply that "besides her bereaved husband, the deceased is survived by one son, William Jr., and an adopted son, Minik, the Esquimo, whom her sympathetic heart loved as her own."

Rhetta died in the Kilmer Sanitarium in Schoharie, New York, near Cobleskill, on March 29, 1904, of "heart failure and a complication of diseases." She was buried in the family plot that William Wallace had purchased in the Cobleskill Rural Cemetery.

It had been a trying three years for William Wallace. Without the museum's salary to depend on, he discovered that his business empire was an empire only in his imagination. It could support him no longer. The debts piled up and creditors demanded payment. Sometime before the death of his wife, Wallace had lost his farms, and with them many of his dreams. In the short space of little more than three years, then, he had lost his job, his business, and his wife. With the job had gone also a reputation for honesty and trust built up over a period of twenty years of apparent devotion to duty. With the business had gone his stature in the local communities of Cobleskill and Lawyersville, and many of his fondest hopes. And with his wife had gone his reasons for remaining connected with Schoharie County at all.

He tidied up the few loose ends of his affairs in the area shortly after his wife's death. His last remaining act there was to sign over his lots in the cemetery — where in better times he had announced that he would build a memorial to his father, who had been killed in the south in the Civil War — to Cyrus Karker, his wife's brother-in-law. For William Wallace, now almost fifty years of age and virtually destitute, the hopes and accomplishments of twenty years had been mercilessly swept away. All that remained were the shame and embarrassment and the responsibility of raising two young sons. There was nothing now to keep him in the picturesque and peaceful hamlet of Lawyersville, for he would only grow to hate it; it had brought him so much anguish and pain. He was a city man, and big-city ideas had brought about his downfall. It was time to start anew. Minik, now in his early teens, and Willie, seventeen, would roam the hills of Schoharie County no more.

With the loss of his other property, William Wallace had lost also his prestigious house in New York City. Leaving Cobleskill, he did not return immediately to New York. What was there to return to? He took Willie and Minik, whose own health was still not robust, and went to Connecticut for six months. In the fall, Wallace and Minik returned to New York and took up residence at a hotel, the Hunter Island Inn in Pelham Park on Long Island Sound.

For Minik this was almost as good as Lawyersville. He was an outdoors boy at heart, despite the frequent illnesses he suffered, and the two years they spent on Hunter's Island were a period in which his health improved remarkably. He played football and baseball, became a proficient swimmer and diver, finishing second in a swimming competition for boys eighteen years of age and under, and won two prizes in a skating competition. He became an excellent horseback rider as well as a crack pistol and rifle shot. He retained his passion for fishing and also took up caddying at the local golf course of

Pelham Park, where he "made a reputation for grit." He liked golf himself and won the trophy in the Caddies Golf Tournament there. He was cheerful and good-natured as usual, but he had developed also a strong streak of independence. When the manager of the golf course ordered the boys to get uniforms, Minik refused and warned the other caddies that he would "thrash the first one who yielded." One of the other caddies, older and bigger, took him up on this challenge and "promptly got a whipping."

The change in Wallace's fortunes meant a decided change in Minik's life as well. When he returned to New York with Wallace, there were just the two of them, for with the death of his mother, Willie had gone to live — temporarily, it was hoped — with relatives in upstate New York. Wallace could no longer afford to pay for Minik's education and had to abandon his plan to prepare the boy for northern work, perhaps as a missionary or a teacher. A newspaper reported that Minik, fourteen years old, had "given up his idea of becoming an explorer and has embarked in the real estate business," working with his foster father, who had found a job selling property for a firm in the Bronx. Eventually Wallace and the boy ended up living in a crowded flat in the city, an apartment that was "like a prison to the wild spirited Eskimo."

From time to time Wallace appealed to Professor Bumpus, director of the American Museum of Natural History, for assistance in the care of Minik. On occasion he swallowed his much wounded pride and contacted Jesup as well. In 1904, as Wallace's world was falling apart, the philanthropist had made another well-publicized personal gift of $200,000 to the museum. Surely, thought Wallace, he would provide a little support for the Eskimo boy. But Wallace's efforts were to no avail. Minik had become an unwitting victim in a clash of personalities. Jesup despised the man who had betrayed his trust, and Minik, who lived with Wallace, would in no way benefit from the largesse of Jesup or the institution he controlled.

Wallace, for all his faults, was devoted to Minik and desperate for the means to provide him the life he had promised. "We had planned much for him," he wrote, "but our dreams seemed doomed to failure. Our only object had been his welfare and his success."

If gentlemanly approaches to Jesup had been to no avail, perhaps a more dramatic approach was warranted.

9

GIVE ME MY FATHER'S BODY

BY 1907 NEW YORK HAD largely forgotten about Minik. He continued living with William Wallace, a quiet if poor life. But all that changed on a Sunday in early January, when the *World*, a New York paper, carried a sensational full-page article in its magazine section. Amid pictures of Minik and an artist's sketch of the pleading boy, his arms outstretched toward the museum, the headline blared, "Give Me My Father's Body." The subtitle read, "The Pathetic Story of Minik, the Esquimau Boy, Who is Growing Up in New York and . . . Who Now Wants Most the Bones of His Father from the Museum of Natural History."

The article shocked the *World's* readership. It read in part:

"Minik, the Esquimau boy, longed for but one Christmas gift, but that one he couldn't have. He asked back his father's bones that he might put them in a quiet grave somewhere, where they could rest in peace forever.

"And Minik wept just a little, stoic that he is, when he found that it couldn't be.

". . . Minik lives here in New York, despairing of ever seeing his people again. He is the sole survivor of six Esquimaux whom Lieut. Robert E. Peary brought here. . . . Four died, including Qisuk, Minik's father, and one went back again to the frozen north, glad to escape from the death and disease of New York.

"The scientists who were delighted to study leisurely the Esquimaux here in New York have long since forgotten these simple folk from the bleak Arctic. True, four of them died here, all of tuberculosis, but not until these wise men had learned everything they cared to know.

"And then, were not the corpses turned over to the doctors for very interesting dissections which added much to our knowledge on ethnological subjects? But, best of all, the perfect skeletons were turned over to the American Museum of Natural History, up in Manhattan Square, where savants who wish to study Esquimau anatomy may do so quite comfortable.

"And that is where the bones of Minik's father, nicely articulated, are now.

"There, too, is his precious kayak — his boat of skins — his gun and his knife and his Esquimau clothes, a most interesting exhibit. . . . Minik thinks that according to the American laws of inheritance these things ought to be his. He has heard at school, too, of fair play and the square deal, and he has in his mind an idea that he ought to be allowed to bury his father as the Christians do, in some quiet country churchyard.

"But an upstairs room — at the museum — is his father's last resting place. His coffin is a showcase, his shroud a piece of plate glass. No quiet of the graveyard is there; the noise of shuffling feet and the tap, tap of the hammers as the workmen fix up other skeletons, is ever present. And when the sunlight fades they turn on the electric lights so that Minik's father may not have even the pall of darkness to hide his naked bones.

"Lieut. Peary has long since ceased to concern himself with little Minik, the Esquimau boy, and others who have assisted the boy have not continued the contributions which at first aided him.

" '. . . I can never be happy till I can bury my father in a grave,' [said Minik]. 'It makes me cry every time I think of his poor bones up there in the museum in a glass case, where everybody can look at them. Just because I am a poor Esquimau boy, why can't I bury my father in a grave the way he would want to be buried?

"'Our poor people are brought up to love their parents and their ancestors. Even the poorest of them up in Greenland can bury their father and their mother in a grave covered with stones. But I can't. And when a man dies his gun and his knife and his kayak always go to his son. Why can't I have my father's things?'"

In February of 1898 when Minik's father, Qisuk, lay dying in Bellevue Hospital, that institution had written to Franz Boas at the museum, "I hardly believe Qisuk will survive the night. The body will I suppose belong to the Museum of Natural History or Mr. Peary and they can of course do anything they wish with it. . . ." Minik was eight years of age. Had he been older and able to read, he might possibly have seen reports in the newspaper two days later, after his father's death, under the heading "The Esquimau's Body" and the prophetic title "Trouble Over the Dead Eskimo." The American Museum of Natural History and Bellevue Hospital were fighting over Qisuk's remains. By that evening the situation had been resolved. The paper reported, "The disposition of the body was adjusted last night. It was agreed that students at Bellevue should make such use of it as possible in the dissecting-room, and that the skeleton should then be mounted and preserved in the Museum of Natural History."

But Minik could not read, nor could he understand more than a few words of English. But had he not been at a funeral for his father after his unfortunate death in Bellevue? Had he not stood in the garden of the American Museum of Natural History on a cold February evening with a group of scientists and museum employees and the only man the Eskimos could speak through, Matthew Henson, and seen his father buried there? How then could his father's skeleton be in a glass case in the museum? With his own eyes, wet and weary from the tears of his father's death, he had seen his father laid to his final rest there in that peaceful garden.

Even had Minik been older and able to read, it is unlikely he would have chanced to see a dry scientific report by the anthropologist, Alfred Kroeber, one of those who had studied the Eskimos while all six were yet alive. Kroeber had written a detailed paper on the Smith Sound Eskimos without ever leaving the comfort of New York!

He based it on the information he had gathered from the museum's six living specimens, under the direction of Boas and with Henson as interpreter. Kroeber continued to work with the Eskimos right through the time of their illnesses, their residence at Bellevue, and the deaths of Qisuk and Atangana. He had ample opportunity, therefore, to observe the Eskimos' manner of mourning their dead, and in the report he published in 1899, there is a startling admission implied in one small word in brackets in the section of the report dealing with the death of Qisuk. Kroeber reported that Nuktaq insisted, some time after Qisuk's death, that Minik "visit the [supposed] grave of his father, and instructed him how to act."

The "supposed" in brackets is Kroeber's. For, incredible as it may seem, the scientists at the American Museum of Natural History had staged a phony funeral for the benefit of little Minik!

Strange reasons are given for this fake funeral. Were they contrived after the fact? Or were they genuine and well-meant, another plan that touched on the life of an unsuspecting Eskimo boy and backfired? William Wallace was later to provide an explanation that somehow fails to ring true:

"It is an Eskimo custom for the nearest relatives of the dead to see that they are properly buried or pay the penalty with their own lives. So the four Eskimos told Minik they would kill him unless he went to the hospital, claimed the body of his father and saw it interred.

"Minik went to the hospital . . . but there the scientists had turned the body over to the museum.

"Then Minik went to the museum with a demand for the burial of the body.

"At first there seemed no way of appeasing the child son of the dead man. Finally this scheme was hit upon. A fake burial was authorized for the benefit of Minik."

This implausible reason for staging a fake burial stretches one's credibility. One can hardly imagine a grief-stricken Eskimo boy of eight or nine, speaking no English, petitioning a New York hospital or museum for the burial of his father's bones. Nor can one put much credibility in the belief that the other Eskimos would have killed Minik had he not succeeded in having his father buried. It is true that Kroeber reported that infanticide was common among the Polar Eskimos and that "when a woman dies who has a child that she is still carrying in her hood, it is buried with her," but Minik, at eight years of age, could hardly be considered an infant. Kroeber reports, too, that "when Qisuk died, leaving a son, Minik . . . without a mother, Nuktaq offered to kill him," but there is no indication that this offer was placed in the context of arranging for Qisuk's burial. This explanation, if it is the real one at all, is probably the result of a misunderstanding or misinterpretation. If so, it was a misunderstanding with tragic consequences.

From Peary, Kroeber had learned some of the characteristics of an authentic Polar Eskimo funeral, and he quoted the explorer in his report: "On the death of a man or woman, the body, fully dressed, is laid straight upon its back, on a skin or two, and some extra articles of clothing placed upon it. It is then covered with another skin, and the whole covered in with a low stone structure. A lamp with some blubber is placed close to the grave; and, if the deceased is a man, his sledge and kayak, with his weapons and implements, are placed close by, and his favorite dogs, harnessed and attached to the sledge, are strangled to accompany him. . . ."

From his own inquiries, Kroeber learned much the same and added: "When a person is dying, he is removed from the house, when possible. . . . The mode of burial is as follows: A hood is put on the corpse. It is then carried on the back to the burial-place of the settlement, which is not far away, the corpses being laid down next to each other with their heads away from the sea. The body is then surrounded by stones, and covered with flat slabs."

The scientists at the American Museum of Natural History decided to duplicate this primitive funeral as best they could on the museum grounds. Years later, William Wallace would recall the bizarre ceremony:

"That night some of us gathered on the museum grounds by order of the scientific staff, and got an old log about the length of a human corpse. This was wrapped in cloth, a mask attached to one end of it and all was in readiness.

"Dusk was the time chosen for the mock burial, as there was some fear of attracting too much attention from the street which might invite an investigation that would prove disastrous. Then, too, the boy would be less apt to discover the ruse. The funeral party knew the act must be accomplished quickly and quietly, so about the time the lights began to flare up Minik was taken out on the grounds, where the imitation body was placed on the ground and a mound of stones piled on top of it after the Eskimo fashion.

"While Minik stood sobbing by, the museum men lingered around watching the proceedings. The thing worked well. The boy never suspected, and when the grave was complete he made his mark on the north side of it. You see that is the Eskimo way. They think that the mark prevents the spirit of the dead coming back to haunt them, and the mark is always made between the home of the living and the resting place of the dead. At that time Minik was living at my place in High Bridge.

"When he got back to the other Eskimos he told them he had seen his father buried, and they were satisfied."

By the time William Wallace recounted this tale, he was certainly no friend of the American Museum of Natural History, and one might suspect that he fabricated or embroidered the tale to discredit his enemies at that institution. Such is not the case, however, for there is verification of the bizarre event from another source, none other than Franz Boas himself. In 1909 Boas, by then at the anthropology department of Columbia University, confirmed to a reporter that the burial had taken place much as William Wallace had described it. The purpose of the burial, Boas claimed, was "to appease the boy, and keep him from discovering that his father's body had been chopped up and the bones placed in the collection of the institution." Not only did Boas confirm the story of the fake burial, though, he also defended it. He said that he saw "nothing particularly deserving severe criticism" in the act. "The other Eskimos who were still alive were not very well, and then there was Minik, and of course it was only reasonable to spare them any shock or uneasiness. The burial accomplished that purpose I suppose."

The reporter questioned the right of the museum to claim the body of a man whose relatives were still alive, but Boas responded, "Oh, that was perfectly legitimate. There was no one to bury the body, and the museum had as good a right to it as any other institution authorized to claim bodies." But, protested the reporter, did not that body belong rightfully to Minik, the son of the deceased? "Well," was Boas's reply, "Minik was just a little boy, and he did not ask for the body. If he had, he might have got it."

The same reporter questioned Dr. Huntington of the College of Physicians and Surgeons, who said that the brain of Qisuk was in preserving fluid at the college and that, following his death at Bellevue Hospital, his body had been shipped to the school, where an autopsy was performed in accordance with the agreement reached with the museum.

What was William Wallace's involvement in this sordid affair? After the story broke, there was an attempt by the museum staff to implicate Wallace as being one of the perpetrators of the whole event. Penciled on the top of a museum memorandum from 1907 is the notation, "Wallace made effort to get skeleton for museum and for burial." But the museum was hampered in its efforts to cover its own tracks and to lay the blame on Wallace by the facts that the events had occurred a decade earlier and two of the key players in the story, Wallace and Boas, had left the institution in the interim. Further, there had been enmity and petty jealousies between Boas and the museum's new director prior to Boas's departure, and Boas lost no opportunity to imply the incompetence of the new man.

It was only later that Wallace was to develop his intense love for Minik, and in 1898 he may not have taken very much interest in the strange affair in which he found himself involved. His name turns up often in the fiasco over the bodies, and although it is apparent that his involvement was a dispassionate one, it is equally apparent that he was merely doing the bidding of his masters at the museum. He was, on paper at least, superintendent of buildings, but memos under his signature make it clear that he was called on by his superiors to be their go-between on many matters that had nothing to do with the buildings. Thus, when the dispute arose between the American Museum of Natural History and Bellevue's College of Physicians and Surgeons over the disposition of Qisuk's body, the newspapers reported that "Superintendent Wallace contends that Lieutenant Peary left the Esquimaux in his care and that he has a right to claim the body," and "Superintendent Wallace . . . in whose care the Esquimaus have been, wishes to dissect the body and have the skeleton mounted as a study."

Later, when Nuktaq died at Cobleskill, Wallace reported by memo to Jesup that "Dr. Boas requested me to have the body sent to New York. . . . I followed Dr. Boas [*sic*] request in regard to the matter of the final disposition of the body."

Wallace was involved too in the preparation of the Eskimos' bodies for the museum. The operation took place in what was known as the "bone-house" on the Wallace farm in Lawyersville. In 1909, looking back on the events, Wallace said, "We were only acting under instructions from the museum authorities. It had all been arranged that the bones should be prepared for exhibition and they had to be cleaned."

Nuktaq was troubled by not being able to go to see the grave of Atangana on the tenth day after her death. It is fortunate for the museum's scientists that he was too sick to leave the little cottage at Highbridge, for the scientists had not arranged a mock burial for the dead lady, nor had they heeded any of the woman's other last requests. Immediately after her death, Atangana's body was spirited away to the College of Physicians and Surgeons, where her brain was removed for study and an autopsy performed. From there, she ultimately made her way, as had Qisuk, to the American Museum of Natural History.

Atangana, Nuktaq, and Aviaq all followed Qisuk through the Wallace "bone-house" and the College of Physicians and Surgeons to the Osteological Department of the American Museum of Natural History. The child, Aviaq, was the last to die. There were no more fake funerals to impress or appease any other members of the party, nor did the press take any interest in the fate of these bodies.

10

IN THE INTEREST OF SCIENCE

D R. ALES HRDLICKA WAS ONE of the scientists who studied Minik and the five other Polar Eskimos in New York. Hrdlicka was born in Bohemia but emigrated to the United States as a young teacher. After earning a degree in medicine in New York, he interned at the State Homeopathic Hospital for the Insane, where he compiled data on the body forms of abnormal individuals. He became interested in the American Indian and from that was drawn gradually from medicine to the young science of anthropology.

Hrdlicka's main interest in his new discipline became the collecting of skeletons and skeletal material, and he went about it with zeal, building up one of the world's largest skeletal collections for the Smithsonian Institution in Washington. Hrdlicka — or Hard Liquor, as he became known to his friends — scoured the world seeking to add to the geographical and racial coverage of that collection.

He was one of the first to examine the Polar Eskimos after their arrival in New York and he saw them often during their illnesses. Yet his interest in them cannot have been the same as that of Boas or Kroeber, folklorists and ethnologists, for to a physical anthropologist obsessed with the collecting of skeletons, one brief but final breath separates a human curiosity from a scientific specimen. In the spring of 1898 Hrdlicka found the opportunity he relished with the deaths, in a space of two months, of four of the Eskimos. Of them, he wrote, "These six individuals the writer was able to examine during life and, in one instance, immediately after death; he further secured and described the brain of one of the men and made a preliminary report on the others. . . . Finally, he was able to examine the skeletal remains of the four who died, as well as several additional skulls and skeletons collected in . . . the Smith Sound region by Mr. Peary."

Perhaps the final indignity for Qisuk was the publication of Hrdlicka's article, "An Eskimo Brain," in 1901. The identity of specimens usually remains unknown, but this one was denied the dignity of anonymity; the article began, "The brain in question is that of Qisuk. . . ." The article contains two photographs, which Minik mercifully never saw; they were labeled "Qisuk's Cerebrum (Dorsal Aspect)" and "Qisuk's Cerebrum (Basal Aspect)."

In the late nineteenth century, anthropology, as a science, was still in its infancy. It had not completely shaken off its early preoccupation with phrenology, an aberrant pseudoscience which held that the conformation of the skull was indicative of mental faculties and character. Phrenologists had busied themselves acquiring skulls from a broad spectrum of humanity. Theirs was a time when heredity, rather than society, was thought to account for most human behavior, and so the skulls of murderers and other social misfits were compared with those of savants in the hope that the differences that were assumed to exist would reveal information to account for the social behavior of the original wearers of those heads. The jingoism of nations also permeated this pseudoscience, and so the skulls of people of different races and nationalities were compared and judgments pronounced on which race or which national group was the more advanced.

Physical anthropology at the time of Hrdlicka's early work had advanced little past phrenology. He and his colleagues collected the skulls and skeletons of people from all over the world. The specimens they secured were cataloged, studied, measured, described, and compared. Indeed, the physical anthropologist of the day measured unceasingly in the vain hope that mere quantifying would lead to an understanding of the nature of humans.

It is easy, with the hindsight of nearly a century, to look back on the work of these early anthropologists and disparage both their activities and their attitudes. Yet Hrdlicka, like his colleagues, was not a "gaunt and dedicated decapitator," drooling with scalpel and calipers in hand at the prospect of another severed cranium on his dissecting table. If his passion for collecting skeletons bordered on obsession, it is because he was a man dedicated to his work, one who intended to leave his discipline a richer field than he had found it.

It is simple to characterize these men as cold, unfeeling, dispassionate scientists who cared little for the human consequences of their work. It is easy to do — too easy — for it is wrong. This stereotype of the early anthropologist is not borne out by fact. Most of these men did care. It was their interest in human beings that had drawn them to the science of anthropology in the first place. They and their colleagues in cultural anthropology — men such as Boas and Kroeber — were proud of their liberalism and open-mindedness. They would have been hurt deeply had anyone suggested that they were, at heart, racists.

They were, nevertheless, products of their times, and the intellectual and cultural traditions from which they had emerged were permeated throughout with an insidious bigotry. The endemic prejudices of the late nineteenth century were racist and sexist. They determined that, to the anthropologist no less than to the man on the street, men were superior to women, and whites were superior to blacks. The Eskimos had inspired intense scientific and popular interest because they had been able to eke out a livelihood, and at the same time develop a rich culture, in the world's most hostile environment. They were remarkable, but they were not white, and that fact alone marked them too as inferior.

An eminent historian of science, in a compassionate evaluation of the work of such men, has suggested that, from our vantage point, "it is a little unfair . . . to criticize a person for not sharing the enlightenment of a later epoch, but it is also profoundly saddening that such prejudices were so extremely pervasive."

93

The bones and brains that gather dust on the shelves of the back rooms of the world's great museums were acquired in the spirit and hope of human enlightenment and betterment. Undoubtedly a great deal of valuable knowledge has been derived from their study. The scientists did not murder to secure specimens; the original owners of these human parts were usually unaware that their naked bodies would be dissected by strangers in the name of science, and in most cases no harm was done.

In most cases. But with the six Eskimos from Smith Sound, science went too far. It was one thing to collect human parts in the far-off corners of the world. It was quite another to bring living specimens, human exhibits, from the far-off corners of the world to entertain the public and allow the scientists of America to do their work in comfort. Was this fieldwork when the field was brought to the scientist? Science had briefly become a sideshow in 1893 when people from all over the globe were exhibited at the World's Columbian Exposition in Chicago. Boas had been chief assistant in anthropology at that world's fair, at which Eskimos from Labrador had been exhibited. Had he not learned anything from the deaths of many of that fair's "exhibits," including some of its Eskimos, whose bodies had become part of the permanent collection of the museum established there? Yet he had encouraged Peary to bring more of these naive and unsuspecting people to America in the interests of his science.

Had it been worth it? Boas's only published statement on the scientific results of the study of the six Polar Eskimos is remarkably brief: "Many things heretofore unknown have been learned regarding their language, their traditions and their personal characteristics. Casts of their heads have been made for the museum."

Bones, brains, anthropological notes, and plaster casts. Peary, as usual, had profited from bringing these people to the United States. But Boas, Kroeber, and Hrdlicka had profited too, for their young careers each received a boost with the publication of their researches on the Eskimos. Four Eskimos paid with their lives for this meager addition to scientific knowledge. Moreover, it had necessitated a bizarre and misguided cover-up, a phony funeral on the lawn of the American Museum of Natural History, to impress a seven-year-old

Eskimo boy. Men of science were both involved in and implicated in this macabre event.

In 1898, no harm had been done. But profound harm would yet be done almost a decade later when the cover-up was revealed and young Minik experienced the trauma of learning the truth of his father's funeral.

In 1899, the museum's staff was still busy acquiring Eskimo bodies. An eleven-year-old Alaskan girl, one of the twins brought to New York by Captain Miner Bruce, a fur trader, had died of consumption in Mount Vernon Hospital. The *New York Tribune* reported that the body would be sent to Columbia University, where it would be preserved and turned over to the Museum of Natural History "as a specimen of the race," there being no relatives to claim it. A letter to the editor questioned the legitimacy of such an act:

"It would be interesting to know by what authority Columbia College assumes to take any such course.

"While it is true that our law permits a person to direct the manner in which his body shall be disposed of after death, there is no intimation that this poor Esquimau child ever gave any such direction.

"'Except in the cases in which a right to dissect is expressly conferred by law,' says section 306 of the Penal Code, 'every dead body of a human being, lying within this State, must be decently buried within a reasonable time after death.' And the same statute imposes the requirement of burial in respect to the remains of a human body after dissection.

"There can be no authority to turn the body of this Esquimau girl into a mummy and place it on exhibition in the Museum of Natural History, unless it be derived from the girl herself during her lifetime. . . ."

Columbia University responded to this charge with a statement issued by Dr. Bern B. Gallaudet: "We think the body of the girl will be an interesting study — an Esquimau, you know — and we would like to examine the internal organs to see how they compare with those of persons reared under other conditions and in other climates. Just what will be done with the body I don't know, but we . . . can do what we please with it."

Boas, then holding down the double role of lecturer in physical anthropology at Columbia and curator of the American Museum of Natural History, arranged the transfer of the body from Mount Vernon. He had reported succinctly to Jesup in a memo a week earlier, "Little Eskimo girl died in Mt. Vernon. I have secured skeleton. $15." Now he commented, "Before Captain Bruce went away he told me, the children being sick at the time, that if either died the college might have the body for scientific purposes." He concluded that "the body will probably be preserved after it has been examined," adding the phrase, a favorite of his friend Peary, "in the interest of science." To Dr. Gallaudet he sent a terse memo: "I am sorry to see that the papers are making so much fuss. Skeleton to be transferred to Mus."

A number of years passed between the death and phony burial of Qisuk and Minik's discovery that the bones of his father were on display in the American Museum of Natural History. During those years, as Minik grew up a loved member of the Wallace family, William Wallace kept the terrible secret of Qisuk's fate from the boy. He regretted his involvement in the whole disgusting affair and he dreaded to think what opinion his foster son would form of him should he chance to become aware of the truth. Then, finally, Minik did learn the truth. Wallace tells the story:

"The newspapers had found out that the bones of his father were in the museum, and though they never knew of the fake burial or the bone cleaning in Cobleskill, they printed stories about the skeletons. At school Minik was thrown in contact with other children, and naturally they talked to him about the Eskimos. Eventually he learned that he had not witnessed the burial of his father's remains, but he kept it to himself for a long time. We noticed that there was a change coming over him, and then one day we learned its cause.

"He was coming home from school with my son Willie one snowy afternoon, when he suddenly began to cry. 'My father is not in his grave,' he said; 'his bones are in the museum.'

"We questioned him and found out how he had learned the truth. But after that he was never the same boy. He became morbid and restless. Often we would find him sitting crying, and sometimes he would not speak for days.

"We did our best to cheer him up, but it was no use. His heart was broken. He had lost faith in the new people he had come among."

Minik's own version of his discovery of the fate of his father is more dramatic, if less truthful: "Unexpectedly one day I came face to face with it. I felt as though I must die then and there. I threw myself at the bottom of the glass case and prayed and wept. I went straight to the director and implored him to let me bury my father. He would not. I swore I never would rest until I had given my father burial."

11

"THE VERY PITIFUL CASE OF MINIK"

FOUR DAYS AFTER THE appearance of the *World's* article, William Wallace wrote to Morris Jesup about financial assistance for Minik. On two occasions the previous summer, he pointed out, he had met with Professor Bumpus at the museum to talk about the original agreement between himself and Jesup, but he had gotten no satisfaction — Bumpus had claimed that the "Esquimaux matter was fully settled." As far as Bumpus was concerned, no agreement had ever been made. The Eskimos had been brought to New York as wards of the United States government, Bumpus insisted, and as for Minik, Wallace had simply picked him up from the street as a vagrant — a startling admission, coming from a museum official. Wallace argued that Jesup's letters to him from years past, and payments, although totaling only a meager $200, did not bear out this contention. Rather, he felt, Professor Bumpus was "simply carrying out your unkindly feelings which I can not accept." He told Jesup that his petty actions were unbefitting "a gentleman of your standing" and asked two concessions: the return to Minik of his father's personal belongings and of his body for burial, and financial assistance for Minik's education, for "it requires more means than I have to provide for his education and maintenance."

The letter contained also just the slightest hint of blackmail: ". . . you too well know, Mr. Jesup, that any part of the collections that were received by the United States Government from the steam ship *Kite*, which I fitted out under your direction, was paid for indirectly to Mr. Peary."

The *World's* article sent the staff of the American Museum of Natural History shuffling through ten-year-old files to ascertain the status of Minik. They had hardly begun the task when another article appeared, this time in the prestigious *Washington Post*.

A New Yorker by the name of Roswell Chester Beecroft had called at the White House on January 11 and had had an audience with President Roosevelt's secretary, William Loeb Jr., in the hope of enlisting the president's aid in providing a proper education for Minik. Loeb heard his guest out and, according to the article, had promised to bring the matter to the president's attention. He had also asked Beecroft to prepare a complete statement on the subject. Beecroft had been quick to oblige; he prepared a lengthy statement on the subject.

That statement began, "I beg to call your attention to the very pitiful case of Minik. . . ." Whereas the *World's* article had discussed simply Minik's interest in getting his father's body from the museum, Beecroft's statement referred to that only in passing. The letter was, instead, a well-reasoned plea for financial support for Minik and for his education. He described Minik as "a National guest and a National prisoner" and claimed that "his condition is rapidly becoming a National disgrace." He characterized the boy as "the most abused and helpless individual within its [America's] jurisdiction."

Beecroft was equal to the task of trying to get a fair shake for Minik and letting the right people know of the boy's plight. He was a professional publicist associated with the Hotel Astor and a motion picture company, but he stressed that his "only interest in Minik is a humane one." He had met Minik three years earlier, before the death of Rhetta Wallace, and since then had maintained a kindly interest in him — one report referred to it as a "particular and peculiar interest." He had become very concerned about the deterioration in the boy's condition since the death of Rhetta Wallace.

William Wallace was, he knew, devoted to the boy — too devoted perhaps, for he had struggled alone to ensure that the boy was given a good education when those others who had once been interested in Minik had defaulted on their obligations. By early 1907, though, Wallace had lost almost all he had once struggled for. He was very poor and worked as a foreman over a gang of laborers making improvements to the New York subway. Wallace had had to give up the house in Highbridge and Minik lived with him in a small city flat. He was "meagerly clad" and, despite Wallace's heartfelt efforts, "improperly cared for." His education had been abandoned.

Beecroft was concerned especially over the physical environment the boy was growing up in. He was in his mid-teens, and his character was "still forming, and, indeed, is probably now in its most critical state." Pointing out that one of the aims of the scientists who had first expressed an interest in him was to see the effects of civilization on an Eskimo, Beecroft stated that "if he is allowed to grope about in the unwholesome atmosphere of the slums, with cigarette-smoking boys and gambling, swearing men as his daily examples, it can scarcely be hoped that he will ultimately turn out a polished gentleman."

Beecroft outlined the circumstances under which Minik and five of his countrymen had been brought to New York by Peary. The government of the United States bore no blame for Minik's current desperate situation, Beecroft suggested, only by virtue of the fact that "the matter has not been brought before the proper authorities." The matter was, however, ultimately a government responsibility and by sending this letter to the president's office, and having a copy published at the same time, he hoped to ensure that the government would assume the responsibility. The government was responsible, he claimed, because Minik had been brought to America by "an officer of the United States." While it was true that Peary had washed his hands of the matter immediately after he turned the Eskimos over to the museum and had expressed no further interest in them, Beecroft reminded the president that the Polar Eskimos, whom he characterized as "gentle, kind and hospitable" had "received Peary warmly, welcomed his people, provided shelter, food and the dogs and guides that made possible the explorer's sledge dash toward the pole." "It would be reasonable to expect," he went on, "that Mr. Peary, if only out of a sense of gratitude for their valuable service, would make it his duty to see that [Minik] . . . was properly provided for. . . ." Peary showed no indication of living up to that responsibility and, if he would not, the government should.

Beecroft alluded to the Wallace affair at the American Museum of Natural History. He claimed that the museum was neglecting Minik because of the bad relations that had developed between William Wallace and the museum, that Minik was suffering because of his continued association with William Wallace. But Minik had not defrauded the museum. And the financial scandal that had so embarrassed the museum's officers six years earlier was, in any case, not Beecroft's concern; his concern was for the welfare of Minik. He wrote, "What private griefs these gentlemen may have had, or what quarrels or disagreements may have come up, between any of them and the man who adopted and cared for Minik, I do not know; but I am certain that they furnish no excuse for the shameful neglect of the boy. . . ." Were these men not quite human, he wondered? ". . . might not the directors of that institution show some slight concern in the welfare of the . . . survivor? . . . These men should have been too big in spirit to allow their own quarrels to put the innocent Esquimo into a state which makes him look upon civilization as a curse."

As an educated and literate young man, Minik had told Beecroft that he admired President Roosevelt, whose "square deal" was the political gimmick of the decade. He had asked Beecroft if he did not think the president would give even an Eskimo a "square deal" if he knew how unfairly that Eskimo had been treated in the United States. Beecroft had assured Minik that the president would indeed see that he was treated fairly and it was this suggestion of Minik's that inspired Beecroft to bring the matter to the White House.

Beecroft closed his long statement on an optimistic note, outlining a plan he hoped would be implemented for Minik's education and expressing confidence that "right shall at last be done."

Two days after the appearance of the article in the *Washington Post* and the composition of Beecroft's outline of the case, a curious event occurred. William Wallace wrote personally to William Loeb, secretary to President Roosevelt. His letter was brief and negated much of what Beecroft had passionately requested. Wallace claimed that he had never asked Beecroft to request the president's assistance and, he said, "I would thank you, if you will kindly not bring the matter before President Roosevelt. Mr. Morris K. Jesup of this City is interested with me in this little lad from the far North, and we hope some day, he may be of great service among his people at Smith's Sound."

To Loeb's office this must have been a confusing turn of events. But in any case, it was not something Loeb was going to blindly lay on Roosevelt's desk without first investigating the matter himself. To an experienced political aide, this was more than the social matter it appeared on the surface; this was also a political matter. And were it not handled properly it could well become a political liability. Morris Jesup was a man of influence, and the institution he had built in New York was a prestigious one. He had impeccable political connections in that city and he could influence votes. He was a man to be treated carefully and not to be offended.

Peary, too, was not to be treated lightly. He had just returned, on Christmas Eve, from his latest Greenland expedition, the first with the clear and single-minded purpose of reaching the North Pole. Jesup had provided a considerable amount of funding for that voyage, on the condition that Peary raise the rest. To do this, Peary had set out to solicit money from the wealthy through a dignified pamphlet outlining the importance of conquering the North Pole; Roosevelt had contributed a statement to that pamphlet: "No better — and I may add, no more characteristically American — work could be done than Peary's efforts to go to the Pole." The ship Peary used on that voyage was one he had designed himself, a ship custommade for ice work. Launched in March 1905, she had been christened the *Roosevelt,* with the president's consent, a sign of Peary's care in ensuring that people in high places would continue to look kindly on his expensive polar obsession. Peary's attempt to reach the North Pole had failed, but he had achieved a new "Farthest North" and was already making plans for his next voyage.

Yes, this was more than a social matter. Loeb knew he had better look beneath the surface of this affair. Loeb contacted the American Museum of Natural History for comment. The matter was handled by Benjamin Strong, the private secretary to Morris Jesup, who handled all of Jesup's affairs, both within and without the museum. The article was unfortunate, Strong thought, but it had already been published and there was little he could do about that now. But the letter from Wallace to Loeb was perplexing. The longer he studied it, the more he thought it out of character for Wallace to write such a letter. Perhaps, he thought, Wallace had not written it at all. Sometime after the death of Rhetta Wallace in 1904, William Wallace had remarried; the previous summer the new Mrs. Wallace had written Bumpus and that letter was on file. Strong compared it with Wallace's letter to Loeb, for both letters were handwritten. The handwriting was identical. Moreover, Wallace's signature on the letter to Loeb did not match his signature on any other letters on file, but it was in the same hand as the text of Mrs. Wallace's earlier letter.

So Mrs. Wallace had written the letter to Secretary Loeb asking him not to bring the Minik matter before the president. But why? One can only guess at the reason. Perhaps she thought that her husband and Chester Beecroft were going just a little too far in championing Minik's cause. She may have thought that William Wallace should wait a little longer in the hope of possible results from his January 10 letter. Perhaps she resented Beecroft's involvement altogether and the public attention that was being thrust upon the family as a result of the sudden revival of popular interest in Minik. Or perhaps she resented Minik himself, for it is clear that she did not show the same warm affection for him that Rhetta Wallace had always displayed. Her reasons are not known. But when Benjamin Strong discovered that she had written the letter purporting to have been written by Wallace, he advised both Bumpus and Loeb.

In Washington, apparently, the letter went no further, although Beecroft would later claim that he had met the president personally and that the president had called the museum's actions an outrage and the Minik affair a national disgrace. Beecroft would claim that "afterward we learned that Capt. Peary . . . had influenced Mr. Roosevelt to pay no attention to Minik."

When Bumpus received from Strong a copy of the Wallace disclaimer and the information that it was not in Wallace's hand, he contacted Franz Boas on January 19 in an effort to learn for himself the circumstances under which the Eskimos had been brought south. This cannot have been a very pleasant task for Bumpus, for he and Boas had never gotten along well. When Boas had been curator of the museum's Department of Anthropology, Boas and Bumpus had often complained, through letters petty in the extreme, about the interference of each in the other's work, and Jesup had been expected to act as referee in these disputes. He had usually sided with Bumpus. For that matter, relations between Boas and Jesup had often been strained. By midsummer of 1906 Boas had left the museum and gone to Columbia University. He apparently gave Bumpus no information at all.

Bumpus also met Peary in the Grand Union Hotel to discuss the matter. Peary was then still basking in the limelight of the publicity surrounding his recent return; he could not be bothered with the Eskimo matter, for he had not devoted more than a passing thought to it since 1898, when he had deposited Uisaakassak safely home on the shores of Smith's Sound. Moreover, he was now engaged in a flurry of activity planning his next expedition to the north, which he hoped, vainly as it turned out, would get away that very summer. He did offer the implausible information that he had brought the Eskimos to New York at their own "urgent request" and that Minik had been urged to return in 1898 but "absolutely declined, presumably on Wallace's or Mrs. Wallace's instructions."

Bumpus was by now more confused than ever. He was at a decided disadvantage in handling any of this matter because he had not been at the museum when the Eskimos were brought there and had only just joined the museum staff when Wallace was fired in 1901.

He went to see Mr. Delafield, the museum's legal counsel, who advised him "to do nothing whatever about the case except to keep all papers on file."

In the midst of this perplexing situation, William Wallace wrote Jesup another letter, this one in his own hand. In it he told Jesup that his friends were "insisting that I lay the matter before the President," but first he felt he should receive some reply from Jesup to his earlier letters. Once again he called Jesup's attention to his letter of August 1898, in which he had asked Wallace to "give Minik a name," and later correspondence between the two in 1902. Benjamin Strong received this letter at Jesup's business office. It is clear that he had been keeping much of the Minik matter from Jesup and it is doubtful if the aging Jesup ever saw any of the 1907 correspondence on the subject. This was partly a museum matter, though, and he contacted Bumpus immediately, suggesting that "the President [Jesup] should be informed of the exact state of the case and that it should be done orally and promptly." Bumpus suggested that Strong inform Delafield of the recent letter, but advised him that Delafield had already disapproved of replying to any letters of Wallace. He did not comment on the advisability of informing Jesup. Jesup at this time was old and in ill health. Perhaps for this reason his staff kept unpleasant matters such as this from him. But if Jesup was not informed about the exact state of affairs in early 1907, he nonetheless knew that there was one Eskimo remaining in the United States who had been brought there at the request, official or otherwise, of his institution. Five years earlier he had corresponded with Wallace briefly on the subject over his own signature. Moreover, with the attention the Minik Wallace matter was given in the press in 1907, Jesup could not have remained totally ignorant of what was going on.

And there the museum left the matter, save for one small malicious act a month later.

The new Mrs. Wallace — Pamela was her first name — was the widow of a former museum employee, Jenness Richardson. Richardson had been one of the leaders of the museum's first field expedition in 1887, an expedition to Montana, financed by Morris Jesup, to collect bison specimens for an exhibit. He had been the museum's first taxidermist and had mounted the first animal groupings ever displayed there. After Rhetta Wallace died in 1904, Richardson's widow married William Wallace. Richardson's son happened to be a museum employee, following in the career of his father as a taxidermist. His only involvement in the affair of Minik, who was many years his junior, was to convey a message from Bumpus to Wallace in July of 1906. But with the events of early 1907, the museum decided that it could scarcely afford to have any member of the Wallace family in its employ. In a terse letter in mid-February, Bumpus informed Jenness Richardson Jr. that his employment would cease at the end of the month, the reason given being that "you are not adapted to the work of the museum." The museum had been cleansed of the Wallace affair.

That same month Jesup, ever solicitous of the welfare of the explorer who had placed his name on the most northerly cape of the world, committed $20,000 to Peary's next expedition.

12

"A HOPELESS CONDITION OF EXILE"

WILLIAM WALLACE PROBABLY never realized that Jesup was not receiving his letters directly. When he had been at the museum, he had direct access to Jesup and it probably never crossed his mind that in the time since he had left, some of Jesup's employees, especially his private secretary, Benjamin Strong, had begun to act as a shield between the aging Jesup and the public. His letters and other efforts of 1907 were to no avail. Jesup was impervious to any solicitations for funds to provide for Minik's education or support.

Nonetheless Wallace continued his sporadic efforts. In an interview, he remarked, "I am unwilling to believe that Mr. Jesup has treated Minik and myself so without having what he believes to be some good reason. I feel quite certain that he has been misled by someone. . . . Mr. Jesup was kind to Minik at the Museum, and it was his own suggestion to finance his care and education with a view to preparing him for Northern work. This he has failed to do, and I am at a loss to understand his action, or rather his lack of action, unless, as I said, he has been misled and influenced by some one whose personal interests prevent him from allowing justice to be done."

That person, Wallace suggested, was Peary. He continued, "As far as Peary is concerned, he soon found out the extent of the wrong he had done in bringing the poor Eskimos to this country, and tried to get himself out of the matter as quickly as possible. During Minik's stay at the Museum and his later illness, Peary never visited him. Since that time he has simply ignored the boy, and once, when Peary was living in a New York hotel, I took Minik to see him and received in answer to our card that he 'did not wish to see us.' "

Both Wallace and Beecroft had some definite ideas about what type of education Minik should be given to prepare him for an eventual return to the north. Neither suggested a conventional approach. Beecroft felt that special tutoring was necessary, while Wallace proposed that an informal group of physicians, scientists, and teachers should be appointed to "ascertain how far it was possible to carry his education so that no stone should be left unturned to fit the boy for the northern work he desired and seemed made for." Wallace said that if his continued guardianship of Minik was the only obstacle to having his education assisted, he would give up all claim to him. Beecroft took up the subject in his overture to President Roosevelt. The only tangible result of the efforts of both Beecroft and Wallace was a suggestion from the White House that Minik make application for admission to the Carlisle School, a residential school for Indians located in Pennsylvania. Minik refused this offer; he wanted preparation for a return to the Arctic and he thought, quite rightly, that he would not receive this in a school whose avowed purpose was the acculturation of Native Americans.

Wallace was very impoverished by this time, although he was working — the construction gang over which he was foreman was working on the subway ventilation system at Union Square. Minik, as he grew older, came to blame himself for Wallace's circumstances. He cannot have known the details of the Wallace affair at the museum that had culminated in William Wallace being fired in 1901; Wallace certainly would not have volunteered any information on this episode in which his own dishonesty had been discovered and punished, though that of his acquaintances in the Peary Arctic Club and their accomplices at the museum went unacknowledged.

In his own tortured mind, Minik blamed all that had happened since 1901 on himself: "I can't be a burden on Uncle Will any longer," he felt. "He has lost his position, lost his money — he is miserably poor, and slaves like a laborer, all for me. He is the only man who has ever been kind to me, and see how I have repaid him. I have made him destitute. For three years I have wanted to leave him and go to work to help him. I am willing to do anything. Each year he has said that the ones who are making us suffer would relent and do what is right and fair; but the condition remains just the same and will always be the same while I stand in his way. If I cannot work or make those who are responsible for my being here do something, I can at least go away off to the Canada woods and lose myself and give poor Uncle Will a chance. But before I go I want to make the Museum give me my father's body to bury, and his canoe and gun to keep. If they don't give them up I will sue them just as soon as I come of age. But think of my father being down there to be stared at and laughed at all that time. I would try to punish Mr. Peary and Mr. Jesup and Prof. Bumpus, only I want them to see how well Uncle Will has brought me up, and how much more just a savage Eskimo is than they are. . . . Here I am, a prisoner in this country. Everything, my home, my father, all has been taken from me. I ask that they pay back Uncle Will what he has spent on me, return my father's body, and give me a preparation for northern work. I can support myself then. . . ."

On January 22, 1908, Morris K. Jesup died at the age of seventy-seven. With him died William Wallace's hope of any support for Minik. Over the years — it was only a few months less than a decade since he had written Wallace in 1898 with a pledge of assistance — Jesup had contributed a grand total of $200 for Minik's support. He left behind him an estate valued at $12,814,894. To his wife, he left over $9,000,000. Another million went to the museum and $100,000 to the Presbyterian Church he attended. Of the sixty-one benefactors, only three were blood relatives. The rest were institutions and individuals. Minik was not among them.

The efforts of Wallace and Beecroft were directed not only at securing some financial assistance to provide for Minik's education, but also at getting the release of Qisuk's bones from the museum so that they could be turned over to Minik for a proper burial. Wallace was not as involved in this as was Beecroft, for he bore a continuing shame over the role he had played in the phony funeral of Qisuk and the

111

deception of the unsuspecting Minik so many years earlier. Although he knew that the boy bore him no malice, he was averse to taking a strong public stance in the matter. It was better to let Beecroft handle most of this, and Minik himself, for he was now in his mid-teens, articulate, and able to state his own wishes and demands.

The man who had to shoulder the responsibility at the museum and respond to Wallace's and Beecroft's efforts was Professor Hermon Carey Bumpus, a zoologist and the museum's director since 1900. He had the misfortune to be saddled with a name that conjured up a vision of a man bumbling and inept, who perhaps fitted the stereotype of the absentminded professor. Unfortunately, reality largely confirmed the suspicion.

He was described by a biographer as a man of "exceptional charm of manner, with dynamic, tireless energy and exuberant vitality. He had . . . an exceedingly lively creative imagination which he relied upon, rather than upon tradition, habit or counsel to direct his course of action." Yet there were few of his colleagues at the museum who shared that opinion. Indeed, in 1910 the president of the museum, Jesup's successor, Henry Fairfield Osborn, would force Bumpus's resignation as a result of another minor scandal that the museum dubbed "The Bumpus Affair"; in the investigation of that scandal, Osborn solicited testimony from many of the museum's staff as proof of Bumpus's bungling incompetence. One of his colleagues described the director as "temperamentally unfit to govern the Museum" and listed his qualities as "uncontrollable temper . . . quick to be overbearing and discourteous. Tactless in infringing departmental etiquette. . . . Inordinate vanity, bad faith, false (or unfair) witness, unclean methods, financial shrewdness at the cost of the Museum, quarrelsomeness, jealousy. . . ." He went on to list his personal characteristics as "very autocratic. . . , very unsystematic. . . , untruthful and unreliable . . . , imperious in his treatment of certain curators and employees."

This was the man from whom Minik sought understanding and assistance, and from the outset Bumpus resented the demands on his time that looking into the matter would take. He felt it was unfair that he should be expected to have or find the answers to questions about things that happened at the museum before his tenure began, but he tried time and again to cover his ignorance of these matters with evasive statements. He bore no bad feelings toward Minik personally but resented the interest in Minik that drew reporters to his door and caused his name to be bandied about in the newspapers.

After Minik discovered that his father had not been buried but was instead a museum exhibit, Wallace had gone to the museum to discuss the matter with Bumpus. This was in the summer of 1906, a good half year before the *World* broke the story of Minik's unhappy experiences in the United States. He put the matter of the return of Qisuk's bones to Bumpus at that meeting. Beecroft and Minik had also visited the professor that same summer at his home in New Rochelle. Bumpus had insisted on having his lawyer present. He was one of those men who takes personally any criticism of an institution with which he is associated, and so he took great pains to deny that he was in any way responsible for Minik's position — even though no one suggested that he was. He listened attentively to the story told by Minik and Beecroft and expressed some sympathy for the boy. He promised the immediate return of the body of the boy's father, and of his canoe and gun. He promised, furthermore, to take up the matter of Minik's education with Jesup just as soon as Jesup returned from his country home. But nothing came of either promise. Wallace called Minik's "pleading for a Christian burial for his father's bones . . . pathetic in the extreme." Minik's people had always been unstinting in their assistance to American explorers and he felt that "out of gratitude the boy's plea for a Christian burial should be granted."

When the *World* first broke the story of Minik's unhappy experiences in the United States in January of 1907, Bumpus had been interviewed about the events. His brief comment covered the gamut of his ignorance: "If all these things happened, they were before I came here as director. I have heard that Mr. Wallace has cared for the boy Minik, but to my own knowledge no formal request has been made for the bones of Minik's father. We have hundreds of skeletons here, and I do not even know that the one he wants is here now."

"Should Mr. Wallace or the boy make formal application for the skeleton to the trustees it will be presented to them at the regular meeting and acted upon as they see fit. Those Eskimos were wards of the United States, and whatever was done for them here was done out of pure generosity. That is all I know of the matter."

In April of 1909, when Minik's demands for the return of his father's body were once again very much in the news, the museum's secretary, Sherwood, said that he did not know of any request having been made for the body of Minik's father, "the skeleton of which is still in the museum."

But five days later, Bumpus expressed himself as being "thoroughly mystified" by the entire story. If the skeleton of Minik's father was in the museum, he asked, would somebody kindly show it to him, and as for the gun and sled, he claimed to know nothing about them. "As for his father's body," he blustered, "I know nothing of it. He made no demands on me for it. . . . We have no bodies here. We have a great mass of Arctic curios in the museum which Peary brought with him on one of his trips, and it is barely possible that the sled and gun of the boy's father are among the collection. If so I do not know of it."

Bumpus showed himself a master of semantics, if nothing else, by the fine distinction he insisted on making between the body and the bones. When asked if the skeleton was in the museum, his reply was always that there were no bodies kept in the museum. Thus he denied the existence in the museum of Qisuk's body — from whose bones the flesh had been removed so many years before at the College of Physicians and Surgeons — while ignoring the question of whether the museum had the skeleton.

But the *Evening Mail* reporter who was pursuing this inquiry was as persistent in his efforts to discover the truth as Bumpus was in evading it. The reporter went to Franz Boas, the lecturer in physical anthropology at Columbia University, who lost no opportunity to make Bumpus look the fool:

"Dr. Bumpus . . . has had some hesitancy about admitting the presence of the bones in the museum," the reporter began. "Are they there?"

Boas replied, "Of course they are. . . ."

Asked whether, in his opinion, Minik had had a fair deal from the museum, Boas refused to comment, suggesting that Dr. Bumpus should be asked for comment on that.

The *Evening Mail* reporter visited Bumpus once again and remarked that he seemed inclined to talk about anything and everything except the skeleton of Minik's father." The interview, which he described as like a game of hide-and-seek, was printed:

" 'Are the bones of Minik's father in the museum?' Director Bumpus was asked.

" 'I don't know where they are,' was the reply.

" 'Are they not on exhibition in a glass case?'

" 'No, they are not.'

"Then Dr. Bumpus was asked where the body of the Eskimo boy's father was.

" 'The body is not in the museum.'

" 'Are the bones in the museum?' asked the reporter.

" 'Well, if they are, I don't know exactly where they are now,' replied the director.

" 'Was not the skeleton of Minik's father brought here after his death in a New York hospital?'

" 'Minik's father did not die in this museum. He never came here while he was alive.'

"Dr. Bumpus finally admitted that he had a faint recollection of some of Minik's father's bones having been brought to the museum, but he declared he did not know whether they were still there.

" 'Who would know if those bones are in the institution?' Dr. Bumpus was asked.

" 'I suppose I would, if anybody.'

" 'Well, don't you know?'

" 'No, sir, those bones were never on exhibition.'

"Dr. Bumpus was reminded that that was not the question.

" 'If you should order the curator that has charge of the skeletons to hunt up the bones of Minik's father and told him that if he didn't find them in fifteen minutes he would lose his job, do you think he would make good?'

" 'Well, yes, I think he could find them all right.' "

That Bumpus changed his story about the bones many times is

shown from Minik's later comment: "I asked Dr. Bumpus for my father's bones when I grew older, and he told me first he didn't know where they were. Then he said I could not have them for they belonged to the museum. I tried many times, but it was no use."

B y this time Minik was no longer living with Wallace. In his belief that he was responsible for the problems of the Wallace family, he had left the home, although he continued to remain very close to William Wallace. For a time he lived with Chester Beecroft at the Hotel Astor, and then he took a room of his own at the Alliance House, a boardinghouse on Forty-fourth Street. This was hardly a fit environment for an impressionable young man. There was no parental authority, save for the kindly and intermittent influence of William Wallace and Beecroft. There is no evidence that he was ever in any trouble, but he certainly became very streetwise.

Although he loved the outdoors and rough-and-tumble sports, he was frequently ill and in November of 1908 was in Fordham Hospital with a serious case of pneumonia; for a time, he was not expected to live. The illnesses had always interfered with his schooling, but by now he had left school and was sporadically employed. At one point, William Wallace found him a job working as a team checker on the construction of the Sixth Avenue subway.

Chester Beecroft was very concerned about Minik's environment. Beecroft was an avid outdoorsman, and he often took Minik with him on camping trips outside the city. On these trips, Minik would often wander off alone for hours. On his own walks, Beecroft would sometimes come across him, sitting in a secluded spot and staring blankly into the forest. On these melancholy excursions into the woods Minik would contemplate running away. He fancied escaping to the wilds of Maine or Canada. Either would be an ideal place to try to put behind the life that had become so sad in New York. He would no longer be a burden to his friends and perhaps, with time, he could forget the traumatic events that had made the past few years such a terrible ordeal.

When he was alone in the woods, his thoughts often went back to Greenland. He did not belong here in New York and had come to believe that he would never fit in. Greenland was a distant childhood memory. What he remembered of his early years there was little indeed — it had been a decade — and when he thought about it, his thoughts were in English, for he had forgotten his native language completely. Nonetheless, he wanted to go home.

Early in 1908 Minik heard that Peary, who had been delayed a year in his departure for northern Greenland, would be leaving for the north that summer. Minik determined to go with him. It proved impossible for Minik and Wallace to get an audience with the explorer, however, for Peary seemed intent on ignoring the boy. But, Minik thought, perhaps Professor Bumpus of the museum could be of assistance. He visited Bumpus at the museum with a request that Bumpus approach Peary for permission for Minik to go north with him. Bumpus noted only, "I attempted to do this but failed."

On June 23, 1908, William Wallace wrote to Peary, "Minik is very anxious to visit his people in the far north and I beg to ask if you can allow him to accompany you on your trip. . . . Kindly let me know by Minik if you can grant his earnest request."

Peary replied on June 26, 1908, "I have your letter of June 23rd, and while I would like to please Minik in this matter, I regret that my ship will be too crowded for me to take him this summer. Some other summer when I may be going north . . . I shall be very glad to give him an opportunity to see his people. Or, if he is very anxious to get some news from up there, I shall be glad to try and send him back a kayak or sledge or whatever he may most desire."

Whatever he most desired was to go home, but Peary was not willing to grant that. This was a crushing defeat. There was no way for Minik to return to Greenland except with the consent of Peary, for no other vessels went that far north.

Minik's response was, "If you expect to find the Pole this time there will be no need of a future trip. . . . You found room enough to bring me . . . here. . . . Why can't you take me back?"

A newspaper commented, "The plight of this poor Esquimau is . . . most pathetic. . . . He was brought here from Greenland in the interest of science. He has served his purpose, and American scientists have cast him adrift. A parallel case probably does not exist the world over. It would be difficult to imagine a more hopeless condition of exile. . . ."

By chance, a Danish newspaper specializing in items of American interest, the *Dansk-Amerikaneren*, picked up an item on Minik's plight from the New York *World* and published a story that attracted the notice of the Danish Ministry of Foreign Affairs. That ministry wrote to the Danish Consulate in New York with a request for more information on Minik, whom it regarded as a Danish subject.

The consul tried a number of times to meet with Minik, but each time the appointment was postponed by Wallace "under one or another pretense." In early September, Minik went to Syracuse for a short vacation and during his absence the consul met with Bumpus, Boas, William Wallace, and several others who knew something of the young man's past.

The information the museum's staff, both past and present, provided the consul was brief and in part incorrect. The consul reported to Copenhagen that in 1897 Wallace, on Jesup's instruction, had "made room for the Eskimos in the basement of the museum, where they remained for not longer than two days, after which they were moved to a large, bright room on the top floor. It must be pointed out immediately that the basement was not an ordinary basement, but a large room in the huge museum building, without any excess of humidity, and that the Eskimos did not remain there any longer than absolutely necessary, and were given the best of care. That winter there was an influenza epidemic in New York and all the Eskimos became sick and were transferred to Bellevue Hospital, where they probably were infected with tuberculosis, if they had not already been infected on board ship. At any rate, after they had been released from the hospital and taken to a farm in the country the sickness developed rapidly and all the members of the little colony died except the boy Minik." Uisaakassak had apparently disappeared from the memories of the museum staff.

Both Boas and Bumpus admitted that Qisuk's body had been autopsied and his skeleton kept, but they denied that it had ever been exhibited. Nor would they accept any responsibility for Minik's trauma on learning the fate of his father's body, claiming that "the boy would never have known anything about it had Wallace not told him and impressed it upon his sick and half-civilized imagination."

Museum officials convinced the Danish investigator that William Wallace was merely generating publicity over Minik's circumstances as part of his "systematic campaign" to get back at the institution for his dismissal, although the consul felt no doubt that Wallace loved the boy deeply and had cared for him well as long as he could.

Upon Minik's return from Syracuse the consul was finally able to have a private interview with him. Minik talked of his desire to return to his home in Greenland but the consul doubted that his wish was based on serious thought. "He has heard so much about his own homesickness," he wrote, "that he believes himself that he has such a burning longing." The Danish government had been considering intervening in the case and sending Minik back to Greenland, but Dr. Boas recommended against it, "at least for the time being," for no apparent reason. Minik was eighteen years old and already an adult by Eskimo as well as American standards. The consul disagreed with the scientist, however, reasoning that "down here, he will hardly become any more than half-civilized," and recommended that if the Danish government did decide to send him back to Greenland, it should consider sending him first to southern Greenland where he could relearn the Eskimo language (albeit a markedly different dialect from his own) before continuing north.

The consul promised to monitor the case carefully and report any further developments to Copenhagen.

13

THE POLAR PLAN

I N EARLY JANUARY OF 1909, the Arctic Club of America met for its Fifteenth Annual Dinner at the Hotel Marlborough in New York. The club, a loose affiliation of men interested in the Arctic and its exploration, had been founded by those who had gone north in the summer of 1894 on Dr. Frederick Cook's disastrous *Miranda* expedition, an accident-ridden tourist voyage to Greenland. When they had returned to America, the veterans of that adventure agreed to meet once a year to perpetuate the friendships they had made on their Arctic cruise. The club had gained members in the fifteen years since its formation. Its members were all successful men, but they were more down-to-earth than the super-rich of the secretive Peary Arctic Club.

Professor William Brewer, retiring as president — he had held the post since the club's formation — and Admiral Winfield Schley, who in 1884 had commanded the party that had gone to the relief of the Greely expedition, spoke enthusiastically about the expedition they were planning to send out that summer in search of Dr. Cook. Cook had gone north in 1907 as a rival to Peary on his own search for the North Pole and had not been heard from since. The Arctic Club of America's expedition would be headed by Dillon Wallace, himself an explorer and a survivor of an expedition into interior Labrador in 1903, on which his partner, Leonidas Hubbard, had lost his life.

Minik was in attendance that night. He was often invited to attend the club's meetings, and sometimes he was asked to come dressed in his furs. These events were exhibitions of sorts, too, but more private and kindly than his earlier exhibitions at the American Museum of Natural History. Minik listened with rapt interest to the plans for the Cook relief expedition, for the club had already agreed that it would give him passage back to northern Greenland on that voyage.

It was no secret to the members of the club that Minik had formulated some ideas of his own about the North Pole. He read voraciously everything he could lay his hands on about the Arctic, and particularly the expeditions that had gone to his Arctic, northwestern Greenland, in search of the Pole. He concluded that neither Cook nor Peary nor any other white explorer would ever reach the North Pole because their methods were all wrong.

But he had gone a step further. He conceived a plan for an all-Eskimo expedition to the Pole. William Wallace once claimed, "Our . . . object had been to educate him to be an explorer, for it had always been his theory and ours that if anyone reached the pole it would be an Eskimo." This was the "northern work" that he would undertake.

Minik explained his plan with cutting sarcasm for the methods used by the most recent spate of Arctic explorers. His frankness must have made the Arctic veterans in the club's membership and the supporters of Robert Peary — for he had his admirers in this club as well — cringe with uneasiness:

"The explorers who are trying to find the North Pole now don't know how to do it.

"They fit out nice comfortable ships, take along a number of useless passengers to eat up their provisions and sail as far North as they can in one summer and passively wait until they are frozen in. Then they while away a winter eating up their provisions until summer comes again, when they make a so-called 'dash,' in which they sometimes cover as much as a mile a day, going as far as they can in half the summer. The other half of the summer is taken up in beating it back to their ship before the Arctic winter becomes too severe. Then they return to the United States in a blaze of glory, announce that the pole is to be discovered 'not yet, but soon,' and start out on a long and profitable lecture tour, telling why they failed and how they will surely succeed next time.

"The North Pole will never be discovered in such a way. The man who finds it will go as far as he can in one season and make a permanent camp there until the next season. Then he will continue on his journey, and in such a way he must succeed. That's what I want to do. Not only do I want to be the first man to find the Pole, so that the honor will go to one of my own race, but I want to explore the vast unknown tracts of Greenland, which contain more country unknown to man than any other land."

Such blunt criticism of Arctic explorers was unheard of in the Peary era, especially from eighteen-year-old youngsters. The press, in the business of creating heroes for an expansionist-minded America, had lapped up almost every detail of Peary's experiences in the Arctic, and seldom was a critical comment printed. But it had not always been so. Those with long memories might have recalled a time, over three decades earlier, when even the prestigious *New York Times* had speculated on the mysterious attractions of the far north:

"The record of recent Arctic exploration is exceedingly monotonous. The expeditions of Kane, Hayes, Hall, and Nares, successively started with well-equipped vessels, ostensibly to reach the North Pole. They stopped at Upernavik, in Greenland, long enough to send word home that they were in excellent spirits, and confident of success, and then proceeded up Smith's Sound, in order to go into winter quarters in the neighborhood of the eightieth degree of latitude. As to how the explorers passed their time while in winter quarters, we have, of course, only their own testimony, but we all know that not one of them ever reached the Pole. On the contrary, they uniformly returned at unexpected periods, with the report that on reaching eighty-two degrees of latitude . . . they found further progress impossible, and so returned home to mention the fact. . . .

"It is impossible that this sort of thing should go on indefinitely without invoking the suspicions of the long-suffering and credulous public. The time has come when people will insist upon knowing what is the attraction which makes most officers so anxious to go into winter quarters in Smith's Sound. Their pretense of wanting to

go to the North Pole is altogether too transparent, and their excuses
for returning home without having achieved their professed object
are suspiciously contradictory. Kane and Hayes asserted that they
found an open polar sea, which they could not cross because they
were unfortunately unprovided with the proper boats. Hall said that
instead of an open polar sea there was a nice overland road to the
Pole, over which he promised to travel in sledges, but as he died before he was quite ready to return home, he avoided the task of explaining why his promised sledge journey was not undertaken. As
for Capt. Nares, he informs us that he did not go to the Pole because
in so doing he would have been obliged to cross a frozen sea, where
the ice was only 160 feet in thickness. What his precise weight is we
are not told, but even if he weighs four hundred pounds, the ice was
thick enough to bear him. The English people may not be very familiar with ice, but they cannot help knowing that ice 160 feet thick
can be crossed, with reasonable care, by even the heaviest naval
officer in the service. . . . When four successive expeditions spend a
winter in Smith's Sound, and return with the report that they could
not reach the Pole because there was too much ice or too little ice, or
because there was an open polar sea or because there was not an
open polar sea, intelligent people cannot avoid the conclusion that
there is something in this business which is kept from them, and will
demand to know the true reason why explorers are so anxious to
spend a winter in Smith's Sound."

At the Arctic Club of America dinner, Minik met another man of
some northern experience and considerable northern interest.
This was the naturalist Harry V. Radford. Radford was to leave shortly
on a northern expedition and the Arctic Club of America presented
him with its flag to carry with him.

Minik listened with interest to Radford's impassioned talk about
his plans. After the meeting he approached the explorer. Would it be
possible, Minik asked, to accompany him north on his expedition
and get back to his people in that way? But it was not possible. Radford's destination was northwestern Canada, and there was no way of
getting to Smith Sound from the area in which he would be traveling.

Radford was impressed with the boy, however, and with his seemingly rational talk about an Eskimo expedition to the Pole. But, asked Radford, if Minik's polar expedition were to be a success and if Minik were to be of service to his people after he had achieved the Pole, would it not be wise for him to learn the use of surveying instruments and the compass and to be trained in the sciences before he left? Radford, by chance, was a graduate of Manhattan College, a local private school run by the Order of Christian Brothers, and he suggested to Minik that he could arrange for his acceptance at that school if he wanted it. Minik now had to decide whether he would in fact go north with the Cook relief expedition in the summer of 1909 or postpone his trip indefinitely and resume his education. He told Radford that he wanted a few days to think over his proposition. It was difficult to choose between his longing for the home he no longer knew and his desire for learning, but two days later, when he came to see Radford, it was to tell him that he had opted for schooling.

He put his decision in the context of his long-term desire to both reach the Pole and serve his people:

"I would like to return to my people and see if I could help them. I have never forgotten my people although I have not seen them since I was taken from my playmates when I was six years old. . . .

"My people, they always have tried to help the white man reach the pole. White men have not reached it, principally because the Esquimaus will never tell the white man all they know. The Esquimaus don't know to-day what Commander Peary is looking for. He isn't able to explain it to the Esquimaus. They have no knowledge of geography. They see his ship and think it from some fairyland filled with crackers and coffee.

"Now, I think I can find the pole, after I get my civil engineering knowledge. First, I will go back to Greenland and learn my language again. My people would tell me things they would tell to no white man about the best way to reach the North Pole. They don't know how great a thing it would be to find it, but I can tell them all that and make them understand that the only way to reach the pole is to hunt for it until we find it. Too much time is spent now by explorers coming back to this country to tell people how cold it is up there and how they had to buck the ice. The Esquimau knows it is cold up there, but he is used to it and he doesn't know anything about writing books about the north. He doesn't know how to lecture. I can learn how to read instruments so that I can know when I have found the pole, and the Esquimaus will stick to me until I do find it. There is a lot of time lost in coming back to this country to talk about the ice."

Radford introduced Minik to Brother Peter, president of Manhattan College. Minik told Brother Peter of his plans and ambitions with the same conviction with which he had spoken to Radford, and the brother was so impressed that he promised Minik free tuition through both the preparatory school and the college, in a course of studies specializing in civil engineering and astronomy and leading ultimately to the degree of Bachelor of Science. His education to date had been sporadic, interrupted often by illness and finally terminated because of William Wallace's financial circumstances. However, Brother Peter was sufficiently confident in Minik's abilities, on the basis of a single conversation with him, to tell him that he would be enrolled in one of the high-school classes and that Minik should take some employment outside of his regular school hours to pay his board and incidental expenses. He could start almost immediately, for the second semester opened on February 1.

Radford was pleased. He commented, "I have known Minik only a few days, but have every confidence in him. I do not think it is too much to say that he may be a veritable Moses among his people — or, should we say, a Peary?"

Minik grimaced. "Just let it rest at Minik," he said.

14

RUNAWAY

MINIK'S EXPERIENCE AT Manhattan College was neither pleasant nor successful.

Shortly after he enrolled there in February of 1909, he was off for quite some time in another round of his recurring bout with pneumonia. This was his third serious attack in the past few years. When he had recovered sufficiently, he went back to school, but he found that he hated it. He later explained, "I cannot bear the confinement of a public school class room — it makes me deathly sick in a few days."

Even at Manhattan College he was a curiosity. The newspapers had gotten wind of his acceptance. When William Wallace accompanied him to the school on the day of his enrollment, they found many of the students waiting on the campus to welcome him. But Minik wanted to fit in to the student body like any of his classmates, and this display of interest, well-intentioned though it was, made him ill at ease. He felt that he had become "more or less a freak to those about me. It was so at Manhattan College and I saw it could never be different. So much for me."

He continued to live on his own in the Alliance House on West Forty-fourth Street, and he visited Chester Beecroft often. His surroundings were hardly conducive to good progress at school, but Beecroft tried to keep a fatherly eye on him and ensure that he maintained his studies.

He made one last effort to get his father's bones from the museum for burial, but failed again. With this failure he went into a severe state of depression, and once again he wanted desperately to be anywhere but New York City.

In January, he had been optimistic that he would be able to return to the Arctic that summer on the Arctic Club of America's Cook relief expedition. The plans for that voyage under the explorer Dillon Wallace had been announced in the city papers that month — they were proposing to charter the *Jeanie*, a small but sturdy Newfoundland fishing schooner. But Minik had put aside his intention to accompany that voyage when Radford had counseled him to attend Manhattan College instead. He could, of course, drop out and take the Arctic Club up again on its offer of passage. It would be a little humiliating, but if nothing else he was by now enured to humiliation and setbacks. But two questions were gnawing at his mind.

The Arctic Club had "promised" to take him north on its expedition if he wanted to go. But would they? He had heard promises before and nothing had ever come of them. And there were strong Peary admirers within the club. Peary had refused to take him back north in the summer of 1908. Might not his supporters object to the Arctic Club taking him back this year?

But the more important question was this: Would there be a Cook relief expedition at all? It was now March and the Arctic Club of America was not having the success it needed in getting public subscriptions to help finance the trip. It was expensive to outfit an Arctic expedition. The club members were well-to-do, but their wealth could not match that of the men of the Peary Arctic Club, and so they could not pay for the charter themselves. They were on the verge of scrapping the entire plan. In fact, they had gone so far as to send a letter to a Dundee firm, owner of one of the few whaling ships that still frequented the fished-out waters of Baffin Bay, offering a substantial reward — most of the subscription money they had succeeded in getting — to any whaler that would bring home Doctor Cook. Minik was well aware of all of this because Beecroft had told him. And Beecroft knew it because it was a situation he was well on top of, for he, too, had planned to go north with Dillon Wallace that summer. And so Minik's depression was more severe than normal, for if the Cook relief expedition did fall through, as it showed every indication of doing, he would have no way of getting back to Greenland at all.

In late March, while Chester Beecroft was out of the city, there was a student strike at Manhattan College. Realizing he would not be missed at the school's morning roll call for at least a few days, Minik packed his few belongings in a single suitcase and left the city on a Monday evening. He had $5 with him.

He headed first across the river to Newark, New Jersey. On April 3, while still there, he wrote Beecroft a letter and left it with an acquaintance to be posted after his departure. When Beecroft received the letter it bore an April 7 postmark. It read:

"When this reaches you I will be well on my way as it will not be mailed for three days.

"No matter what happens, I won't forget what you have done for me, my good old friend. You made a brother of me when all the others that were responsible for my being stolen from my own country failed. There was no reason why you should have been so kind to me when you just happened to meet me, but you have a big heart and understand what the others can't.

"I don't see any chance in New York, and I don't want to be a burden to you any longer. You would go on helping me . . . and I feel horrible about it, so I am going away to give you a chance. They won't give me my father's body out of the museum and they never keep their promise, so I am disgusted and will leave it all if I can. You and Mr. Wallace have been true friends and I would die for you, but I won't stay and bother you.

"Never mind where I am. I am just working North. I am homesick and disgusted and when Commander Peary . . . told me he had no room for me on his ship I lost hope; and then when Prof. Bumpus, of the museum, refused to give me my father's body so that I could bury it, or give me even his sled and gun, I gave up believing that your

129

Christian belief which was taught me was meant for a poor Eskimo. After all, my own people are more humane and kind and I am going home; your civilization has done nothing but harm for me and my people. Good bye."

William Wallace received a similar letter.

When Beecroft received his letter he immediately wired the police of various towns that he thought Minik might pass through, asking them to detain the boy if they found him. Beecroft suspected that Minik was heading for Ottawa. Sometime before Minik fled, Beecroft had received a letter from Harry Radford; from it he knew that Radford was in Ottawa making the final preparations for his trip into the Canadian northland. Minik knew that Radford's trip would take him to northwestern Canada, far from the northern part of Greenland that he wanted so desperately to reach. But perhaps he would try to accompany Radford anyway. Perhaps he had decided that any north was better than the existence he was suffering in New York. Or perhaps he merely intended to visit Radford briefly to borrow a little money to continue his trek, with the ultimate goal of reaching Greenland. It was possible, too, Beecroft thought, that Minik was trying to reach Brigus, Newfoundland, the home of the seagoing Bartlett family, on his own. If he got there he might try to secure passage on a northbound vessel. This possibility frightened Beecroft, for he knew that, except for a Cook or Peary relief voyage, no Newfoundland ships were likely to go as far north as Smith Sound. "If Minik is making for Newfoundland and he succeeds in getting passage further north," he said, "I am afraid that he won't get much nearer to his home than a point about 800 miles distant."

He added, "I want Minik to return to his home, but I want him to go in the right way."

In fact, Beecroft found it impossible to speculate, with anything other than sheer guesses, on the boy's destination, for the young man was very depressed and very confused. He wanted to reach Greenland, but what direction was Greenland from New York? It was north, of course, but by what circuitous route could he reach it?

On April 9, Minik arrived in the small town of Deposit, New York. He knew that Chester Beecroft had a brother, Will, living there and that evening he showed up at Will Beecroft's door. He was wearing an old overcoat and sweating profusely; he had no suitcase or indeed any belongings with him. He spent the night with Beecroft. The following morning, before he left, Beecroft gave him $2 and he borrowed $10 from another man. When he left, he told Will Beecroft that he was heading for Albany, where he thought Chester was on a business trip.

He passed the following night, a Saturday, in the Crandall Hotel in Binghamton, and from there he continued to Albany. The state legislature was in session and on Monday evening Minik visited the assembly and secured a floor pass from the speaker of the house. He had been to Albany once before to visit a member of the state legislature in the hope of getting some assistance for his education and in securing the release of his father's bones, but he had failed on both counts. This evening was a final attempt to reopen the matter, but he received no encouragement. Depressed, he left the legislative building and went to the home of Maggie Arned; she had been a servant in the Wallace home for many years and had taken care of Minik when he was just a child.

But the next morning he was off again. He went to Schoharie, near Cobleskill, the area of his boyhood bliss. But no sooner had he arrived than he realized that there was nothing to draw him there anymore, and he abruptly left for Troy.

Chester Beecroft, in the meantime, had been busy. His brother, Will, had called him, concerned after Minik's departure, and told him about the boy's intention to visit Albany. Beecroft called a number of people that he knew were acquainted with Minik and he picked up the trail. He followed him through Albany, Schoharie, and Troy, but he was always one step behind him, and at Troy he lost the trail. There was nothing to do except return to New York in the hope that Minik might change his mind and contact him.

He felt that there was a good chance that Minik would return or at least call, for even to the supportive Beecroft, this flight of Minik's was a strange one. If Minik was definitely trying to escape and not be found, he was doing a mighty poor job of it. He had visited people that Beecroft knew were his acquaintances, paid a call to Beecroft's own brother, and gone briefly to the area of his youthful summers in Schoharie. This young runaway was leaving a definite trail. One would think that he was crying out to be caught.

Chester Beecroft was incensed that the neglect of Minik by the museum and the Peary Arctic Club's members had driven the boy to the desperate and futile measures he had taken. He let the New York newspapers know about the runaway and he pulled no punches in telling the press exactly what he thought of society's shoddy treatment of Minik: "The treatment which has been accorded this child by men who, besides being learned scientists, hold reputable positions in society, is not barbaric, it has been inhuman."

And was it any wonder Minik had given up the Christianity that had been the religion of the devout Morris Jesup and the other men who could afford to patronize Peary but could not manage to send one young Eskimo boy to school? "Everywhere Minik looked for help," continued Beecroft, "he got none. Old men and women patted him on the head and told him to love Jesus and have faith in God, but as far as giving him a real lift was concerned they had nothing in that line to offer. He asked for bread and he got a stone."

Minik knew Chester Beecroft well enough to know that, with his superb connections, he would have contacted the authorities to be on the lookout for him. Small and swarthy in complexion, he knew too that as the only Eskimo in America he was very conspicuous. And so he trekked northward cautiously. In the daytime he slept in barns or anywhere else where he could find some shelter from the still-cold northeastern spring. At night he walked or rode freight trains. He begged food along the way and worked a day or two on farms in return for a square meal and a bed for the night.

At the Canadian border he was mistaken for a Chinese. He was detained for a time, but his usual charm saw him released in a few hours.

By the time he reached Montreal, Minik was half-starved and quite ill. He spotted a half-sunken derelict boat in a river he crossed. The cabin was still above water and he crawled in and slept. It wasn't a comfortable spot, but it was at least safe, and he was exhausted. He remembered, "When I woke up, I was so stiff I could not stand. I was sick, too, and oh, so hungry. I lay down in the dryest spot, and slept again. For three days I stayed on that boat, and I thought I was dying. It was there I decided to kill myself."

Finally he had enough strength to leave his half-sunken refuge, and he made it to a cottage nearby. There a woman gave him a sandwich and he wrote another letter to Chester Beecroft:

"This is probably the last letter I will ever write. I know that you will feel awfully bad when you read this, but I must let you know. Please forgive me, and this will be the last favor I will ask of you, who have always been my big, kind brother.

"I guess I will never swim with you or camp with you, or sail with you, or suffer with you again. You see, Dob [his nickname for Beecroft], I worked my way up here, and you can guess how hard it is to work your way, or beat your way as far without money, and many a day I have been hungry and many a night I have cried. Now I am in Canada, and am sick and weak, and have no more strength to fight off this awful want to die.

"What is the use, Dob? I can't get to Brigus in time now to catch a whaler and if Capt. Moses Bartlett is going to run the relief ship for Dr. Cook I will be too late to catch him, even if I could keep well to make the trip.

"You can't know the sad feelings I have, Dob. No one can know unless they have been taken from their home and had their father die and put on exhibition, and be left to starve in a strange land where the men insult you when you ask for your own dear father's body to bury or to be sent home.

"These are the civilized men who steal, and murder, and torture, and pray and say 'Science.' My poor people don't know that the meteorite that they used till Peary took it fell off a star. But they know that the hungry must be fed, and cold men warmed, and helpless people cared for, and they do it.

"Wouldn't it be sad if they forgot those things and got civilized and changed kindness for science? I can't get home to them, but I can die. I remember that you told me that the sure way to get revenge is to be unlike the one that hurt you. I am going to do that now. I am going to die smiling at Peary and Prof. Bumpus, and the scientists and others in the Government that you know.

"Good-by, dear Dob. If I don't find some health and some way positive to get me home by next Monday I will kill myself. I will wait just long enough, not just because I am afraid, but because I want to

133

use up every chance first; but Monday will be the last, and you know that I will keep my word.

"Good-by, dear friend. Two things I have to be thankful for. One, because I was educated enough to write this letter to tell you. The other is that I knew you. Tell them to let my people alone to live the way nature made them to live.

"When they are perfect themselves, then let them tell everybody else that their way is the only way. If you ever get a chance, warn my poor people against proud hypocrites and save what few are left. Don't cry for me, Dob. Be glad. Stay like you were to me and don't get like the rest.

"The rich build homes for cats, but who offered to even let me work? Only you and Uncle Will.

"My last word will be thanks. On Monday, Dob, good-by, good-by, good-by."

This melodramatic letter was not a suicide threat. This was a pathetic plea for help from a boy deeply traumatized by the events that had surrounded him. Elsewhere Minik had written, "Think of the injuistice [sic] of it all. Think of that burial of stones or a piece of wood instead of what I thought was my father's body. When I found out, can any one imagine what I felt?"

Beecroft received the letter at the Hotel Astor. At about the same time as he received it, he received a telegram from William Wallace. Wallace had gone to Lynn, Massachusetts, where he knew that Minik had friends, in the hope that Minik would contact them. He did, and Wallace telegrammed the information that Minik was in Montreal, confirmation of the letter Beecroft had just received.

Some of the New York newspapers had published articles about Minik's desperate flight, and Beecroft had allowed them to print Minik's first letter to him. Vesta Tilley, an entertainer on Broadway, had read the letter and, sympathetic, she publicly expressed her indignation at the way the young man had been treated. Miss Tilley was a lady of means. Although she used the stage name Vesta Tilley, she was in fact Lady Matilda Alice Powles de Frece, the wife of Colonel Sir Walter de Frece, a former member of the British Parliament. She had initially made her reputation on the stage as a male impersonator, but at the time she took up Minik's cause, she was playing the lead role in "My Lady Molly" at Daly's Theatre. Through Acton Davis, editor of the *New York Sun*, she met Chester Beecroft and offered to defray the cost of his search for Minik. Now, with Vesta Tilley's money, Beecroft left for Montreal.

Beecroft had earlier telegraphed the police in Montreal to be on the watch for Minik. In fact, they had already found him once, but Minik had convinced them that he was an Indian from the nearby Caughnawaga Mohawk reservation. This ruse was successful with the police, so Minik decided to employ it again. He met a man named William Green and convinced him that he was one of the Indian athletes who was to take part in a marathon race on May 24 in Quebec City. But he lacked the train fare from Montreal to Quebec, so Green gave him $6 to buy his ticket. He also gave him a letter of introduction to a priest in Quebec City who would look after him on his arrival.

When Minik arrived in Quebec — a few hundred miles closer to Newfoundland — the priest took this bedraggled Eskimo traveler to a boardinghouse for a much needed rest. Even had he been an Indian athlete, he was certainly in no position to compete in a marathon. And it was in this boardinghouse that Chester Beecroft, through good luck and good connections, found him.

With the characteristic understatement with which he often closed his stories, Minik summed up his adventure. "I went to a boarding house," he said. "I was very sick. As I was lying in bed, who should come in but Mr. Beecroft. I was glad to see him and here I am."

Beecroft brought him back to the Hotel Astor and to the questions of eager newspapermen. He was in poor health, disillusioned, and bitter. But he made time to explain his position to the reporters:

"I left New York six weeks ago determined to get home to my people. Mr. Beecroft and Mr. William Wallace had done all they could for me, and I was tired of waiting for the Arctic Club to send me back. I beat my way by foot and on freights to Montreal, and realizing that I could not get North in time to reach Capt. Bartlett's whaling expedition, I made up my mind to kill myself. I still want to get back to my people.

"Yes, I had a hard time, but it was worth trying. There is nothing for me to do here. Nobody cared what became of me. I was a curiosity, that's all. And what good could I do by being that?

"I was not strong like American boys, and I could not have worked, because I have pneumonia every little while. They would not take me back to my people. They had used me for what they wanted; they had stolen my father's body for their science. They did not want me any more, and it was too much trouble to take me back."

Vesta Tilley, the entertainer who had financed Beecroft's search for him, visited Minik at the hotel. Beecroft was now almost certain that the Arctic Club of America would not raise enough money for its Cook relief expedition. Both he and Miss Tilley thought that the United States government must be called somehow to act in the matter of sending Minik home. Vesta Tilley promised that if the government would not do something for the boy, she would personally organize a benefit concert to raise money to send him home to Greenland.

But if anything was to be done, it would have to be done fast. It was now late May and the brief Arctic summer was rapidly approaching.

15

"AN IRON-CLAD AGREEMENT"

AFTER MINIK HAD FLED New York but before he had been brought back by Beecroft, a newspaper printed the most sensational article yet on his plight. Illustrated with photographs and a sketch of Minik gazing in horror at his father's skeleton mounted in a glass case, it bore the title, "Why Arctic Explorer Peary's Neglected Eskimo Boy Wants to Shoot Him."

Based on interviews with Minik from before his disappearance, and with Wallace and Beecroft, the article gave a complete summary of the whole sordid affair.

In it, Minik posed the rhetorical questions: How would Peary like to have his daughter carried off to the Arctic and abandoned to the charity of some kindly Eskimos? And what would the explorer do if he were walking through the museum and came across his own father staring blankly at him from a glass case? The article also quoted Minik as having said, "I would shoot Mr. Peary and the Museum director, only I want them to see how much more just a savage Eskimo is than their enlightened white selves." This, coupled with the readers' knowledge that Minik was already trying to make his own way north, made another comment particularly relevant: "I can never forgive Peary," he said, "and I hope to see him to show him the wreck he has caused."

The report concluded provocatively, "And if he does meet Peary, what then may follow?"

Almost all the articles that had been published about Minik were critical of the roles that Peary, Jesup, and the museum had played in his tragic life. Yet this was the only one known to have gotten a reaction in print out of the Peary family. Robert Peary was in the Arctic, but his wife, Josephine, saw the article and dashed off an enraged note to Herbert Bridgman, secretary of the Peary Arctic Club, in which she said that she was "hopping mad" and wanted to know what could be done about the article. Bridgman contacted the American Museum of Natural History to ask what its reaction would be. But the museum maintained its remarkable consistency in the treatment of the Minik affair; its brief reply was that "our policy of paying no attention to these [reports] seems to be the wisest."

But more was to follow. It was as if Minik had saved up a final barrage of invective to heap upon the Peary forces and their sympathizers.

A few days after his return to New York, he told a reporter what he suspected may have been Peary's real reasons for refusing to take him north the previous summer. He said, "Peary suspected I would tell my people just how he and members of the [Peary] Arctic Club have treated me, and knew that if I did, he would never reach the Pole."

His friend Beecroft had earlier told a reporter from the *New York Times*, "Minik is you know somewhat of an Indian, so he can hate, and I do not think he has any too much love for Commander Peary. Bearing this in mind, I am not so sure but that he has some scheme in mind to try and defeat Peary in his hunt for the north pole. . . .

" . . . If Minik were to tell them of his treatment here they would, I think, believe the boy and do all in their power to hinder Peary. . . .

"I once heard Minik say, If I get north and see my people before Peary gets there [the Pole], it will be the last move he will make in the north.'"

These comments are telling. They reveal far more than Minik's despondency and hatred for Peary, however. They show also that Minik and his well-intentioned adviser, Beecroft, knew really very little about Eskimos, how they think, and the conditions under which they live. They knew that Peary depended heavily on the Eskimos — but that was no secret, for anyone could read it in the newspapers when

Peary returned periodically to America in his brief flashes of glory. What they did not know was how heavily Minik's people in north-western Greenland had come to depend on Peary, the man who singlehandedly controlled the influx of trade goods into the district. The relationship that had developed between the Polar Eskimos and Peary, although uneven, was mutually beneficial, a very lopsided symbiosis. In assuming that the Eskimos, no matter how sympathetic, would abandon Peary en masse, Minik and Beecroft underestimated the essential pragmatism of the Eskimos, the one quality above all others that enabled them to survive as a people in one of the world's harshest environments.

Yet to the Peary forces Minik's claims, however implausible, were damaging just the same. They were getting increasing coverage in the press and the public was slowly developing a righteous indignation at the treatment meted out by wealthy individuals to a helpless foreign orphan.

The articles of the previous few years had been ones in which Jesup and the museum were slandered and Peary merely mentioned, disparagingly to be sure, but only in the context of having brought the boy here in the first place. But the most recent coverage was rapidly turning it into a different matter altogether. With Jesup dead, Robert Peary, isolated in his Arctic domain, was now bearing the brunt of Minik's criticism. Mrs. Peary, the staunch protector of her husband's reputation during his absences, was genuinely mad and getting madder.

The Minik affair was becoming an embarrassment and, potentially, a liability. Neither Herbert Bridgman nor Mrs. Peary had any way of knowing if Peary had reached the Pole on his present trip, but of one thing they were certain — if he had not, he would want to try again. In that event, there would be money to be raised, and that meant politicians to be influenced. This Minik affair was a potential liability, for it could tarnish the public's view of Peary and perhaps hinder his efforts to raise the money to pursue his polar obsession. Bridgman was well aware, too, that the Danish consul in New York had earlier expressed official interest in the treatment of Minik and was continuing to follow the situation and report to his government in Copenhagen. A serious formal complaint from the Danish government might adversely affect

Robert Peary's reputation in Washington. Bridgman and Josephine Peary turned over the possibilities in their minds and discussed them at length. It was well that Peary himself was not here, Bridgman knew, for the explorer had a way of making intemperate statements in public when angry. Finally Bridgman and Josephine Peary concluded that it would, after all, be better if Minik were sent north to Greenland, so that the American public could, they hoped, quickly forget him. With Jesup dead, the task of raising money would be difficult enough without any unnecessary hindrances.

The Cook forces had failed to raise enough money through subscriptions to charter a vessel to go to the doctor's relief. They had to throw in their lot — and their paltry $1,000 — with Bridgman, who was now Peary's master strategist. Bridgman purchased the *Jeanie*, a small, two-masted schooner of ninety-eight tons, the same ship that the Arctic Club of America had proposed to use for a supply voyage to provision Peary's *Roosevelt* for her return voyage south. Her commander and a partner with Bridgman in her purchase was Captain Samuel Bartlett, uncle of the *Roosevelt's* captain, Bob Bartlett. Samuel Bartlett, like all the Bartletts of Brigus, Newfoundland, was an experienced sailor in icy waters and had been north for Peary on three previous occasions. This expedition, Bridgman was clear in pointing out, would not be jointly sponsored; it would be a relief voyage for Peary sponsored by the Peary Arctic Club. That club agreed to accept the Arctic Club of America's money to inquire after, relieve, or bring back Cook.

General Thomas Hubbard, a wealthy contributor to Peary's expeditions, had replaced Jesup as president of the Peary Arctic Club, but Bridgman, secretary and treasurer, was clearly the man with the most knowledge of Peary, the only member of the club to have actually been north himself, and the most capable manipulator of both the press and the people.

Bridgman was a most remarkable man. In 1909 he was sixty-five years old but powerfully built, and with the sturdy chest and shoulders of an athlete. He had a large head and a luxurious, flowing mustache. His eyes, deep-set and probing, gave a look of brooding asceticism to his otherwise handsome face.

He had been in the news business all his adult life. In 1887, he had become the business manager, and later part owner, of the Brooklyn *Standard Union*. As one of the founders of, and three times president of, the American Newspaper Publishers Association, it galled him that he was unable to exert influence on some of his colleagues in New York and stop their troublesome coverage of the plight of Minik Wallace. He was a fastidious man and seldom wasted a moment. A journalist as well as publisher, he was a superb manipulator of public opinion and prided himself on his ability to find elusive items in the least likely places.

Behind this austere front hid a man with a passion for the exotic. He indulged it in travel. Bridgman had a reputation, well deserved, as both an explorer and a patron of exploration. He had a particular interest in the Arctic, although he explored also in Africa and other parts of the world. He first met Robert Peary in 1892 and had become an unwavering supporter of the explorer. He went to the Arctic on Peary relief voyages on three occasions. In 1899, after he returned to the United States from the voyage of the *Diana*, he formally organized the loose club of gentlemen who had earlier been brought together by Morris K. Jesup as the Peary Arctic Club. While Jesup, until his death, had been the president of that club and its wealthiest patron, Herbert Bridgman was happy to remain in the background, attending to the details as secretary and treasurer. He was often simply described as Peary's press agent. He didn't mind the description at all. He was an unassuming man who took his private pleasures in the respect of the wealthy and influential rather than the masses. He was a modest man of simple tastes. When he died in 1924, his wife was surprised to discover that he was a millionaire.

Both Bridgman and Jesup were respected for their interest in young people. Jesup had been a founder of the Young Men's Christian Association, and Bridgman was active in many organizations that supported young people's activities. What could have been their reasons, then, for maintaining their resolute opposition to any of the requests that had been made by Minik and on his behalf for the return of his father's bones for burial and for assistance in securing an education? It was simply this: Jesup's and Bridgman's America was the land of opportunity for all who wished to seize it. Its population was still rapidly expanding westward and immigrants were pouring in by the shipload to build America and their own fortunes. Bridgman and Jesup were both self-made millionaires. Was there any reason why Minik could not embrace their work ethic and become one too? There should be no need for special treatment. People of other countries scrimped and saved for their passage to America. To live in the United States was a privilege. Why, they asked themselves, could Minik not understand that? Just being in America was enough! These single-minded men did not understand trauma, and because of that they could never understand Minik.

Minik's friends had been agitating for the boy's repatriation to Greenland. But the Arctic Club of America's planned expedition under Dillon Wallace had fallen through, and there would be no way north now unless the Peary Arctic Club agreed to take the boy north. Bridgman and his colleagues had already decided that they would be happy to see the last of him. Perhaps it had been part of Minik's strategy to ensure that decision by launching his torrent of abuse at Peary through the press in May of 1909. Mrs. Peary agreed, too, but she had her own concerns — after all, the Eskimo was on record as saying he would like to shoot her husband. And so Bridgman determined to send the boy north—but there would be a few strings attached.

Bridgman and Beecroft met in early July and Bridgman, very much in charge, outlined the facts of Minik's repatriation in a general way. He concluded the conversation by reminding Beecroft that "the conversation counted for nothing, and that I would make no commitment, except in writing."

Bridgman drafted an agreement that he proposed must be signed by William Wallace, Beecroft, and Minik himself before Minik would be allowed to travel on the *Jeanie,* and he forwarded a copy of it to Mrs. Peary for her approval or, for that matter, her disapproval, for "we are under no obligation in any manner. . . ."

On July 9, the day before his departure, Minik and his two closest friends in the United States signed what Bridgman referred to as "an iron-clad agreement."

142

1. The earliest known photograph of Minik, being carried in the parka of his mother, Mannik, June 1892.

2. Qisuk

3. Nuktaq

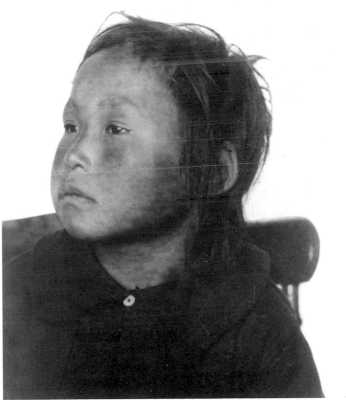

4. Minik

5. Atangana, Nuktaq's wife

6. Uisaakassak

7. Aviaq

8. Robert Peary

9. Robert Peary

10. Peary and a group of Polar Eskimos aboard ship.

11. Mathew Henson

12. Minik and Marie Peary

13. Peary's daughter, Marie,
the Snowbaby.

14. Minik, posed in Eskimo costume shortly after his arrival in New York.

15. Avaiq

16. Minik and foster brother, Willie Wallace, 1898.

17. The house in Lawyersville where Minik and the other Polar Eskimos were cared for in 1898. Nuktaq and Aviaq died in this house.

18. Minik and his foster mother, Rhetta Wallace, with an Alaskan Eskimo girl, "Zaksriner," and her foster mother Miss Meagher, an artist at the American Museum of Natural History.

19. Minik in Lawyersville, New York.

20. Minik, dressed in Eskimo costume in Lawyersville, New York, about 1900.

21. The house at Wallace's Cold Spring Farm.

22. The Reformed Church of Lawyersville, where Minik attended Sunday school in his early years in America.

23. William Wallace

24. Minik, standing outside the Augustin Hotel, Cobleskill, New York, about 1904.

25. Professor Bickmore in his study at the museum.

26. Franz Boas, who asked Peary to bring a Polar Eskimo to America.

27. Morris K. Jesup, president of the American Museum of Natural History.

28. Dr. Henry Carey Bumpus, of the American Museum of Natural History.

29. Herbert L Bridgman

30. Capt. Bradley S. Osbon, of the Arctic Club of America.

31. The first newspaper article to describe Minik's attempt to have his father's body released from the American Museum of Natural History was published in *The World*, Magazine Supplement, January 6, 1907.

The Pathetic Appeal of Little
Mene Wallace, Who Was
Brought to New York "in the
Interest of Science," Turned Adrift After All His Unhappy Re[latives]
Had Died Here and He Had Seen His
Skeleton Grin at Him from a Glass [Case in]
the New York Museum of Natural [History]
and Who Has Abandoned "Civiliza-
tion" Because He Cannot Get [...]

WHY ARCTIC EXPLO[RER]

By Mene Wallace, Last Survivor of Peary's Wretche[d ...]

Peary's Daughter in Eskimo Costume.

Little Mene in His Very Earl-
est Days, with the Bicycle
Mr. Wallace Bought for Him.

Mene
as He
Looked
When
Peary
Found
Him.

The Meteorite Peary Brought from the Arctic.

The Eskimo Boy
Nine, Pleased
His Clothing of
Civilization.

32. The most sensational of all articles to appear on Minik in American
newspapers was entitled "Why Arctic Explorer Peary's Neglected Eskimo
Wants to Shoot Him." It appeared in the *San Francisco Examiner*,
Magazine Supplement, May 9, 1909.

35. The mission station at North Star Bay under construction, 1909. The supply ship *Godthaab* is seen in the bay.

36. The completed mission station at North Star Bay, August, 1909. On the left is the missionaries' house, on the right a warehouse. In the background is the mountain, Uummannaq, later to be known as Thule Mountain.

37. Polar Eskimos at Uummannaq, July, 1909.

38. An Eskimo man, Ittukusuk, and his sister, Kassaaluk, outside a summer tent at the Eskimo village at Uummannaq, July 1909.

39. Three Polar Eskimo hunters. Left, Maissannguaq, aged about 45; center, Ittukusuk, aged about 24; right, Ulloriaq, aged about 35, at Uummannaq, July 1909.

40. Arnarulunnguag, Navarana and Inugaarsuk, three Polar Eskimo women. Arnarulunnguaq married Minik's first cousin, Iggiannguaq; Navarana was the wife of Peter Freuchen; Inugaarsuk was Minik's first cousin, a daughter of Amaunnalik.

41. Eskimo children at the mission and trading station at Uummannaq, July 1909.

42. Soqqaq, the
Polar Eskimo
shaman, who took
Minik
into his home at
Uummannaq
in 1909.
Photographed
before 1898.

43. Eri, son of the
shaman, Soqqaq,
who became Minik's
"guardian" in 1909.
Eri is about 35 in
this picture, taken
in July 1909.

44. Qaarqutsiaq, son of Eri and grandson of the shaman Soqqaq, at
Uummannaq, July 1909. Qaarqutsiaq, who lives today in Qaanaaq,
Greenland, was one of the author's informants in his research on Minik.

45. Two Polar Eskimo women. Standing, Arnaruniaq, aged about 21; seated, Inalliaq, aged about 24.

46. Missionaries at Uummannaq, 1910. On the left are Emilie and Sechmann Rosbach. In the center is Ane Sofia, wife of Gustav Olsen, who is on the extreme right. The others are a Polar Eskimo man, Uusaqqaq and a woman, Antonethe.

47. Gustav Olsen and his family and a group of Polar Eskimo children.

48. Three Eskimos in the house of the Thule Trading Station, about 1910.

49. Arnannguaq, who was Minik's wife for a time at Uummannaq, photographed in 1916. The child is Peter Freuchen's son, Meqqusaaq.

50. Peter Fruechen and a group of Eskimos at the Thule Trading Station, Uummannaq, about 1915.

51. Minik hitching his dogs.

52. Minik in kayak, at Uummannaq.

53. Minik and some of the men of the Crocker Land Expedition in MacMillian's house at Etah. From left to right, Minik, Small, Allen, and Tanqueray.

54. Minik sitting with his gun and binoculars in the doorway of the Crocker Land Expedition quarters at Etah.

55. Minik and Sigluk, with two women, on the ice in the Parker Snow Bay in front of the *George B. Cluett*, winter, 1915–16.

56. Donald B. MacMillan, leader of the Crocker Land Expedition.

57. Group of Eskimos at Etah during the Crocker Land Expedition.

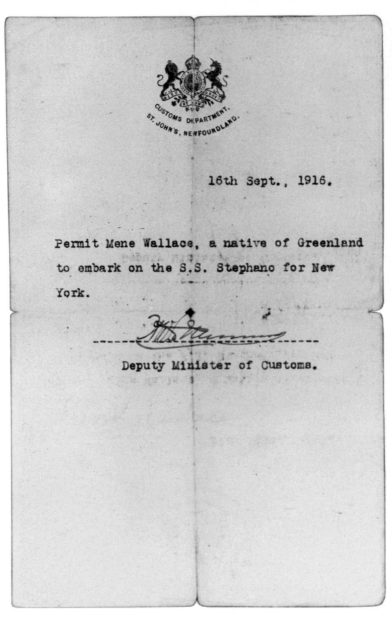

16th Sept., 1916.

Permit Mene Wallace, a native of Greenland
to embark on the S.S. Stephano for New
York.

Deputy Minister of Customs.

58. Permit from the Customs Department, St John's, Newfoundland,
allowing Minik to embark for New York, 1916.

59. Copy of Minik's Military Registration Certificate. June 1917.

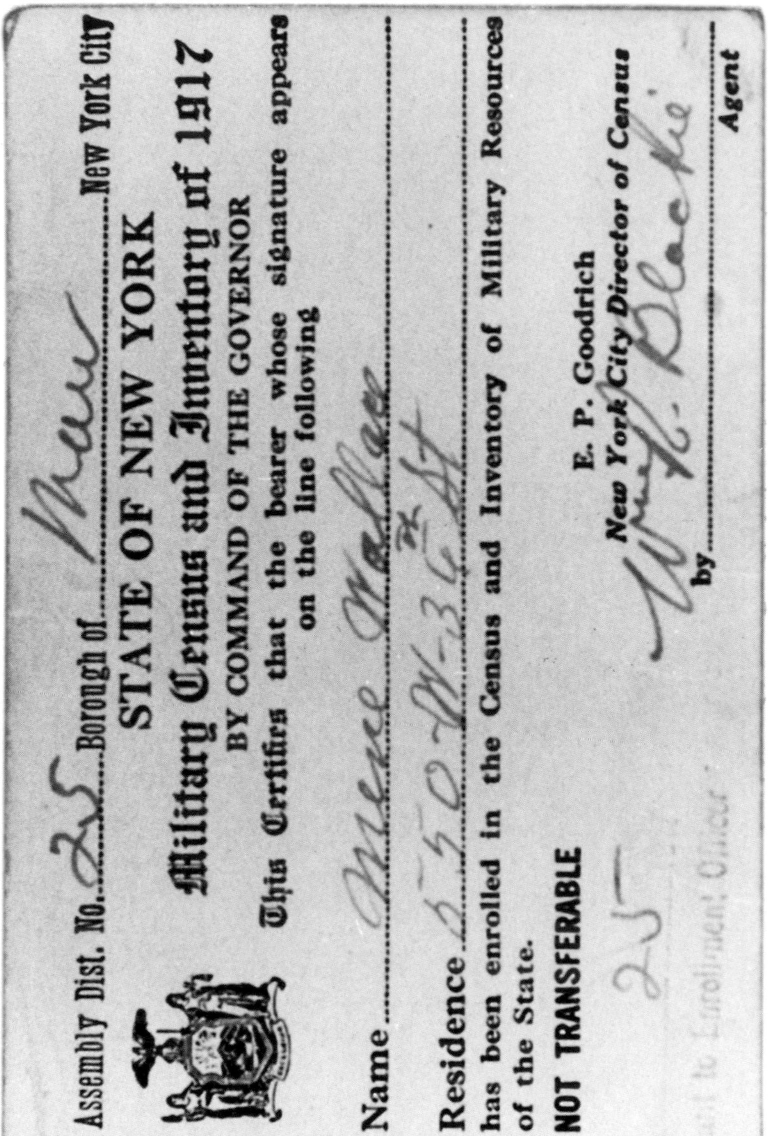

Assembly Dist. No. 25 Borough of Man New York City

STATE OF NEW YORK

Military Census and Inventory of 1917

BY COMMAND OF THE GOVERNOR

This Certifies that the bearer whose signature appears on the line following

Name Mene Wallace

Residence 550 W-36 St

has been enrolled in the Census and Inventory of Military Resources of the State.

NOT TRANSFERABLE

E. P. Goodrich

New York City Director of Census

by Wm H. Blackie

Agent

25

60. Minik's Military Census Card, State of New York, 1917.

U. S. DEPARTMENT OF LABOR
NATURALIZATION SERVICE

No. 146312

JRO-288-77

TRIPLICATE
[To be given to the person making the Declaration]

UNITED STATES OF AMERICA

DECLARATION OF INTENTION

☞ **Invalid for all purposes seven years after the date hereof**

State of New York, }
County of New York, } ss:

In the Supreme Court of New York County.

I, Mene Peary Wallace , aged 27 years,

occupation Clerk , do declare on oath that my personal

description is: Color white , complexion dark , height 5 feet 6 inches,

weight 155 pounds, color of hair black , color of eyes brown

other visible distinctive marks none

I was born in Etah, Greenland

on the 5th day of August , anno Domini 1 889 ; I now reside

at 550 Third Avenue (Give number and street.) , New York City, N. Y.

I emigrated to the United States of America from Parker Snow Bay, Greenland

on the vessel George B. Cluett (If the alien arrived otherwise than by vessel, the character of conveyance or name of transportation company should be given.) ; my last

foreign residence was Etah, Greenland

I am unmarried

It is my bona fide intention to renounce forever all allegiance and fidelity to any foreign

prince, potentate, state, or sovereignty, and particularly to Christian X.

King of Denmark , of whom I am now a subject: I

arrived at the port of New York , in the

State of New York , on or about the 21st day

of September , anno Domini 1 916 ; I am not an anarchist; I am not a

polygamist nor a believer in the practice of polygamy; and it is my intention in good faith

to become a citizen of the United States of America and to permanently reside therein:

SO HELP ME GOD.

Mene Peary Wallace.
(Original signature of declarant.)

Subscribed and sworn to before me in the office of the Clerk of

said Court at New York City, N. Y., this 30th day

of January anno Domini 191 7

[SEAL]

WILLIAM F. SCHNEIDER

Clerk of the Supreme Court.

By *Thomas J Shalvey*, Special Clerk.

Special Deputy County Clerk

61. Minik's copy of his Declaration of Intent to become a citizen of
the United States, January 1917.

62. Minik's grave in the Indian Stream Cemetery, Pittsburg, New Hampshire. His date of birth is incorrect.

PEARY'S NEGLECTED ESKIMO BOY WANTS TO SHOOT HIM.

Eskimo Garments of Fur, Was Dressed When He from Greenland.

Mene's Father, Whose Bones Are Now in the Museum as an Interesting "Scientific Exhibit."

SKELETON OF AN ESKIMO PRESERVED BY ROBERT E. PEARY

"What would Mr. Peary do if he was walking through the museum and suddenly came face to face with the skeleton of his father staring at him from a glass case?"

How the "Scientific Subject" Struggled Against His Destiny.

33. Vesta Tilley, the actress who befriended Minik.

34. Herbert Bridgman and Josephine Peary, in Sydney, Nova Scotia, 1909.

There were actually two agreements. The first, signed by William Wallace, who was identified as "Foster Parent," and by Chester Beecroft and Minik Wallace, read, "Minik and his friends, guardians in fact though not in law, hereby agree that he will accept the discipline of the Jeanie and obey the orders of its captain; that he will land and remain at some point of call, agreed on by Commander Peary and himself, or in Commander Peary's absence by Capt. Bartlett and himself; that he will take on shore for himself and for his people only such arms, ammunition, and other goods as Commander Peary or Capt. Bartlett may approve, and that all claims of every kind against the 'Jeanie' and her owners are hereby expresly [sic] and forever waived."

William Wallace was made to sign an additional statement. It read, "Thirteen years ago I became the foster parent of Minik at the request of the late Morris K. Jesup and as a parent I accept the kindly interest offered by H. L. Bridgman to allow Minik to again see his people in the far north, feeling that it will aid the boy and his people."

This statement, drafted by Bridgman, Jesup's closest associate in the Peary Arctic Club, belatedly acknowledges what Jesup had steadfastly refused to admit, that Wallace had assumed the care of Minik at Jesup's request. Bridgman's eye for detail had not noted, though, that Minik had been in the United States for only twelve years, nor that for the first of those years William Wallace was not his foster parent. But such details were of little consequence now; the agreements were signed, for their signing was the condition for Minik being given passage.

One further condition was exacted from William Wallace: In a telephone conversation with Bridgman the night before Minik's departure, he agreed that he would give the captain permission to examine Minik's baggage before the boy embarked in St. John's, and added that "Minik's feelings toward Peary and all of the Americans were kindest." One wonders why Bridgman went on extracting hollow statements of loyalty and kind feelings from a young man who had no reason to do anything but despise Peary, for there was no chance that Minik or Wallace would disagree with anything Bridgman said at this point. One suspects it was a means for Bridgman to humiliate William Wallace as much as possible. Bridgman advised Mrs. Peary by letter of Wallace's concession and added that he would ask Captain Bartlett "to avail himself of this permission to the fullest extent and endeavor to hold him, in Peary's absence, personally responsible for anything that Minik may land."

Was there reason for this paranoia? What did they expect him to take with him? It seems that Bridgman and Mrs. Peary were concerned that Minik might actually try to make good on his threat to shoot Robert Peary. Peary had been in the north since the summer of 1908 and had no way of knowing the events that had occurred since then. He had been in the north through all the turbulent events of early 1909 — Minik's unsuccessful flirtation with higher education at Manhattan College, the desperate attempt to escape northward and homeward via Canada, the plaintive plea for help and understanding in the suicide letter from Montreal, and all the sensational press coverage bannering for all the world to see how Peary and his cronies had mistreated and neglected a helpless boy in a foreign environment. Peary would not even know that Minik was aboard the *Jeanie*, let alone that the boy had publicly stated that he would like to shoot him. Bridgman, whose responsibility was to effect the relief of Peary, could not afford the possibility, however slight, that an unsuspecting Robert Peary might be shot on sight by the Eskimo boy he had ignored.

Bridgman sent Bartlett a copy of the agreements, with the instruction that he should transmit them and any other relevant facts on the matter to Peary as soon as he should meet him, although he added, "I will endeavour to cover the ground in my own letter to him." One can be sure that letter was a lengthy one.

A few days later, after Minik's departure, Bridgman would gloat in a letter to Mrs. Peary, "Minik Wallace still has no contract nor anything else signed by me. They all signed the memorandum of which I sent you copy."

Since his return from Quebec, and his recovery under Beecroft's care at the Hotel Astor, Minik had been living with William Wallace again, on Long Island. He had maintained his friendship with Vesta Tilley, the Broadway actress. She would later claim in her autobiography that "he had become my devoted slave, and both my husband and myself were loath to part with him. We rigged him out and he left us in tears." He made a request to see his father's remains one last time before he went north, but his request was denied. "They say they are not on exhibition any more," he complained, "so I can't see them!" He spent the day before he left the United States at Chester Beecroft's camp on Hunter's Island, swimming and trying to relax.

Although he had just recovered from another attack of pneumonia, he had some fighting spirit remaining for his last visit with the press on the day before his departure and gave them his parting thoughts on America. "You're a race of scientific criminals," he charged. "I know I'll never get my father's bones out of the American Museum of Natural History. I am glad enough to get away before they grab my brains and stuff them into a jar!" Incredible as it may seem, someone had, just before he was to leave, made the suggestion, duly reported in the *New York Times*, that he should "bequeath his brain to science for anthropological purposes." The *Times* could not seem to understand why Minik was shocked and offended by such a suggestion; it commented, ". . . to Minik, the polite request seemed chilling, and suggestive of early and sudden demise. He could not catch the scientific point of view." Small wonder!

Minik continued, "I sail north tomorrow and I am tickled to death to get away. . . .

"About the only persons I regret to leave are Mr. Beecroft and the Wallaces, my foster parents. I don't know what I should have done, but for them. They have been most kind to me."

In overdone language, replete with stereotypes about both the north and his own people, he outlined again his plan, naive and pathetic as it was, to conquer the North Pole himself with an all-Eskimo expedition:

"You Americans never will discover the north pole. You are not physically constituted for the work. Only an Eskimo can live for any length of time up there.

"When I get back to Etah in the north of Greenland, I am going to organize an expedition of my own and go in search of the pole myself. I'll find it, too.

"You folks down here have done one thing for me. You have given me a scientific education. I understand navigation and the use of the sextant, so I'll know when I do reach the pole.

"My people will have many advantages over your polar expeditions. When the six months of darkness set in, your explorers have to go into camp and stay there until it grows light again. If they didn't they'd get lost. We are accustomed to the darkness and go straight ahead.

"We won't need to bother much about supplies, either. People who are brought up on blubber and fish don't worry much about canned peaches and other delicacies like that. We will be able practically to live on the country as we go along.

"The only reason the Eskimo hasn't discovered the north pole is that he is not able to realize that the world is curious about it. He thinks Peary and the rest of the explorers are crazy.

"From what I have seen down here, I think I understand the restless spirit of scientific competition that drives you on. So I am going to get into the game myself."

He didn't balk at talking to the press about the agreement he and his guardians had been forced to sign, either, and he put it in the context of his plan for a North Pole expedition: "It is this fact which caused the signing of the agreement never to return to this country, because other explorers are jealous and do not wish me to inform the world of possible success. This, however, will not deter me and the world will know what I discover."

Could he have done it? There is very little likelihood that he could ever have succeeded in carrying out his plan for a polar expedition. The Polar Eskimos' sole interest in the North Pole was that Robert Peary paid those he trusted reasonably well in trade goods for their services as sled drivers and camp helpers. Other than that, they had no desire to reach the Pole. It is impossible they would be convinced to join Minik in such a senseless undertaking simply for the glory of their race, for such ethnocentrism was a white man's idea that Minik had learned in the United States and one not shared by his fellow Polar Eskimos. He was, in fact, correct in stating that the Polar Eskimos suspected that white men, at least the ones they knew, were indeed crazy because of their single-minded quest for a remote geographical point. Although Minik could not have known it at the time, in April of that very year his people's suspicion had been confirmed, they felt, when Robert Peary claimed to have finally reached the Pole in their company and the Eskimos observed, to their utter amazement, that there was nothing there! The Eskimos would not partake in such a senseless undertaking except for a just reward, and Minik most certainly did not have the means to pay them.

But to the meticulous Bridgman, it was probably a cause for concern. Peary, as he had demonstrated repeatedly in his statements of virtual ownership over his "American Route" to the Pole, was paranoid over any threat, real or imagined.

Minik's bravado, his flare for publicity, and his apparent self-confidence belied a terrible insecurity that had grown within him. Four months earlier, as he trekked desperately northward in his futile attempt to reach the Arctic and live the life of an Eskimo again, a perceptive newspaper report had asked, "But even if he gets there, can he do it? He has been in America since he was seven, and even though he is unfit here, it is probable that his life has made him equally unfit for that environment. If so, it will be his crowning tragedy and the crowning injustice of the heartless science that made of him a subject. He will be literally a boy not without a country, but without a place on earth."

The experiment begun by the museum's scientists and sanctioned by Jesup had been set aside and never completed, for reasons not the fault of its unfortunate subject. It had drawn itself inexorably to its own sad close. As far as the museum and the Peary Arctic Club were concerned, the experiment, abandoned years ago, would be formally ended on the following day.

Wallace bid farewell to Minik that night at Beecroft's camp at Pelham Bay Park. He brought with him his son, Willie, Minik's one-time playmate in the halcyon days at Cobleskill. Now twenty-two, Willie was about to become a father — his young wife, Matilda, would give birth to their first son in only four days. Some time after the death of Rhetta Wallace and the virtual collapse of William Wallace's world, Willie had gone to live with relatives; this tearful departure from Minik was also their first reunion in a number of years.

On the following day, July 10, Minik sailed from New York for St. John's on the Red Cross Line steamer, *Rosalind*. The line had given him free passage. Once in St. John's he would transfer to the *Jeanie*.

Bridgman was at the pier to see him off and, to be sure, to make certain that he left. It was not a pleasant farewell, but the Peary Arctic Club had to keep up appearances. Minik carried with him a few unlikely gifts — a set of dentist's tools given him by a dentist in New York, who had instructed him in their use, and a medical kit, the last-minute gift of a doctor.

Bridgman, never one to leave affairs half finished, wrote to William Wallace that evening, "I bade Minik good-bye this morning on the 'Rosalind' and was glad to see him looking so well and cheerful. I hope the journey will be agreeable and that he may ultimately be of real service to his people."

16

RETURN TO GREENLAND

MINIK HAD A THREE-WEEK wait in St. John's before the *Jeanie* left for Greenland. There was nothing for him to do except wait for her departure in a local hotel, for Bridgman had arranged that Captain Bartlett would not take charge of him until the actual sailing.

The down-to-earth people of St. John's, unlike those of New York, had seen "too many Eskimos in their native state . . . to be very much impressed with one," but they did note with sarcasm that Minik could "smoke cigarettes, play billiards and drink brandy neat, along with other evidences of . . . higher education. . . ."

But there was one man in St. John's at the time who took a more compassionate view of Minik. He was a minister of the Church of England bound for the Canadian Arctic. His name was Archibald Lang Fleming and he would later become the first Bishop of the Arctic.

Fleming had arrived in the city in early July to attend to the outfitting of the *Lorna Doone*, a small fishing schooner that the church had chartered for the voyage to Lake Harbor on Baffin Island. While there he chanced to meet Minik. Fleming described the encounter: "Shortly after my arrival in the city an immaculately dressed young man came up to me in the lobby of the Crosby Hotel where I was staying and said, 'Excuse me, but are you the man who is going to the Eskimo in Baffin Land?' Almost before I could answer he surprised me by saying in a pleasant, soft voice, 'I go back to my home in Greenland.' I was startled and for a moment speechless. Before I had recovered and while I was still studying his face, noting his copper skin, brown eyes, black hair and high cheekbones, he smiled gravely and said, 'I am Minik Wallace.'"

Fleming had heard of him and read of his escapades in the Canadian newspapers, but he was surprised to find him in St. John's, for in his mind he had associated him only with New York. Nonetheless he greeted him warmly. This was to be Fleming's first trip to the Arctic, and Minik Wallace was the first Eskimo he had ever seen. The missionary took a kindly interest in him. "My surprise and delight at encountering him were very real," he wrote. "We soon became friends and because Minik had nothing to do but await the arrival of the ship that was to take him north he was glad to come with me on various errands when I was purchasing our supplies. He was very lonely and talked with great freedom about his experiences in New York. . . ."

Minik had had some second thoughts about leaving the south for the unknown of Greenland, especially since he, Wallace, and Beecroft had been forced to sign Bridgman's agreements. He was "discontented and even bitter," Fleming thought. In his tormented mind he had begun to look upon the move as an exile rather than as a repatriation. He had decided also that William Wallace should share some of the blame for the way his life had turned out. And he had started to fantasize, so that his life in New York, barely behind him, had begun to take on elements even more fantastic than the events that had already occurred — the sad and defeated William Wallace had become Dr. Wallace and was "just waiting for him to die so that his skull might be put in the museum alongside that of his father!" Vesta Tilley, the actress more than twice his age whom he had met only in May, became his girlfriend and constant companion.

Fleming felt sorry for this young man who was searching so obviously for friendship and love. The rough exterior was not convincing. Behind the bragging and boasting that peppered his talk hid an insecure young man pleading for understanding, for if Minik were really the cold, uncaring fellow he professed to be, why had he sought out the company of the missionary, helped him on his errands, and spent countless hours in conversation with him? Fleming wrote, "My heart went out to him but I found him hard and void of any love for his own people. This may have been understandable after the adjustments he had been required to make, but it was distressing. He was completely lacking in religious faith of any kind, whether pagan or Christian."

On July 30 Minik was at the dock to wave farewell to Fleming as the *Lorna Doone* bore him out of the protected harbor of St. John's to begin his Arctic odyssey.

On August 3 it was his own turn. On that day, the *Jeanie* finally sailed, the latest a ship had ever left for the High Arctic. Minik was aboard, taking with him "a fine assortment of the vices that are supposed to be necessary evils which go with civilization."

Three weeks later, the *Jeanie* was in Melville Bay. Sunday, August 22, she was steaming ahead under dead reckoning. The fog was thick but now and then, when it lifted, Bartlett was able to pick out some familiar landmarks. It was important to be able to recognize every significant feature of the shoreline in this treacherous body of water, the grave of so many experienced seamen. When the fog lifted late in the morning, a stretch of pack ice miles wide could be seen rafted against the shore to the east of Cape York. Bartlett gave the pack a wide berth and, picking his way delicately past some monstrous icebergs, passed Cape York and the crimson cliffs beyond it. Here icebergs were numerous as they calved off the three-mile-wide marble wall of the Pitugvik Glacier.

The weather remained clear. In late August the sun sinks lower in the sky as fall approaches, but at midnight it still skimmed the edge of the horizon. Coffee was served in the cabin at midnight, and no one felt like turning in, even though there was no real reason for staying up, except that the ship was well into the Arctic, the scenery was spectacular, and the weather splendid.

Minik was the first to sight the *Roosevelt*. It was half past one in the morning when the distinctive rigging of Peary's specially designed Arctic ship came into view on the horizon. As the *Roosevelt* drew near, the fur-clad figure of Peary could be made out on the bridge standing beside Sam Bartlett's nephew, Bob, the *Roosevelt's* master. The sailors, too, recognized one another, for they were all Newfoundland men, almost all from Brigus.

The two Bartletts decided that they would head for North Star Bay to coal the *Roosevelt* in the protected waters there. The cargo of coal that the *Jeanie* carried for Peary was vital to him, for the *Roosevelt* had used up most of her own fuel and the precious cargo of the *Jeanie* was what she awaited before making her departure down Davis Strait for the south.

As the two vessels entered North Star Bay, kayaks appeared from the shore as the Eskimos of Uummannaq hurried to discover the reason for the *Roosevelt's* return and to inspect the unknown ship that accompanied her. Aboard the *Roosevelt* were a number of Cape York Eskimos — "Peary's People" — on their way back to their homes. And on the *Jeanie* stood one Eskimo, small, frightened, back home at last, but feeling very much alone.

The Eskimos were curious about this dark-skinned young man aboard the *Jeanie*. He looked like one of them. But he was reticent about stepping forward and making himself known, for he could not speak a single word of the native language. There were a few white men aboard the *Roosevelt*, however, who could speak the Eskimo language after a fashion and they explained to the curious crowd of Eskimos that had gathered that this was their long-departed countryman, the son of the great Qisuk, who had sailed south with Peary so many years earlier. This was the orphan Minik.

Harry Whitney, the sports hunter who had gone north on the *Erik* the previous year, and who would shortly leave for bear hunting on Ellesmere Island aboard the *Jeanie*, had picked up enough of the local language to make himself understood, and he tried to tell them that "Minik was now a 'qallunaaq,' a white man." The Eskimos wouldn't hear of it. Eskimos did not become white men. If he was the son of Qisuk, he was one of them. Through signs, smiles, and gestures of friendship, they welcomed him home.

The *New York Herald* correspondent aboard the *Jeanie*, Royal K. Fuller, noted the next day that, although Minik could not understand the language, "he soon fraternized with them and last night was again a full-fledged 'huskie,' sleeping in a tupiq."

Fuller also wrote, "Commander Peary has given to him two guns and an elaborate outfit, and when he gets his fur clothes he will be one of his own again."

In another report, the correspondent said that Minik "made his peace with Mr. Peary when the ships were lying side by side at North Star Bay, and Minik received a shotgun, a rifle, ammunition for both, and complete outfit of good tools and supplies, which he declared was all he asked and which was entirely satisfactory to him."

These dispatches from the *Herald's* correspondent cannot be entirely trusted. On July 15, before the *Jeanie* had left St. John's, Herbert Bridgman, the master strategist, was putting the finishing touches on what he referred to as a "scheme" involving the *Herald*. Whatever the scheme was, documentation of it, as with most of Bridgman's dealings where Peary was concerned, has not survived. But it was important enough that it required Mrs. Peary's approval. He drafted a memorandum to her and in a covering letter that has survived he drew her attention to the third paragraph as being "of special interest." He explained, ". . . besides the obvious advantage to the owners of the 'Jeanie,' I am rather inclined to think that the 'Herald' man on the spot, with what I should be able to give him beforehand, would get 'the rights' of this whole Cook-Minik, etc. business, in a way, which would be advantageous. . . . I have had the 'Herald's' formal assent to the scheme." Whatever this undisclosed plan was, it was in part designed to make Peary look charitable and ungrudging in his treatment of Minik.

The first thing Samuel Bartlett gave Peary was the thick letter he carried from Herbert Bridgman. It gave Peary a complete rundown of everything that had transpired to date in the matter of Doctor Cook's preemptive polar expedition as well as informed him of the events that had led to the repatriation of Minik. It suggested to Peary strategies for handling both. Before Minik left the *Jeanie* and was finally free of Peary, he was made to sign one more document:

> I hereby acknowledge the receipt from Commander Peary
> of the following items of supplies and equipment. The same
> being all that I have asked for and all that are needed to
> make me entirely comfortable.

4 cases biscuit.

1 case tea.

1 case coffee.

1 case sugar.

1 case beans.

1 case oil.

salt and pepper.

1 double barrel 10 gauge shot gun.

1 — 100 loaded shells.

1 40-82 Winchester repeating rifle.

200 rounds ammunition.

11 pieces lumber for sledge, kayak and paddle.

1 pair steel sledge shoes.

6 dozen screws for same.

2 pieces lumber for harpoon and lance shafts.

250 primers.

1 hatchet.

1 saw knife — 2 knives.

2 pair scissors.

2 files.

2 fox traps.

4 papers needles.

12 spools thread.

14 thimbles.

2 pair smoked glass goggles.

1 cooking pot.

1 cup.

1 plate.

1 bowl.

1 knife and fork.

3 pipes.

3 or 4 lbs. Tobacco.

2 dozen boxes matches.

1 sweater.

This, the final document in the humiliation of Minik, was Bridgman's last thrust at the unfortunate Eskimo boy and undoubtedly part of the plan to have the *Herald* make Peary look generous in his treatment of him.

But there was one other observer of Minik's return from America. This was an educated Greenlander, Gustav Olsen, who had arrived on the Danish vessel *Godthaab* only a month earlier as the first missionary to the Polar Eskimos. Neither Herbert Bridgman nor Robert Peary had any control over what Olsen wrote, and of Minik's return he made a brief entry in his diary, "On this day another small ship . . . arrived. It was the Jeanie and had come from Newfoundland. . . . On that ship was an Eskimo named Minik who was returning home. He was one of the ones that Peary had taken away when he was a child. He has completely forgotten his language. He came ashore here but we have seen very little of him. He has only the clothes on his back."

17

AN ESKIMO AGAIN

THE DEPARTURE OF THE *Roosevelt* and the *Jeanie* marked the end of an era for the Polar Eskimos. Robert Peary, who had dominated their lives for almost twenty years, would return no more. It was twelve years since he had taken six Polar Eskimos to New York, and in those years he had returned to northwestern Greenland on three major expeditions and had come to regard the area even more as his exclusive preserve.

Now, in 1909, he was claiming the elusive geographical point to which his ego had driven him. The Pole, he wrote, was "MINE . . . to be credited to me, and associated with my name, generations after I had ceased to be." He did not intend to share the credit with anyone. Yet if the Pole belonged to Peary, it belonged equally to Matthew Henson, of whom Peary had said, "[He is] as subject to my will as the fingers of my hand," and to the Eskimos Uutaaq, Ukkujaaq, Iggiannguaq, and Sigluk, whom he belittled with the backhanded compliment that ". . . although they were not qualified to lead, they could follow another's lead and drive dogs much better than any white man." They were the ones who had brought him to his farthest north. But the glory would be Peary's.

With each return of Peary, the Eskimos had become more dependent on him, and he on them. With his usual arrogance, he described his feelings about the relationship in this way: "I had come to regard them with a kindly and personal interest, which any man must feel with regard to the members of any inferior race who had been accustomed to respect and depend upon him." He had needed them for their services as dog drivers and hunters and as providers of the skins and ivory tusks he sold for a good profit in America. They had depended on him for payment in material goods — guns, ammunition, knives, needles, and utensils of various sorts.

Peary would boast, "I have used the Eskimos to a greater extent than any other explorer." In so doing, he had moved them about his northern domain at will, as if they were so many chattels. On each of his last two voyages he had taken between seventy and eighty Eskimos, including all the best young men in the tribe, north on the *Roosevelt* to the tip of Ellesmere Island to act as support for his attempts to reach the Pole. Knud Rasmussen would later comment, ". . . can anyone think of a more serious and extensive contribution to scientific exploration than this wholesale sacrifice of the supremest?"

The glory was Peary's. But there is no denying that the Eskimos had benefited too. When Peary left them, their material standard of living was far higher than it had been when he first came among them. It was much higher, too, than that of the *qavangangnisat* — the West Greenlanders, many of mixed blood, who lived south of Melville Bay. Gustav Olsen, the first missionary to the district, was one of them, and reported, "The Eskimos here have a large number of articles of utility of various kinds, which they have obtained from Peary, so that they, in regard to arms, tools, etc., are better provided than their countrymen in the southern part of the country."

Peary prided himself on this. But it was a selfish and irresponsible pride, for having ensured their almost total dependence on him for the acquisition of material goods, in 1909 he abandoned them without so much as a passing thought for their future. The Polar Eskimos would no longer be Peary's People.

It was fortunate, then, that the year of Peary's departure, while marking the end of one era, marked also the beginning of another in the history of the Polar Eskimos. Since 1906, the Greenland Church Cause had been anxious to establish a mission to the Polar Eskimos, but it had not proven possible to actually begin the work until 1909. The establishment of that mission marked the beginning of a long evolution during which the northwestern part of Greenland would gradually become an integral part of Danish Greenland.

On July 23, 1909, a small ship, the *Godthaab*, anchored in North Star Bay near the Eskimo village of Uummannaq. Captain Schoubye and his crew remained for two weeks to help the missionaries with the hasty construction of a mission station-cum-trading post and a small house for the priest, the catechist, and their families.

The church's choice of priest was fortunate. Usually a Dane was sent as missionary to the outlying districts, but to Uummannaq the church sent Gustav Olsen, a native Greenlander from Jakobshavn in Disko Bay. He was thirty years old and had been ordained into the priesthood only a month earlier. The Polar Eskimos called him Guutak. He was accompanied by his wife, Ane Sofia. With them was a catechist, also a native of Disko Bay, the thirty-one-year-old Scchmann Rosbach, and his young wife, Emilie.

It was only a month after the establishment of the North Star Mission that the *Jeanie*, following closely behind the familiar *Roosevelt*, arrived and deposited Minik on the shores of North Star Bay. Minik held back shyly on board the *Jeanie*, afraid to step forward and present himself, but finally he stepped gingerly into a kayak to be taken ashore. He hadn't uttered a word yet, but the sailors said that he was Minik, son of Qisuk.

Word spread quickly through the small village. Minik was back! Twelve years is not such a long time for people of an oral culture, whose minds do not need the crutch of the printed word to aid their memories. Of course they remembered him. They had never failed to inquire of Peary, whenever he returned, of the child who had been taken from their midst so many years before, and if the replies had been evasive or difficult to comprehend, it had been enough to know that he was yet alive. But they had long since given up any idea that he would return.

When Peary's Eskimo companions had spread the message that Peary had reached the Pole and was now leaving the district for good, those who still cared had felt for certain that now Minik would never return, for there would be no way of getting from America to Greenland. And now, miraculously, almost at the last minute of the Peary era, here he was!

He had been orphaned in 1898, but he would get no sympathy at Uummannaq on that count, for by Eskimo standards he was already an adult. It was unusual, though, in an Eskimo society, that he had been an only child; as a result, besides being an orphan, he had no siblings to rely on. His mother, Mannik, had had two older sisters, however, and both had married and had children of their own. Mannik's eldest sister, Siuleqatuk, had become the wife of Angutilluarsuk and had borne him two sons, Ivik and Iggiannguaq. The other sister, Amaunnalik, had married Qujaukittoq. They had a daughter, Inugaarsuk, and a son, Inukittoq, whom white explorers had nicknamed Harrigan. He had been one of Peary's men. So Minik had first cousins, and in an Eskimo community that was just as good as having siblings. He would not be alone.

But — *nallinnaq!* — he was certainly to be pitied. For this young man, this relative of theirs, was something that the Eskimos of Uummannaq had never imagined, an Eskimo who could not speak a single word of the Eskimo tongue!

The Polar Eskimos had long since learned to take change in their stride. Times were changing for them, they knew. If Minik was unusual, if his ways were to prove a trifle eccentric, perhaps he was just a bit ahead of his time, a sign of the times to come.

He came ashore wearing a light sweater and a thin overcoat. He was wearing his only pair of pants. On his feet he wore a pair of short socks and everyday shoes, fit for New York but hardly appropriate for the Arctic. He carried with him his medical and dental kits. He had nothing else.

He was taken to the tent of Soqqaq, one of his relatives. Soqqaq had been one of the greatest hunters in the district and a powerful shaman as well. He was one of the few who had always resented the migration of the Eskimos from Baffin Island, led by the mighty Qillarsuaq, to the land of the Polar Eskimos half a century earlier. They brought with them new customs and reintroduced technology long forgotten by the Polar Eskimos, but Soqqaq never adopted their ways, and the newcomers usurped some of his influence and a great deal of his glory. He was an old man now, lame in both arms, but he still had a reputation as the best dog breeder in northern Greenland and he was the proud owner of a team of black dogs far superior to those of his tribesmen. He welcomed this pitiful kinsman into his home and vowed to teach him the language and the ways of his people and help him to make up, as best he could, for his lost childhood.

Under the guidance of the old shaman, Minik learned quickly. In his last few trying years in New York, he had found true enjoyment in the camping trips he had taken with his friend, Chester Beecroft; to the extent that his precarious health permitted, he had always been an athlete and an outdoorsman. Back in the crisp climate of Greenland, he took readily to the life of a young hunter. Today, among the oldest of the Polar Eskimos, there are those who knew him in 1909 and remember, still with a trace of awe, how quickly he learned the ancient skills.

The theme of the neglected orphan, mistreated by his own people and abandoned to find his food among the scraps left by the dogs, is a common one in Eskimo mythology. In these myths, the orphan invariably survives and grows to adulthood to become a mighty hunter who ultimately wreaks his vengeance on those who had most badly mistreated him. A Polar Eskimo summed up the merits of this harsh philosophy with the following logic: "An orphan who has a hard time should never be pitied, for he is merely being hardened to a better life. Look, and you will see that the greatest chief hunters living here have all been orphans. . . . I can remember how Qisunnguaq was left behind by starving foster parents and still made out by seeking out the winter depots of the foxes and at the same time training himself more in hunger than people thought possible. Today, it is impossible for Qisunnguaq to feel cold. Look at Angutilluarsuk, who always manages to cross the tracks of the game animals, and who endures all hardships and can live without sleep more than anybody else. His childhood was spent in constant starvation, and for several winters his only food was stolen from the hunters' meat graves. . . ."

The deprivations of Minik's youth had been of a different kind, not physical, but cultural and emotional, and they had hurt him deeply. There was no one at hand for him to take his revenge on, but within two years of his arrival he had become a hunter the equal of any of his people and the superior of many. Seal, walrus, polar bear, narwhal — Minik would tackle them all. It was as if he had to prove to his people that he had at last, if belatedly, found his place in the world.

Immediately on his arrival at Uummannaq, Minik found a friend in the catechist, Sechmann Rosbach. At first the two could barely communicate and relied on an improvised sign language to converse. In fact, Minik, Rosbach, and Olsen all shared one problem — that of how to communicate with the Polar Eskimos. Although Rosbach and Olsen were native Greenlanders, the Eskimo dialect they spoke was radically different from that of the Polar Eskimos, and until they were used to it, they could barely understand the local language. But they set about to learn it soon after their arrival. Minik was at even more of a disadvantage; he spoke no Eskimo dialect at all, but in the tent of Soqqaq he too learned quickly.

On August 25, only two days after his arrival, he went on his first hunting trip, to the head of Uummannaq's fjord, by boat with Sechmann Rosbach and a party of Eskimos. Just before the *Roosevelt* had left, Peary, perhaps feeling a belated twinge of conscience, had given the boy a rifle and a shotgun — although he did not provide him the other articles on the long list he made the young man sign. On this hunting excursion, Minik took to a kayak and, with his rifle, killed his first seal. To the great surprise of Rosbach and the Eskimos, he tried to skin it without slitting it down the belly. Rather, he cut it around the head and tried to remove the flesh, bones, and fat through that opening, in effect hollowing it out, leaving a huge skin bag complete with flippers. What on earth was he trying to do? they wondered. Through signs they asked him. He pointed inland, to where the caribou roamed, and finally, through a series of gestures, he made them to understand that he intended to put a caribou skin inside this sealskin and use it as a sleeping bag! It proved impossible and he gave up the attempt. But his relatives thought him all the more unusual for this innovative approaching to skinning a seal.

How lonely he must have been, despite the kindly help of old So-qqaq and his other relatives! For despite his rapidly acquired hunting prowess, he remained in many ways a stranger at home. Although he had quickly acquired fluency in his native tongue, he missed the English language, the companionship of Beecroft, and the attention of William Wallace. If his room at the Alliance House had been small, then Soqqaq's tent was minuscule — and squalid to boot! Still, he loved the old man for the care he showed him and the wisdom he shared with him.

One day he borrowed Soqqaq's team of powerful black dogs and left inland to hunt for caribou. He was gone for several days, alone with his thoughts in his homeland, a land almost as foreign to him now as New York City had been to him as a child. Finally he returned. He was dead tired as he trudged dejectedly toward the mission house. He stood nervously outside until Emilie noticed him and beckoned him in. Rosbach and his wife, unable to speak with him, nonetheless made him welcome through their smiles and gestures. They made him tea and fed him. By the time he had eaten his fill, tears were streaming silently down his face. Embarrassed, he dried his eyes and got up to leave. As he was going out, Emilie handed him some food to take with him.

He turned and spoke to the couple but they could not understand what he said. Then he left.

Much later, when all of them had learned the language of the Polar Eskimos, Minik told the Rosbachs about the thoughts that had raced through his mind on that critical day. He told them:

"The life I have led has been so embarrassing that I have been unable to tell anyone about it. But I would like to tell you because the two of you care and you have opened up your hearts. Here, among people who are heathens, you have shown me that there is still a God who loves the poor folks and cares for them. In America, when I found out what they had done to my father, I gave up the beliefs that I had had and I didn't think I would ever want to go back to them. But when I was out caribou hunting, I felt like I was the loneliest person in the world. There, for the first time in a very long time, I cried when I was alone, and I prayed to the God of whom I know so little, and

163

asked that he lead me back to the village while I was yet alive, for I had given up hope and I was so weak and hungry.

"And he led me back to the village. And as I approached your house, I thought, 'if they just ignore me, then I will know for sure that I am no more important than a mere animal.'

"I had already decided that it would be better if I took my own life very quickly. When I was standing outside your house, I saw the priest [Olsen] but I couldn't even talk with him because we couldn't understand each other. I tried to say to him. 'I am so miserable and useless that I didn't even see one caribou.' He just looked at me and gave a little smile, and I didn't say anything more. Just as I was about to go back to the tent, your wife came out and beckoned me in. That touched my heart and I was trembling when I came into your house.

"When you treated me so kindly and let me eat my fill and had coffee with me, I just couldn't do anything else but cry, because I realized how much God still loved me and wanted to save my life. When I had finished crying, what I said to you was, 'I abandoned my heavenly father along life's evil road.' Many times after that I often thought that I had led such a terrible life that he would never take me back to him again. But a few days ago, I realized again that he still loves me and has pity on me, and he has shown me all this through you. So I want to thank you, man and wife, because you saved my life, and for the rest of my life I will always remember you and always love you."

Sechmann and Emilie Rosbach remained in the district until the early summer of 1916. For all that time, Minik was their close friend and he never failed to bring them a gift of fresh meat whenever he returned from a hunting trip.

But the loneliness and the feeling of anomie continued. In September of 1910, after a full year in the Arctic, Minik finally had a chance to send letters to a few friends. He sent one to Vesta Tilley, addressing her as his "Great White Queen." But the longest was the one he wrote to Chester Beecroft. He referred briefly to the controversy that had broken in America in 1909, shortly after his return to Greenland, over whether Cook or Peary had been the first to reach the

North Pole, and he offered a cutting comment on whether the effort to find the Pole had been worth the price that had been paid. Already his English was a little rusty:

"I am still alive, how or why I can't tell you. First, let me explain that you would have heard from me long ago only I couldn't get them to take a letter to you. Peary had them land me at North Star Bay a long way south of my home. We had to sign their agreement, you remember, that I would land when Peary said, but they promised in return for the black-hand papers they made you sign, to take me back to Etah.

"But as they had broke faith and human rule with me when I was there [*sic*] stolen gest [*sic*] I was not surprised when they dump me off, by Peary's orders, in a strange part of Greenland, with no furs, gun, sleg [*sic*] dogs, or equipment to battle for life in the desolit [*sic*] ice.

"They refused to carry my letters back to you, though they took my card to Mrs. Cook. . . . In a letter I will tell you a wonderful interesting story of my meeting with the people of my father whome [*sic*] the Americans murdered in the name of science, how they live, how I efected [*sic*] them, how the new-old life efected [*sic*] me, what chanhes [*sic*] I made in them and them in me; later, because the ship is waiting.

"Whitney also refused to take a letter home to you, and mails [malice?] seems to follow me even beyond the North Wind. So to get a letter to you at last I had to make a trip to Cape York. . . . I wanted to prove how I love the only tie that binds me to the land of warmer climate and colder hearts. . . .

"I know you will expect something about Cook. Well, Dob, I have gone to the bottom of the matter. No one up here believes that Peary got much farther than when he left his party. His name up here is hated for his cruelty. Cook made a great trip North. He has nothing in the way of proofs here that I can find. I believe that he went as near as anyone, but the pole has yet to be found. Cook is loved by all, and every Eskimo speaks well of him and hopes that he has the honor over Peary — has he? I will know all soon and will let you know.

"I don't think both ends and the middle of the earth are worth the price that has been paid to almost find one pole. See all the white bones. Where is my father? Why am I no longer fit to live where I was born? Not fit to live where I was kidnapped? Why am I an experiment there and here — and tormented since the great white Pirat [*sic*] interfeared [*sic*] with nature and made a failure and left me helpless orfin [*sic*] — young, abandoned 10,000 miles from home?

"I do not know if this will reach your hand and be looked at with your eyes, but I wish my hand and eyes were taking the same chance with it. I have no friend here or anywhere. I am lonely, lonely. Come up here and I will show you how to find the pole. I will make you king. Then if you want me I will go back to New York with you or stay here or go to hell for you, my friend when there was none."

The letter ended with a postscript: "I expect a white Xmas, Dob."

18

THE THULE STATION

IN 1910, KNUD RASMUSSEN arrived in Uummannaq to establish a trading post alongside the mission in North Star Bay. He named the site Thule, the name the ancient Greeks had given to a mythical archipelago far to the north of Europe. As European knowledge of northern waters had gradually increased, so Thule had moved farther and farther north, always cloaked in mystery, always at the outer edge of European man's geographical knowledge.

A man needs some excuse for putting down roots, and Rasmussen had become a trader as a reason for being in northern Greenland. He was part Eskimo himself and his first language was Greenlandic. Born in Jakobshavn on Disko Bay, he had passed his childhood there, hearing occasional tales of the wild and untamed Inuit of the little-known part of Greenland north of Melville Bay. He became deeply interested in the folklore and history of his people and he determined that he would go to these far northern Eskimos who still lived the lifestyle of his ancestors. After an education in Denmark and a spell working as a journalist in Copenhagen, he had taken part in Mylius-Erichsen's Literary Expedition to northwestern Greenland in 1903. On that expedition he had met the Polar Eskimos for the first time. He was hooked. He knew he must return.

Rasmussen reasoned that Peary would not remain in the district forever. And he knew also that the Eskimos had developed far too heavy a dependence on the American and his trade goods. When Peary eventually found the Pole, he would abandon the Eskimos who had served him so faithfully. They would be even more isolated, thrown roughly back into the Stone Age from which they had so recently emerged. There would not even be the whalers to fall back on, for the *upernaallit* — those who come with the spring — had failed to live up to their name; they had virtually exterminated the bowhead population of Baffin Bay and seldom came to these waters anymore. Only the *Morning* and the *Diana* came now from Scotland to the waters of Melville Bay — in a few years, they too would come no more. Without Peary, the Eskimos would have no source of the trade goods on which they had come to rely. Survival may not have depended on them, but they certainly made a harsh life more tolerable.

So Rasmussen had nurtured a dream of establishing a trading post in the district. The profits from the trade would support his real ambition of mapping what remained uncharted of northern Greenland, of recording the folklore and history of the Polar Eskimos, and ultimately, he hoped, of supporting a mammoth undertaking: a trip through the heartland of the Eskimo world, the central Canadian Arctic, and via Alaska to the Bering Strait, recording ethnological information and folktales the whole way and bringing back an immense collection of artifacts for study in Denmark. It was an ambitious and idealistic hope. Ultimately it worked. But it had its humble beginnings at Uummannaq on the shores of North Star Bay.

In 1909, Rasmussen had helped the Greenland Church Cause, a branch of the Danish Lutheran Church, to found its North Star Mission at Uummannaq. The priest it sent, Gustav Olsen, had been his childhood friend in Disko Bay. And in 1910 he followed, building his trading post, the Thule Station, in the shadow of Mount Dundas, afterward known as Thule Mountain.

With him he brought a giant of a man from Denmark. Peter Freuchen was twenty-four years old and had already been on one Greenland expedition. He too had become hooked on the Arctic. He met Knud Rasmussen in Denmark after his return and the two had become fast friends. When Rasmussen outlined to Freuchen his plans for the Thule Station, Freuchen expressed his willingness — indeed his eagerness — to go. He would manage the Thule Station for the next ten years and go on to earn a reputation as one of the Arctic's most entertaining and prolific writers.

Minik had been living at Uummannaq for a year when Freuchen arrived. He had learned quickly the hunting skills that most boys learn as they grow to manhood and had proved himself a capable hunter. But Freuchen thought him listless and sullen. He had been influenced by stories he had heard about the young man's unusual life, and he wrote, "Minik was a great nuisance to all of us. He was an unhappy lad with a bad disposition. . . . He was absolutely destitute when I first saw him."

Freuchen was at Uummannaq when Minik decided to get married. The young lady was Arnannguaq. She had been offered to Peter Freuchen the previous year by an Eskimo, Majaq, who had been Freuchen's host at a small camp where the Dane had stopped for the night on a trip. Majaq pitied this healthy young man, for everyone knew, he said, that it was not good for a man to be without a woman. He had a girl in mind and immediately brought her forth. Freuchen describes the rest:

"In a whisk Arnannguaq was completely undressed, and her master stood her before me and pointed out, like a slave trader, her especial qualifications, leaving nothing to my imagination. It was a great recommendation, of course, that she was cross-eyed, which would make her the more valuable to me — I would not have to waste my time fighting over her. Her body was not without its virtues, and her manager would have us marry immediately.

"I was both young and bashful, and was more embarrassed for the girl than for myself. Without giving too much offense, I tried to explain my reasons for not wanting to marry her, and finally lay down to sleep. . . . She went away and I did not go to her."

Now Arnannguaq was living as the joint mistress of four young men in one of the houses set aside for the youth of Uummannaq. The missionaries were concerned about this seemingly immoral arrangement. Knud asked Freuchen what he thought they should do about the situation.

Support for the church was one of the few subjects on which Freuchen and Rasmussen differed. Freuchen had an abiding dislike of missionaries and he was sorry that there were any in Uummannaq at all. He wrote, "We must realize that missionaries are going to violate all manner of racial rules and traditions, and even trample upon what the pagans have already believed to be decent.

"Usually they set to work on the question of sex. It is strange how sex has always interested the church. . . . I have always been a little embarrassed for preachers, who seem to wield such small influence over their own flocks at home, daring to interfere with the ways of an alien race."

At one time, when he was traveling with a Polar Eskimo man on an extended trip through southern Greenland, Freuchen heartily concurred when the Eskimo, Ajaku, explained to a local minister, "Up in our country, we consider it wedding enough when one gets the pants off the girl."

Freuchen told Rasmussen that he thought the matter was none of their business, but Rasmussen went to talk with the girl about the situation anyway. Her reply was one of charming innocence. "Don't you think," she asked, "that I would rather marry one single man? This is the only way I have of getting in touch with them."

That same evening, however, Minik came to the house and told the two Danes that he wanted to marry Arnannguaq. The problem was that he had no house of his own to offer her. He wondered if the Danes would allow him and Arnannguaq to move in with them for the winter and in the spring he would build a house of his own.

Freuchen and Rasmussen agreed. They decided that Minik was "probably a good enough fellow and only needed a break." The next day Minik and Arnannguaq left for the north on a honeymoon trip. There was no ceremony.

On their return Minik and Arnannguaq moved into Freuchen's and Rasmussen's home. Freuchen had been concerned by Minik's preoccupation with America and his recounting of a number of improbable adventures there. After the marriage he said, "I saw Minik working at last, adjusting to conditions and trying to make a living for himself and his wife. He had exaggerated his own importance, he said . . . and he promised to begin over again and forget the outside world." He became the handyman for the Thule Station.

The following summer Minik and Freuchen built another house, a smaller one, beside the larger trading post where they had all lived with Rasmussen. The old house would serve as office, dining room, and trading post, and Rasmussen would sleep in the attic. Freuchen would live with Minik and Arnannguaq in the newer and smaller building.

But Minik's marriage to Arnannguaq was less than blissful. She liked nothing better than to spend the whole day asleep. In describing her laziness, Freuchen claimed that she was the most resourceless girl he had ever met. As a result, Minik began to remain away longer and longer on his hunting trips, and in so doing, he inadvertently played a role in Freuchen's own famous marriage to Mequpaluk, who later took the name of Navarana.

One day Minik, tired of Arnannguaq's laziness, announced that he was going north on an extended trip. He left Freuchen living alone in the house with his young wife. Even so, he let Freuchen know that "he did not want to make appointments for exchange of women" with anyone, contrary to the general wife-exchange that took place throughout the district, which the missionaries were trying to end. Freuchen describes the events that ensued:

"To circumvent any whisper of scandal Arnannguaq invited Mequpaluk to spend the night with her. Each evening after the girl had done her chores at home she came running down to the house. . . . She was always in the best of humour and our room became a cheerier place when she entered it. . . . Each night we awaited her arrival with impatience.

"Finally one evening when she came Arnannguaq was absent, and I told Mequpaluk that she had better stay with me. She looked at me a moment and then remarked simply:

"'I am unable to make any decisions, being merely a weak little girl. It is for you to decide that.'

"But her eyes were eloquent, and spoke the language every girl knows regardless of race or clime.

"I only asked her to move from the opposite side of the ledge over to mine — that was all the wedding necessary in this land of the innocents."

Shortly afterward Freuchen and Navarana set off north on a honeymoon trip of their own. They wanted to find her aging grandfather, one-eyed Meqqusaaq, and bring him back to live with them. On their way northbound, they encountered Minik, finally returning from his long hunt. They told him that his wife was expecting him. He appeared, said Freuchen, "none too enthusiastic."

Shortly after, he left her. He was an alert and active young hunter and he told his friend, the catechist Rosbach, "Some of the women are very clever, but others are just lazy. Arnannguaq is nothing but sleep in disguise and I don't want to be married to her."

19

UISAAKASSAK: THE BIG LIAR

IT IS LIKELY THAT MINIK MET Uisaakassak, the only other Polar Eskimo to have survived the year in New York, some time after his return to Greenland, for in 1909 Uisaakassak was living in Inglefield Bay, the next major fjord north of Uummannaq.

In 1898 the *Windward* had taken Uisaakassak back to Greenland, leaving Minik behind in America. Uisaakassak was twenty-three years old when he returned to his people, the first adult Polar Eskimo ever to visit the land of the white men and return to tell about it. That telling was to color his fellows' perceptions of him for the rest of his life.

Uisaakassak had been away for only one year, so language was not a problem for him on his return. Once back among the Polar Eskimos he assembled an audience of his campmates and began to describe to them his experiences among the "man-made mountains" of New York:

"The ships sailed in and out there, like eiders on the brooding cliffs when their young begin to swim. There weren't many free drops of water in the harbor itself; it was filled with ships. You'd risk your life if you tried to go out there in a kayak, you'd simply not be noticed, and you'd be run down unmercifully. People lived up in the air like auks on a bird cliff. The houses are as big as icebergs on a glacial bank, and they stretch inland as far as you can see, like a steep chain of mountains with innumerable canyons that serve as roads.

"And the people. Yes, there are so many of them that when smoke rises from the chimneys and the women are about to make breakfast, clouds fill the sky and the sun is eclipsed."

Encouraged by his listeners' incredulous expressions, he went on. He told about "the streetcars, big as houses, with masses of glass windows as transparent as freshwater ice. They raced on without dogs to haul them, without smoke, and full of smiling people who had no fear of their fate. And all this just because a man pulled on a cord."

The amazement turned to amusement and finally to disbelief. The final straw was his description of the "distance shrinker": "He, Uisaakassak, had stood and talked to Peary, who was visiting another village. Without shouting to one another, they had talked together through a funnel, along a cord."

This was too much. Old Soqqaq rose and told him, "Uisaakassak, go tell your big lies to the women!" He got the message. A few years later an Eskimo commented to a white explorer that Uisaakassak "can tell a lot from over there (America), but he really doesn't want to, for nobody believes him. To begin with, when he came home, he told us so much about Peary's land that it can't possibly be true. Now he's fortunately stopped trying to make us believe more of his tales."

From that point on Uisaakassak was known by the unfortunate nickname, "The Big Liar." He was an excellent hunter, but he was relegated to a position of low prestige within the community because of his tales.

The winter following his return, he worked for Peary as a dog driver and hunter. That winter he almost lost his life far north in Kennedy Channel. Peary recorded that ". . . a biting wind swept down the channel and numbed the Eskimo who had spent the previous winter in the States to such an extent that to save him we were obliged to halt . . . and dig a burrow in a snowdrift. When the storm ceased, I left him with another Eskimo and nine of the poorest dogs and pushed on."

When Knud Rasmussen visited the district on the Literary Expedition in 1903, Uisaakassak was living in the rich hunting grounds of

Inglefield Fjord with his wife, Aleqasinnguaq. With her, he participated in the district's general wife-exchange; that winter he and Piugaattoq, whose wife was named Aleqasina, often exchanged wives,
sometimes for a night, but often for longer periods.

This wife-exchange with Piugaattoq may have been responsible
for Uisaakassak's falling-out with Peary, for although Uisaakassak
worked for Peary in 1898 and 1899, there is no evidence that he ever
worked for him again. And on March 31, 1900, while at Fort Conger,
Peary, in written instructions to his men at Etah on which natives
were to be taken on board his ship there and brought north, included the statement, "The following natives are not to be allowed
on board ship under any circumstances. . . . Should they get on board
by 'mistake' you will see that they are put off at once." The list included the name "Uisaakassak, the young man who was in the
States."

Peary had been enamored of Aleqasina since at least 1896, when
he had described her as "the belle of the tribe," and he had long been
sharing her with her husband, Piugaattoq. He was known to be extremely jealous whenever any other man showed an interest in her.

But Piugaattoq's wife was not the only object of Uisaakassak's attention, for the Eskimos described him to Mylius-Erichsen in 1903 as a
man "who has a bad habit of borrowing other men's wives in an irregular way — that is, without the permission of the man in question."

Uisaakassak was an intelligent man but temperamental. While he
could be good-humored and entertaining, he was at the same time
greedy and acquisitive and "not the kind of person who would offer
to help people who could not be expected to do something for him
in return — he had, unfortunately not for nothing, spent a year in a
civilized people's land!"

In 1905, Uisaakassak, with a few of his kinsmen, moved farther
south than Polar Eskimos had ever lived, to Tuttulissuaq, the great
caribou land. On the shores of Melville Bay, it was a haven for caribou, polar bear, narwhal, and seal. Uisaakassak was the unques-
tioned leader of the small camp he established there. A fearless man
of many talents, he did not hesitate to challenge a bear with only a
harpoon and a flensing knife. He was, moreover, a man of imagination and a bit of a dreamer. He had always felt himself superior to his

fellows, and his stay in America had confirmed that, indeed, there were places in this world where individuals could depart from the norm and excel, while incurring not the wrath but the respect of their countrymen. He had been badly humiliated by the sharp tongue of Soqqaq shortly after his return; but here at Tuttulissuaq he had found a place where he might restore his reputation, so unjustly ruined through the ignorant consensus of his countrymen.

Rasmussen visited Uisaakassak at Tuttulissuaq in 1907. His host regaled him with hunting stories, recounted over generous feasts of polar bear, narwhal, and caribou. Uisaakassak was a man whose meat racks were full and he was proud to display this evidence of his prowess to the infrequent guests who chanced to pass by. Rasmussen continued on northward and tried to restore the reputation of Uisaakassak, for whom he felt a great deal of sympathy, by assuring the Polar Eskimos that he was, after all, not such a fabricator of tales as they had thought. But he was cautioned, "Yes, Uisaakassak was a great hunter, he had the best dogs, and was awfully good company; but you could never believe what he told you, for he was incorrigible and full of lies."

For some reason, Uisaakassak and his band moved back to Inglefield Bay sometime after Rasmussen visited them. He was there in 1909, and it is possible that Minik may have met him after his own return from America. Uisaakassak and Aleqasinnguaq had separated before the move to Tuttulissuaq and Uisaakassak had taken another wife. But the new wife died and soon after his return Uisaakassak decided that he needed not just one, but two, wives. He stole Aleqasinnguaq back from her husband and took the wife of another hunter as well. Worse, he arrogantly taunted Aleqasinnguaq's husband, Sigluk, deriding him for his loneliness while reminding him publicly of his wife's erotic abilities. But he had picked a formidable enemy. Sigluk had recently been with Peary to his farthest north and had received rich rewards from the explorer for his services. Such a man could not lose a wife to an incorrigible liar like Uisaakassak! So Sigluk bided his time.

One day in the summer of 1910, the great Uutaaq, Peary's chief guide, arrived at the village by kayak. He too had a problem. His wife had died the previous year and it was proving hard to find a new one, for men outnumbered women in the district by quite a number.

One day narwhal were seen in Inglefield Bay. The men of the village took to their kayaks. But it was not narwhal that occupied the thoughts of Sigluk and Uutaaq. Here they had the chance for a simple solution to both their problems. Sigluk shot Uisaakassak, but hit him only in the shoulder. Uutaaq finished the job with a bullet through the head. Uisaakassak rose momentarily as if to speak, then slid from his kayak into the frigid waters of Inglefield Bay. He was thirty-five years old and left two wives and no children.

20

WANTED: DEAD OR ALIVE

MINIK WANTED TO BE SOMEBODY too. But unlike Uisaakas-sak he was unable to talk with his kinsmen on his arrival at Uummannaq. It is true that a few of the Eskimo men could speak and understand a very little bit of English, but it was expedition and trade jargon and not the sort of vocabulary that would help one comprehend tales of life in America. Until he relearned his native tongue well enough to communicate easily with his own people, he had to keep the memories of his troubled life bottled up, festering in his mind. And there, like an insidious cancer, they fed on the trauma he had experienced in America and the loneliness he was enduring in Greenland and grew into an extravagant melding of fact and fantasy. But the emphasis was on the fantasy. His countrymen, inured to the tales of Uisaakassak a decade earlier, and reassured by Rasmussen that many of them had in fact been true, listened and believed. By the time he was able to recount the adventure he had concocted to his fellow Polar Eskimos and to his friend, Rosbach, Minik may have believed it himself.

The beginning of his tale was credible enough. He had boarded Peary's big ship with his father and the rest of the Eskimo party to make the trip to America. On their way south they stopped at Godhavn on

Disko Island; he had not forgotten it, for it was in the land of the Kalaallit, the West Greenlanders of whom he had heard. But to a small boy the only thing worth remembering about the place was that the houses were beautiful and the people friendly. From God-havn they crossed Davis Strait and made a brief stop at Cape Haven, a whaling and trading station on southern Baffin Island, and from there they made for America and the wonders of New York.

He told of his first impressions of the city. "There are many large ships and huge buildings there," he said, "and between the tall build-ings the streets are crowded with people. Vehicles with many people inside them go every which way and at first I didn't realize that we were going to get inside one of them and travel a great distance." The people of the big city had never seen an Eskimo before and came in throngs to gawk and stare. Minik remembered, "If I hadn't had a white person looking after me, I'd have been stepped on just like a mosquito."

Finally they reached the large building where they were to stay. They were pleased at first, for they had never been inside such a huge structure. But soon the pleasure turned to discomfort and they were all down with colds. "It was so hot that we could hardly breathe," said Minik, "but I got used to it quickly and got over my cold."

The others were not so fortunate. Soon Qisuk was dead — some of the survivors said he had been murdered in the hospital — and Minik had gone with the white people to see his father buried. With the deaths of the others, save Uisaakassak, he was alone in a world of strangers.

That part of the story his kinsmen already knew, for they had heard as much from Uisaakassak. In fact, Minik's account was far more down-to-earth than Uisaakassak's description had been. Per-haps that is why they unquestioningly believed the rest of the story.

A rich man named Jesup had taken him in first, he told them, but shortly after had decided, for unknown reasons, not to keep the boy. Another wealthy man, by the name of Wallace, had then taken him in as a son. Minik told them about his early life with the Wallaces: "Unlike Jesup, my new father was a good man, kind and helpful. When I lived at his place, he taught me everything; he took me to the movies and to the zoo to see the animals. And I also started to learn how to read and write — I found it hard at first and sometimes I cried. It was difficult for me sometimes because I didn't know the language very well."

Wallace had hired a tutor for him, a friend who also happened to be a minister. One day, when Minik had been in America for almost two years, Wallace decided to teach Minik a peculiar lesson about the importance of learning English well. He taught him a new phrase that he should use to greet his tutor the next time he came to the house. Minik practiced the phrase until he could repeat it well. When the priest visited again, Minik ran to him, took his hand, and uttered the greeting. The priest drew back in surprise and the smile vanished from his face. He hurried into an adjoining room to fetch Wallace, leaving Minik standing alone wondering what he had done wrong. The priest and Wallace came into the room laughing and Minik found out that he had said, "What are you doing here, you silly old fool?" Minik was crushed. He didn't realize the purpose of this cruel and heartless joke. But it seemed to work nonetheless. Minik threw himself into his studies and soon he was able to speak English just like an American boy.

Finally Minik had learned enough of America's language and customs that Wallace felt him ready for baptism. He suggested that Minik take a new Christian name at his baptism, but Minik replied, "I have never met another person anywhere as kind as you are. I want to keep the name, Minik, that my parents gave me as a baby, but if you agree I would like to take your surname to go with it." Wallace did agree and the following Sunday the boy was baptized Minik Peary Wallace. At a quiet reception at the Wallace home that afternoon, Minik claimed, William Wallace made him a gift of $20,000, but Minik was not to receive it until he reached the age of twenty-five years. In explaining to his countrymen Wallace's generosity, he conveniently forgot about Willie, his Cobleskill playmate, and told them that Wallace was a wealthy man who had no children of his own.

The figure of $20,000 can not have meant anything to the Polar Eskimos who heard this story. Fox and bear skins and ivory tusks were their only currency. But Sechmann Rosbach knew that it represented a very large sum of money indeed. He was impressed. But was this sum real or another figment of Minik's free-wheeling imagination?

There is no doubt that Minik was given a Christian upbringing in the Wallace home, at least until the death of Rhetta Wallace. The Wallaces were churchgoers. In Schoharie County, the family attended the Reformed Church of Lawyersville, and in New York they attended Park Presbyterian Church. Minik attended Sunday school regularly and often sang solos in the Lawyersville church, but in the records of neither church is there any evidence that he was ever baptized. Nevertheless, baptism or not, there is a possibility that Wallace may, at some point, have promised him a large gift in the future. If so, it would have happened while Wallace was still living his flamboyant life of deception. He loved the grand philanthropic gesture, and if there had been the promise of a gift it would have been made publicly. It may not have been $20,000, but it would undoubtedly have been a large sum. But if such a promise was made, it is certain that it was nothing more than just that — an empty promise. The money would not have been put in a trust fund to await the day when Minik could claim it, for Wallace would not have tied up a large sum in a way that he could not use it himself to keep his business enterprises solvent. With the disappearance of the Wallace financial empire, the promise of any substantial gift disappeared too, from all but Minik's fertile mind.

His story continued. It was now time for Minik to choose a career and embark seriously on a course of studies. He decided that he would become a dentist. His Eskimo listeners found this easy to believe, for other than the clothes on his back, his medical and dental kits — gifts given him just before he left New York — were all he carried on his return. He enrolled in a university, he said, where the students at first thought he was Japanese. When they discovered that he was an Eskimo, they began to make fun of him and suggest that it was impossible for a person of such a primitive race to succeed. Minik took that only as a challenge and excelled even more in his studies.

One day he went to the museum to study the teeth of the various animals whose skeletons were on display there. He recounted: "There were many human skeletons on exhibit. Above each one was a little sign identifying the person and where he was from. I went from case to case, looking at the teeth of the exhibits. And in the corner of that room I came across a box containing a skeleton and bearing a label which read 'The Skeleton of Qisuk, a Polar Eskimo.' I thought that perhaps it was the skeleton of another man who had had the same name as my father and had gone to America before us and died there. But from all the books I had read, I couldn't recall any such thing having happened. My heart began to pound and I was trembling. I think I already understood the truth. But I went to the curator's office anyway and asked him when that particular skeleton had arrived at the museum. The curator didn't suspect that I was an Eskimo — he too thought I was Japanese — and he gave me the information. I fell into a chair and began to cry. With my own eyes, I had seen my father's body buried in the ground, so I certainly never expected to find his skeleton displayed in a museum!"

Minik talked to the curator for some time and poured out his grief to him. He asked him if it would be difficult to have his father's grave opened to confirm what he had just discovered. The curator could only suggest that he contact the museum's director to discuss the matter.

Minik then described his visit to the director and it is obvious, although he gave no name, that he was describing the bustling, confused Hermon Bumpus: "He lived in a large, fine house. His servant showed me in. The director was a fat man and very friendly. When I told him I wanted to speak with him, he put his arm around my shoulder and ushered me into his sitting-room. We sat down and he turned to me and asked, 'Now, what can I do to help you?' I replied that I wanted to ask him how the museum had acquired the skeleton it had on display of a Polar Eskimo named Qisuk. He asked me to wait a few minutes while he went to fetch some books. When he came back in with his books, he asked me, 'What was the number of the exhibit?' I answered him, 'Exhibit No. 5 in Room 3.' He thumbed through the book and finally found the information he was looking for. He read aloud, 'Jesup sold it to the museum. It is the skeleton of a Polar Eskimo, Qisuk.' Then he turned to me and asked, 'Why do you want to know about that?' And I told him, 'Because he was my father. He died when I was just a child and I cried at his graveside as he was buried. I wasn't expecting to see him in the museum!'"

The museum director was taken aback. He had also taken Minik for a Japanese. Minik asked him if he thought it would be possible to

183

have his father's grave opened to see what had been buried there. Yes, the director told him, it would probably be possible, but it may be very expensive. Did Minik have any money to pay for it? Minik did not, but after some discussion they decided that if the grave proved to be empty then Jesup could be forced to pay all the costs incurred.

When Minik left the director's house, he claimed, he went home to tell William Wallace of his heartbreaking discovery and what he had decided to do about it. Wallace advised him, however, to do nothing; he thought the effort would be emotionally disturbing and ultimately unsuccessful. But Minik persisted. He remembered where the burial had taken place and he went there and had the coffin dug up. Inside were his father's guts and a bit of flesh!

With that discovery, Minik's life in America changed drastically. He left school and the Wallace home and gave up the beliefs he had held. "If Christian people can be such hypocrites," he said, "then I don't need Christianity anymore." He had only one goal in life now: to take his revenge on Jesup.

He became a drifter and a ne'er-do-well. One night he and fifteen accomplices dug up all the plants from Jesup's huge garden, put them in cases, and drove them away from Jesup's country estate. He drew up a timesheet purporting to be for the removal of weeds, then plied Jesup's foreman with alcohol and got him so drunk that he signed the sheet. The next day, with his face made up so he would not be recognized, Minik went to Jesup's financial office and had the cashier honor the timesheet. With the money in his pocket he began to leave. Just outside the door he met Jesup himself, but the old man failed to recognize him. Jesup continued in and asked the cashier who the man in the doorway was. He was someone who came in with a timesheet for work the foreman had ordered in the gardens, the cashier told him. Jesup just nodded in Minik's direction. Minik returned his nod — and left.

The next day Minik and his accomplices took all the boxes of plants to a rail freight depot with instructions that Jesup was sending them to a dealer in another city. He even managed to get paid for the delivery job, and Jesup would foot the bill for that too.

Soon the newspapers began to mention the swindle that had been perpetrated on Jesup. A reward was promised for the apprehension of the thieves. Minik was even audacious enough to take part in the search himself and would have turned in some of his partners for the reward. Later he met Jesup on two occasions. The last time he met him, he beat him unconscious and stole his wallet and watch.

The fantasy continued. He used Jesup's money to buy alcohol. At that time there was a strong movement in New York against alcohol use — ironically Jesup was one of the leaders of the movement — and bars had to close at nine o'clock. Naturally, illicit drinking establishments flourished. Minik, by his account, became a regular customer of these grog shops and made many unsavory acquaintances there. One day he and three friends were surprised in a bar after closing hours when police burst in. Minik and his friends tried to escape, but the policemen overpowered them and hauled them off to jail. They could sleep off their drunkenness and appear in court the next morning. But by the next morning they were gone, for during the night they had broken out of jail.

Minik stuck with his three fellow escapees. The others were bigger and stronger, but Minik was the smartest. He became the leader of this small but dangerous band of thieves. They roamed freely, beating up people at will and stealing their property. Minik planned the crimes and his henchmen carried them out. They stayed in hotels, or in summer in the open air. And they spent considerable time after hours in the illicit bars of New York City.

Minik and his gang devised a clever scheme whereby they could visit a certain bar after hours without fear of being seen entering the building. At some distance away from the bar stood an old hollow tree. Working only at night, under cover of darkness, and with a policeman they had plied with liquor to stand guard, Minik and his band dug a secret tunnel from the tree to the cellar of the bar. Now he and his comrades, with whatever friends they chose to share their secret, could visit the establishment whenever they wished.

One night in 1909, he and his three companions sat drinking in the cellar waiting for the bar upstairs to close. It was only eight o'clock in the evening. Suddenly they heard the sound of scuffling and shouting above them. Minik and his partners rushed up to see two knife-wielding men fighting violently. Minik was carrying a club with

185

him and jumped drunkenly into the fray. He knocked the stronger of the two over the head. The man fell to the floor. The other man pounced on his fallen foe and killed him with a thrust of his knife through the breast. The bar owner had called the police and suddenly three uniformed officers rushed in, locking the door behind them. But Minik was quick; he broke a window, jumped out to the street, and escaped through the confusion of the crowd that had gathered at the scene.

A few days later Minik's Eskimo features graced the front pages of the city's newspapers. He was being sought as a dangerous criminal. A reward had been offered for his capture — dead or alive!

He was alone. His henchmen had been caught and were in jail, along with the shop owner. Wanted posters bearing Minik's likeness were being distributed throughout North America. Minik was an outlaw! He fled the city, traveling only at night and sleeping in the forests during the daytime.

One day he was roused from his sleep by a sharp kick to his foot. He awoke to see two strong men standing over him. They asked if he was Minik. He tried to escape but they seized him and began to tie him. He fought back desperately and managed to grab his club. He struck one of them a fierce blow across the side of the head, knocking him unconscious. He told the other one to stand aside or he would receive the same treatment. The man fled, but he shouted back to Minik that, now that he had found him, he would not get away. He would be back for him the following day and Minik would not be so lucky the next time.

To avoid being followed, he changed direction. Avoiding the roads and public places, he traveled for three days and nights without meeting a single person. Finally he approached a small town. That night, when it was dark, he went into the town and found a hotel. Starving, he entered the restaurant. He recalled:

"I was the only one in the dining room. I ordered a cheap meal and when it came I gulped it down like a hungry wolf. While I was eating I heard someone walking up to me from behind. I turned and saw a fat, kind-faced lady standing there. I turned away from her. She came closer, tapped me on the shoulder and asked, in a low voice, 'Are you Minik?' I said that I was not. But she insisted, 'I think you are

Minik.' Just then we heard footsteps and she left me quickly. She went to a table in the corner and sat down and ordered coffee. When her coffee was served, she brought it to my table and sat down with me. She started to talk about her husband. He had been travelling for a few years in the Arctic, she said. In fact, he was still away in the north at that time, on an expedition. If I had not already met Peary's wife, I would have thought it was she. As it was, I didn't know who this woman was with whom I was speaking.

"She asked, 'Weren't you living in New York earlier?' I said that I had not been. But she answered me, 'This picture I have is a picture of you. But I am not here to capture you. I have come here to help you. You will understand why later.' . . . She gave me money so I could stay overnight in the hotel, and left. When I had finished eating, I took a room and fell into a deep sleep.

"Suddenly I was woken from my sleep. Two men were in my room and they bound me up. They warned me not to make a sound or they would kill me."

They hustled him outside to a waiting car and traveled in silence for some time. Finally they stopped at a train station. Minik thought for certain that they were about to take him back to New York City and to jail; he looked about frantically for a means of escape. But there was none. They took him into a railway car, unbound him, and went out, locking the door securely behind them. After a seemingly endless fifteen minutes, the train began to move.

Minik sat there, alone and helpless, staring blankly out the window as the train sped through the darkness. Suddenly he heard the sound of a key in the door to his compartment. He looked around, hardly knowing what to expect. To his utter surprise, he saw the lady who had befriended him in the hotel. He described what followed:

"She was smiling, and asked me if I was frightened. I was terrified, but I am a man and so I replied, 'No, I'm not afraid.' She closed the door and sat down beside me. She took my hand and began to talk. 'At the hotel you didn't recognize me,' she said, 'but now I have time to tell you. I am the wife of Dr. Cook who is in the Arctic, in your country, on an expedition. Everyone knows how much my husband has been helped up there by the Eskimos. When I read about your escapades in the newspapers, I decided to help you, to show my thanks

GIVE ME MY FATHER'S BODY

for what your people have done for my husband. I clipped a picture of you from one of the papers and set out in search of you, and I was lucky to find you."

The train took them to Quebec City, where, Minik claimed, Mrs. Cook lived in a fine house. Is it just a coincidence that, when Minik ran away from New York in the spring of 1909, Chester Beecroft had finally found him in Quebec City? Minik was weaving into this incredible fantasy odd details from real life. But Marie Cook, a tall, thin lady, lived comfortably in Brooklyn while her husband was trying to reach the North Pole. Minik probably had met her at some time during his stay in America. It is also probable that she had played a part in the decision of the Arctic Club of America in early 1909 to take him back to Greenland if the club sent a ship for the relief of Dr. Cook that year.

The incredible story continued. Mrs. Cook had a plan to send Minik back to his people. There was a small ship leaving for the Arctic from Newfoundland, she said, and she had already contacted the captain to arrange discreetly for passage for Minik. The captain had agreed. The only problem would be in getting Minik from Quebec to Newfoundland, for as a fugitive whose face was on wanted posters throughout the continent, he could not simply go to the dock and board a ship. But Mrs. Cook had solved that problem, too.

He was smuggled aboard ship in a large wooden box. It was padded on the inside to make it comfortable, and holes had been bored in one side to allow him to breathe. There was even food enough for three days in the box.

The trip to Newfoundland took two days and one night. When the ship docked in St. John's, Minik could feel the box being carried ashore. It was put into a vehicle and driven away from the harbor. Finally it was opened and Minik stepped out to greet the ship's captain, who would take him home. The next day he wrote a note of thanks to Mrs. Cook and boarded the little ship that had brought him to Uummannaq.

There the fantasies had ended and he was thrown roughly back into the real world, a world he had never known. Physically, he had taken to it well. But emotionally and intellectually, he had turned his thoughts inward during that painful period when he was unable to

188

communicate with his own kin or with Rosbach, his friend. He had blended fact and fancy until he ceased to be Minik, the Eskimo boy so misunderstood and hard-done-by in America, ultimately seen aboard ship and exiled back to his native land by the publicity agent of the despised Peary; instead, he had become Minik, the tough and reckless outlaw, smuggled out of North America with a price on his head.

The Eskimos and Rosbach never tired of hearing the stories. Minik told and retold them, embellishing them with each retelling. This was his way of getting some of the attention he had been accustomed to in New York. And with each telling of his imaginary adventures, he longed more and more for America. He had become neither fish nor fowl, the true marginal man, condemned to exist in two opposing cultures and feel at home in neither.

Peter Freuchen, a master raconteur himself, could never finally make up his mind whether he liked Minik or not, but he apparently believed many of his wild adventures. He wrote, "In America he had been adopted by very decent people and been given every opportunity, but he was a born good-for-nothing. He felt that rules did not concern him, and laws were made for him to disobey. After countless attempts to get him interested in something — anything — he was given the opportunity to choose a profession. His choice was to steal money and run away. He was apprehended at the Canadian border, sent back to New York, and finally brought home to Greenland. . . . He returned to the north with no property or money — he had been given plenty in America but had spent it all during the trip for liquor and such."

Freuchen carped occasionally about Minik's obsession with America: "He believed that the world had been bad for him and blamed others for his lack of character. In America he had longed for Greenland, and now that he was in Greenland he wanted to be back in America."

Freuchen should have known better. One other Polar Eskimo had been to America and returned to her people while still a child. This was Eqariusaq, who had accompanied Mrs. Peary south in 1894 and returned the following year. The Americans had dubbed her "Miss

Bill." Unlike Uisaakassak and Minik, when she returned to Greenland, Eqariusaq had refused to tell anyone about her trip. When asked, she said only that she could not remember, or did not feel like talking about it. Once, while on a sled trip bound for one of the distant Danish colonies in a more southerly part of Greenland, Freuchen and Navarana had passed a few days at Cape Seddon with Eqariusaq and her husband, Miteq. Navarana had never been south of Melville Bay and was looking forward eagerly to the trip. One afternoon she and Eqariusaq took a stroll on the ice. Suddenly Eqariusaq turned to Navarana and said, "When you go to the white man's country, be careful not to absorb too much of their spirit. If you do, it will cause you many tears, for you can never rid yourself of it." When Navarana told him this, Freuchen felt that he finally understood the young woman's reticence to speak of her year in America. "Poor woman!" he wrote. "I understood then that it was a desperate, hopeless longing that stilled her voice."

21

THE CROCKER LAND EXPEDITION

IN THE SPRING OF 1913, Americans returned to northern Greenland. Donald Baxter MacMillan, who had been a young assistant on
Peary's last expedition, had felt the magnetism of the Arctic drawing
him back again, as it was to do repeatedly for the rest of his life. An ardent Peary supporter, MacMillan's primary purpose on this expedition
he commanded was to "reach, map the coast-line, and explore Crocker
Land," the land Peary claimed to have seen far to the northwest of Axel
Heiberg Island in the Arctic Ocean. The expedition, poorly organized
and even more poorly supported by its sponsor, the American Museum
of Natural History, spent four years in the Arctic and disproved, much
to MacMillan's chagrin, the existence of his mentor's fantasy island.

Ice conditions prevented the supply vessel *Erik* from reaching
Flagler Bay on the Ellesmere Island coast, where MacMillan had
hoped to establish his headquarters, so the supplies, scientists, and
support staff of the Crocker Land Expedition were dumped at Etah
on the Greenland coast, in the protected bay that had been the home
of so many Arctic expeditions. MacMillan had put in at Cape York on
the northward voyage to pick up three families of Eskimos — Peary's
People — and these joined the nineteen men, women, and children
who were already camped at Etah when the ship put in.

Eskimos from the surrounding district soon heard of the arrival of the Americans and many of them headed for Etah to offer their services to the expedition. The camp jack-of-all-trades, Jot Small, had put together a sturdy building thirty-five feet square; soon after it was completed MacMillan wrote in his journal, "Our home was overcrowded with the bodies of sixty Eskimos, sleeping in our attic, in the carpenter's shop, in the dark-room, under our beds, and under the floor."

One of these was Minik. He had been living at Uutaaq's camp in Kangerlussuaq when he and Uutaaq heard of the arrival of Naalagapaluk — the little boss — and both men decided to make the trip to Etah. Uutaaq had spent many years in the service of Peary and had been the explorer's most trusted native assistant on his final North Pole expedition. Minik, for his part, was overjoyed at the possibility of meeting Americans with whom he could speak English, for he was tiring of the broken English of Freuchen at the post at Uummannaq.

On December 1 Minik visited the house that MacMillan had christened Borup Lodge in honor of George Borup, a colleague on the last Peary expedition who had recently drowned in New York. He introduced himself. The expedition's members had heard of him, of course. Most were impressed with him, especially so because of his fine command of English — he would be a unique asset to them, they thought, a strong young man who could double as an interpreter. But MacMillan was not so sure; after all, this was the young man who had had so many unkind things to say in the American press about the great Peary. But he did not hesitate for long. That same day Fitzhugh Green wrote in his journal, "Mac feels that he will be of great assistance as an interpreter and has told him to stay."

Minik wasted no time in finding some men of the expedition to speak English with. That same day Jerome Lee Allen, wireless operator and electrician, wrote in his journal, "Minik Wallace, the English-speaking Eskimo, and Uutaaq arrived today. Minik is an interesting character to us — he has talked a great deal and we have learned a great many new things about the Eskimos from him. He has mastered the Eskimo language and is now as much of an Eskimo as any of them. He says he would like to get back to New York, but says also that his health was never good there and he doesn't want to stay there always. It seems very funny to us to suddenly have this man, in appearance no different from the ordinary Eskimo, suddenly come to us and talk to us in our own language and with us about our own land — for Coney Island is as familiar to him as Etah."

Dr. Harrison Hunt, the expedition's surgeon, remarked, "He seems to be in good health and prosperous. He is to stay with us. He talks the Eskimo and English well and will be a help to us in learning the language."

Minik reported a sick child at Uummannaq and MacMillan gave Dr. Hunt permission to go to attend to it. On December 6 Minik, Uutaaq, and Hunt left on the three-day trip to North Star Bay. On their arrival, Dr. Hunt attended to routine medical tasks for the native population and the following day, by the light from a native lamp, he amputated two fingers from a hunter; they had been shattered by an exploding rifle cartridge. Hunt reported that Minik ably assisted him in this operation by administering ether to the patient. He also hunted for the party. On the 15th they were off again for Etah, this time traveling via Kangerlussuaq, where they spent two days in Uutaaq's house. It was three times as large as any native home Hunt had seen, testimony to Uutaaq's prestige and the prosperity he had gained through the rewards given him by Peary. The party returned to Etah on December 21, the darkest day of the year.

Hunt was impressed with Minik and pleased with his service. Early the following month, he wrote in a letter to his wife, "Last month I took a trip to North Star Bay with Minik Wallace, of whom you have heard, and who proves to be a nice fellow in his native environment. . . . From there we went to Kangerlussuaq. . . . There I stayed with Uutaaq and Iggiannguaq, two north pole men. They are fine fellows and it is with them that Minik lives."

In February, MacMillan left on his futile search for Crocker Land. The advance parties, comprising 19 men, 15 sleds, and 165 dogs, had already proceeded to the Canadian coast when MacMillan, with Piugaattoq and Minik, left Etah on Friday, February 13. MacMillan professed not to be superstitious, but it was an inauspicious day to begin an expedition, and as it turned out, it was a false start. Before they had reached Sunrise Point, MacMillan discovered that Minik had forgotten the tobacco and sent him back for it, commenting dryly, "Can't discover new land without tobacco."

The weather was bitterly cold. At their first camp, the thermometer registered forty-eight degrees below zero Fahrenheit. Traveling through Rice Strait behind Pim Island, the wind was so cutting that the men were forced to lie down on their sleds with their faces buried in their furs. Alexandra Fiord was so windswept that there was insufficient snow for a snowhouse, so the three built a fire of their biscuit boxes and slept in their sleeping bags beside it. When they finally reached the advance party in Hayes Fiord, many of the men were sick and the Eskimos did not want to go on. Minik spoke with them and reported to MacMillan that they all wanted to return to Etah, feed up the dogs on walrus meat, and try again. Reluctantly, the entire group turned back for Etah.

With a smaller group, the expedition departed again on March 11. They planned to cross Ellesmere Island via Beitstadt Fiord and the awesome glacier that forms its head. When they reached it, MacMillan described it as "an almost vertical wall of ice" and wondered how they were ever to get up it. They slept in a shelter carved out of a snowbank at the foot of the glacier; Piugaattoq and Qajuuttaq spent the entire next day cutting steps and handholds in the face of the glacier. The following day the laborious task of hauling the supplies the fifty feet up the glacier face began. Ittukusuk, "who simply loved hard work," set the pace when he put a tumpline on his 125-pound sled and started up the face. Only one man was able to duplicate his feat. Nevertheless, by nightfall four thousand pounds of supplies had been ferried to the top of the glacier.

That night, the Eskimos gathered around Piugaattoq, the only man of the party who had ever crossed Beitstadt Glacier, to learn the conditions that faced them on the other side. Minik slept on what he heard. The next morning, instead of climbing the glacier to head west with the rest of the party, he took to his sled and returned to Etah. MacMillan did not try to dissuade him.

But as Minik rounded a headland almost an hour later, Elmer Ekblaw, expedition botanist and geologist, noticed from the top of the glacier another sled also heading eastward. He called to MacMillan, asking him if he knew that Tautsiannguaq had left for Etah as well.

194

MacMillan did not know it, nor at first would he believe it; he thought Tautsiannguaq was on the glacier, but when a hasty search failed to find him, he had to concede that the man had deserted.

Minik's departure and Tautsiannguaq's desertion put the success, perhaps even the survival, of the expedition in jeopardy, for they took with them sixteen strong dogs; the amount of food that could now be drawn by the remaining members of the party was substantially reduced. Their survival would depend on finding game on the west coast of Ellesmere or beyond. That night after supper, "when gossip and tobacco smoke were equally thick," MacMillan learned the reason for Tautsiannguaq's desertion:

"Tautsiannguaq had a pretty wife. Minik certainly thought so; therefore he decided to return to Etah, where he might enjoy her company. Tautsiannguaq, unsuspecting, would go on with me and be absent for several weeks. After Minik had gone, one of the boys whispered into Tautsiannguaq's ear; as a consequence, I lost Tautsiannguaq. He didn't bother to climb the glacier and state his reasons for going. His wife was at stake and off he went."

MacMillan commented in his report that hard work at fifty below zero did not agree with Minik. Perhaps the drudgery of expedition work did not. To him and to most of the other Eskimos, this pointless pushing to the limit of both man and beast to find distant geographical points made no sense. For Minik it had a more personal meaning as well. He had nothing against MacMillan, but the whole exercise reminded him too much of Peary. And MacMillan was wrong in thinking him lazy. The Eskimos who knew him are unanimous in their recollection that Minik was, on the contrary, a very active young man who had learned well the skills he needed to survive in his northern home. In fact, he fit well MacMillan's description of the ideal type of sled driver to take along on a lengthy trip: "Young Eskimos for a long and dangerous trip are much to be preferred, as they are fond of adventure and willing to take a chance. . . ."

Minik may have been very lucky that he did turn back. Once the descent to the ice of Bay Fiord had been made safely, MacMillan sent back most of the men to Etah while he and Fitzhugh Green, along with Piugaattoq and Ittukusuk, continued on in search of Crocker Land. Had Minik still been with the party, there is every likelihood that he would have been asked to go along, if only because of his fluency in English.

Having explored the area where Crocker Land was alleged to be, the party of four men returned to Axel Heiberg Island. MacMillan sent Green and Piugaattoq south to explore a portion of the Axel Heiberg coastline that was as yet uncharted. Six days later Green returned — alone. He and Piugaattoq had taken refuge from a storm in a snowhouse. A snowslide had buried Green's sled and killed his dogs. The following day, when the storm worsened, Piugaattoq had insisted on turning back. He forced Green to walk, knowing that the activity was necessary to keep his toes from freezing, as his feet were very wet. Green was on the verge of giving up. Piugaattoq kept his dogs going at a steady pace. Green complained that he could not keep up but Piugaattoq, knowing that the pace was necessary for survival, insisted that he follow his trail. Green was inexperienced in dealing with natives and in his nervous despair he misunderstood Piugaattoq's speed and his exhortations to continue the journey back to MacMillan's camp as an attempt to abandon him. Green snatched the rifle from the sled and warned Piugaattoq to keep behind him. When he turned a few minutes later he saw a frightened Piugaattoq whipping the dogs frantically off in another direction. Green reports the rest in a matter-of-fact manner in his journal: "I shot once in the air. He did not stop. I then killed him with a shot through the shoulder and another through the head."

Piugaattoq had been a trusted travel companion of Peary on all his polar expeditions. He had been one of Peary's favorites. Knud Rasmussen described him as "not only a man whom one could trust, but he was a comrade who in difficult or dangerous circumstances was ready to make personal sacrifices in order to help and support his companions." Piugaattoq had tried to save Green's life. Green had taken his.

MacMillan and Green determined to keep the truth from the Eskimos. They concocted a story that was half true: There had been a snowslide and Piugaattoq had suffocated under it. But Ittukusuk knew enough English that he understood the truth from the beginning, for he had overheard the distraught Green telling his dismal tale to MacMillan. Ittukusuk told the others on their return to Etah;

they should know that these were men easy to anger and who must be treated cautiously.

MacMillan and Green never knew that the Eskimos knew the truth. And Minik, who could have told them, never did, to him it was just one more example of the cheapness of Eskimo life to a white explorer. He wasn't surprised. But it hurt him deeply to reflect on it.

Minik and Tautsiannguaq returned to Etah on March 22. A few days later, Minik left with a hunting party for Neqe, farther south along the coast. In early April, he returned to Borup Lodge in company with Peter Freuchen, who was paying his first visit to the Americans. Relations had been strained between the Danes and the Americans, for they were competing for the natives' furs. Minik, the only Eskimo who was fluently bilingual, heard frequent grumblings from some natives who thought the Americans miserly, and he often had to become involved in defusing potentially volatile situations. Allen wrote in his journal about Freuchen's visit: "We cooked up some beans for Minik and Mr. Freuchen, and gave the eskimoes [sic] only tea and dog-biscuit. Mr. Freuchen told us that he had overheard Minik sticking up for Mac and the expedition several times — especially when Qajuuttaq thought he was treated badly about the gun — and he thinks that Minik wishes the eskimoes [sic] to help us and does not think he would try to influence them the other way."

Minik spent the summer of 1914 at Uummannaq. Elmer Ekblaw and Maurice Tanquary of the Crocker Land Expedition passed part of the summer there too. Ekblaw, still recovering from toes badly frozen during the winter, hunted seal with Minik occasionally. Minik was of great assistance to Ekblaw. Freuchen, in whose house the two scientists were staying, had gone bear hunting in Melville Bay, and as Ekblaw said, "Our supplies were gone, the Eskimos were short of meat, and we had no dogs to go out hunting. Had not Minik helped us out by killing occasional seal for us at this time, we should repeatedly have been hard pressed for food." Finally Sechmann Rosbach, catechist at the mission station there, invited Ekblaw and Tanquary to share the mission house with him and his family. For the rest of their stay at Uummannaq, the scientists were comfortable.

197

In February of 1915, Dr. Hunt traveled to Pitoraarfik to attend to some sick Eskimos. Pitoraarfik is a famous gathering point for the Polar Eskimos in the late winter of each year as the first light is returning. Open water is not far away and walrus and bearded seal are plentiful. People from far away traveled there to renew old acquaintances and fill their bellies after the hardships of the winter's dark. Hunt met Minik there and when he returned to Etah, Minik accompanied him. He was "very repentant over his failure of the year before. He urgently requested that he be given another trial. . . ." MacMillan took him back.

On April 10 MacMillan accompanied Torngi, Taliilannguaq, and Minik on a hunting trip. MacMillan described Minik's part in a walrus hunt over thin ice in a way that indicates that Minik had learned well the tricks of the trade and had become a tough and resourceful hunter, but that even an experienced hunter could make embarrassing mistakes: "At length a large walrus was discovered asleep on the rapidly moving drift ice some 300 yards away. I thought it was positive suicide to approach him over such a treacherous surface. Yet Minik and Taliilannguaq, without the slightest bit of hesitation made their way from cake to cake, now and then carefully gliding across dark, bending ice, up to within twenty yards of the ponderous, sleeping bulk, and here they were blocked by an impassable stretch of water. We saw them now flat on their breasts with sighted rifles. Two sharp reports were followed by a tremendous splash as the 2,000 pounds of meat disappeared, to be lost beneath the surface."

Not only had they lost the walrus, but the ice they were on had drifted slowly away. There was no way back. MacMillan and Torngi ran along the edge of the fast ice and indicated with frantic gestures a spot through where they thought the two men could make it back to firmer ice. They made it, dripping with perspiration and breaking through the ice and filling their boots on the very last step.

Yet they did not give up. Within a few minutes a herd of ten walrus appeared on the surface nearby. The Eskimo men seized their harpoons; MacMillan grabbed his camera: "The action began with a swirl, followed by a mass of grim, ugly faces at the very feet of the hunters — so near, in fact, that the men, astounded, were caught unawares, delayed action for a few seconds, and then excitedly hurled their harpoons. The harpoon of Torngi plunged over their heads and backs; that of Minik stopped suddenly in mid-air and fell harmlessly flat down. Torngi, disgusted and ashamed, expressed himself as befitted the occasion. Minik grinned sheepishly upon discovering that he was standing upon a flake of his coil."

The party returned to Pitoraarfik empty-handed after a trip of thirty-six hours.

Undaunted, Minik left shortly afterward with Qajuuttaq and Aserpannguaq on a musk ox–hunting trip to Ellesmere Island on the opposite side of Smith Sound.

How strange it must have been for him on these trips, when the men whiled away the hours of storm-bound days recounting the tales of their heritage, stories that they had learned from parents and grandparents as they grew to adulthood. Minik had missed out on those carefree years and had nothing to contribute to these smoke-filled hours save fantastic tales of his life in America, and the details of these stories were incomprehensible to his hunting companions, most of whom had never been south of Melville Bay. He was doing his best to learn the traditions of his ancestors now as an adult. But one cannot hope to learn in a few years everything that a child takes all his formative years to learn, and these long days, pleasurable though they were, can only have strengthened his sense of anomie.

Minik was often MacMillan's personal guide. MacMillan liked him, and there was the added advantage that Minik, with his superb command of English, could interpret accurately for MacMillan and provide him with information on a variety of subjects that the explorer would otherwise understand imperfectly or not at all.

On a trip between Etah and Neqe in late March of 1916, the two became separated from their traveling companions, Ulloriaq and Nukappiannguaq, and were in considerable danger. Neither Minik nor MacMillan knew exactly where they were:

"We hardly knew what to do in our dilemma. To await the men and have them pass unseen would result in our sleeping on the icecap with no sleeping-bags — not a warm outlook. There were ominous discomforts and no small amount of danger in going on. A descent by the wrong glacier might result in a drop into one of the

numerous intersecting cracks, or we might bring up against a vertical face blocking our course completely.

"We went on. The *sastrugi* (wind-carved ridges) cut our path at
right angles, and the intervening hollows gave to our sledges the motion of a ship in a heavy sea. I was too much occupied with the an-
tics of my own sledge, and I soon lost Minik as he disappeared in the
darkness, stern first, after running over his dogs and capsizing his
sledge. He was waiting for me at the bottom of the Clements
Markham Glacier, having made record time.

"Even here, where sea ice generally exists, there was open water,
which forced us to take to the ice-foot along the shore until we were
blocked by a projecting buttress . . . we could plainly see phospho-
rescence on the surface of the ice, indicative of only a few hours'
freezing.

"We made tea and ate a piece of chocolate — all we had — under
a shelf of rock. Within an hour the other two men overtook us, ex-
claiming that they thought we were back on the glacier.

"As we were about to prepare for the night, to my astonishment
we saw a light out on the ice. Nukappiannguaq was looking it over
with a candle, and he declared it to be perfectly safe. We drove on at
once to Neqe and remained three nights."

In the summer of 1915, a three-masted auxiliary schooner, the
George B. Cluett, arrived at Uummannaq. Under charter to the
American Museum of Natural History, she had come to the relief of
the Crocker Land Expedition. The vessel was a floating wreck. Captain Pickles refused to take her north of Uummannaq, and those
who were due to leave the Arctic that year had to travel from Etah in
Peter Freuchen's motor launch to join the vessel there. But ninety
miles out from Uummannaq, the ship drifted, disabled, into Parker
Snow Bay and was frozen in for the winter. MacMillan described the
vessel as "absolutely unfit for Arctic work."

Equally unfit for Arctic work was one of her passengers. Dr. Otis
Hovey was curator of the museum's Department of Geology and In-
vertebrate Paleontology, but he was also chairman of the Crocker
Land Expedition. He had come north for the summer cruise to check

on the activities of the expedition and, incidentally, to secure material for a book of his own on the Arctic. Relations between him and MacMillan had been severely strained even before the expedition left New York in 1913, and he was generally disliked by everyone he met in the Arctic. He was aghast at the prospect of overwintering.

He unintentionally insulted Peter Freuchen on first meeting him. As Freuchen recounted, with his characteristic good humor, ". . . He asked me what crime I had committed that had banished me to the Arctic. I was, he said, a fine fellow and ought to be able to find a decent job somewhere in the outside world, even if I were guilty of a misdemeanor." Freuchen's opinion of Hovey was no more flattering; he thought he was probably "a mild little man at home," but in the Arctic he was "a tactless, impolite person" who "whined and expostulated" over every adjustment he was compelled to make because of the misfortune of being stranded so far from home.

Hovey had little regard for the natives. Hunt says he "called the Eskimos savages and treated them with contempt."

Freuchen, as usual, provides more detail:

"He showed me the gifts and trinkets he had brought along to please the natives and to pay them for their favors — empty rifle shells of two different makes, one a little larger than the other so that they would fit together.

" 'These can be polished and used for needle cases,' he said. 'Eskimos like to sit about during the winter and polish things to make them shine. They will be delighted with these.'

"Evidently he had believed, and still did believe, that the natives were anxious to be permitted to give everything away to white men. A needle, he said, was more precious to an Eskimo than a dog. They need only be told what to do, not paid for it."

But even more chilling is another piece of information about this petulant and foolish man, for, if Hovey was at all indicative of the caliber of men employed in responsible positions by the museum at the time, it shows that the museum had learned nothing at all from the tragedy of 1898, when four Polar Eskimos had died in New York as a result of Peary's foolishness, with the complicity of the museum, in bringing them there in the first place. Nor had it learned from the sad follow-up to those events, the trauma experienced by a lonely Eskimo boy as he grew to manhood in involuntary exile from the homeland from which he had been taken. For Hovey, it seems, made a startling suggestion to another young Polar Eskimo, Imiina, with whom he traveled in the Arctic.

The story was recounted to the French anthropologist, Jean Malaurie, by his friend Kuuttiikitoq in 1950. Kuuttiikitoq had casually remarked to Malaurie in their tent one evening that he could have been very rich if he had wanted to be. "I would have sat on a little chair," he said, "dressed in bearskin pants — my most beautiful quilittaq. As Uve [Hovey] used to tell Imiina every time they stopped. . . . I would have held a large harpoon in my hand, and all day long well-dressed, perfumed qallunaat would have filed by in front of me. I'd have been well paid. Tollar amerlaqqaat — bundles of dollars!"

Malaurie thought dryly, "Not just a mannequin but a real live display: what a godsend for a natural history museum!"

Kuuttiikitoq continued, "We could all be rich, you see. . . . For the Inuit, sapinngilaq, nothing is too hard. But not one of us agreed. That's not fit work for Inuit. . . . And yet, and yet, Piulersuaq certainly managed to drag us down there. How could you say no to such a great leader? Six Eskimos left with him on his big boat. Only two of them ever came back. . . ."

But one Eskimo did want to go to America. Minik was still longing for New York. The companionship of English-speaking explorers over the past few years had only heightened his desire to return. In 1911, he had asked Captain Adams of the *Morning,* on the last-ever whaling voyage to Melville Bay, to take him to England, but Adams had refused.

The presence of the *Cluett* at Parker Snow Bay ensured that there was considerable sled traffic that winter and spring between the ship and Etah; much of that traffic passed by Uummannaq, and there were many visitors at Rosbach's house. One day Minik sat talking for a long time with a few of the Americans there. When the conversation was over, Minik, obviously pleased, came out and told Rosbach, "Now I am only waiting for passage. Those men in there have already written a letter about me and have received a reply that I can go to America. They have agreed to take me with them when they go."

Rosbach's American guests had written to Hovey at Etah, and he had given permission for Minik to return to America on the *Cluett*.

Rosbach was happy for him. He had believed all of Minik's tales of his earlier life in America, and he felt sure that his young friend would be able to claim his $20,000 baptismal gift immediately upon reaching New York.

When the *Cluett* broke free of the ice in Parker Snow Bay on July 29, 1916, she had few passengers to take south. Hovey had sent a letter out by dog team via Upernavik in the winter, requesting the museum to send up another relief ship. Anticipating that that ship would arrive, Hovey and Ekblaw, who were due to return south, had refused to sail on the *Cluett*. Even George Comer, the veteran whaling captain who had come north as the *Cluett's* ice pilot, found her so unsafe that he too remained behind. But Minik Wallace was aboard, bound once again for America, this time voluntarily.

22

BACK ON BROADWAY

I N MARCH OF 1911, THE United States Congress passed an act placing Robert Peary on the retired list of the Corps of Civil Engineers of the Navy with the highest retired pay of the rank of Rear Admiral. The act also tendered Peary the thanks of Congress for "various alleged Arctic explorations, which he claimed resulted in his reaching the North Pole." Thus Peary, who had been in the Navy for twenty-nine years, was simultaneously promoted and retired. He had been on active duty for only twelve years and nine days, and on leave or awaiting orders for the balance of that time, yet he had been on the payroll for all except six months in 1896!

In 1915, Congressman Henry T. Helgesen of North Dakota launched an exhaustive analysis of the evidence that Peary had presented to justify his claim of having reached the Pole. The following year Helgesen spoke extensively in the House of Representatives on the subject, and on July 21, 1916, claiming that "Robert E. Peary's claims to discoveries in the Arctic regions have been proven to rest on fiction and not on geographical facts," he introduced a resolution that the 1911 act be repealed and that Peary's name be stricken from the retired list in order to save the taxpayers his stipend of

$6,000 per year "for services which he never performed" and to ensure that "historic and geographic truth may prevail."

Many who were accustomed to the virulent partisanship that characterized the polar controversy in 1909 assumed that this belated attack on Peary automatically made Helgesen a Cook supporter, but the representative denied it, claiming that he was "not a defender of Cook's claims, but . . . a champion of fair play" who believed simply that Cook was "entitled to a hearing."

Nonetheless, the work of debunking the Peary mystique led him to be very interested in Cook's claim to prior discovery of the Pole, and in August of that year Helgesen began to investigate Cook's claims. It was a brief investigation. On September 4, he made a report on the subject and concluded with a question rather than a statement: ". . . Is it possible for anyone who gives this matter any thought or study at all to believe that Dr. Cook ever attained or remotely approached the Pole?"

This was not quite his final word on the subject, however, for he continued his investigation into the merits of the Cook claim and delivered another speech in the House, denouncing Cook as a fraud, in December of that year.

On September 21, in the midst of Helgesen's renewed interest in the polar controversy, Minik Wallace arrived in New York aboard the Red Cross Line steamer *Stephano*, on which he had embarked at St. John's, Newfoundland, a few days before.

He took a room at the McAlpin Hotel and immediately called a press conference.

Minik knew that the polar controversy had been big news in 1909. That story had broken shortly after he had arrived back in the north, but in subsequent years he had heard much about it. He had heard some of the details from the two Danes at North Star Bay, Peter Freuchen and Knud Rasmussen. Rasmussen had vacillated between pledging support for Cook or Peary, but Freuchen had been a staunch Peary man from the beginning. But it was from Donald MacMillan and the members of the Crocker Land Expedition that Minik heard the most detail about the controversy. This had been strongly partisan information, for MacMillan had been with Peary in 1909, and the purpose of his Crocker Land Expedition had been to vindicate Peary's reputation by proving the existence of the land he claimed to have discovered in the Polar Sea. From the talk he had heard at Etah during his time with the expedition, Minik knew something of the intensity of the controversy that had ensued when Cook and Peary had each claimed the Pole within a space of six days. He assumed, as did many in America, that Cook and Peary had both made big money selling their respective stories of their adventures. Minik thought it was now time that he got a piece of that action.

He told the reporters, "I've got a big story about Peary and Cook. After I get a lawyer for a manager, you know, the same way as you would open up any show, I'll tell you the price. . . .

"One fellow on a Brooklyn paper asked me what I would take for my big story. Just to put him off, I told him a million dollars. He said that he would have to call up his office before he could talk business. . . ."

Of course, Minik had to provide a bit more information than that to entice the newspapers to compete for his story. He offered them this:

"No, I don't know who discovered the North Pole. I don't know that it was ever discovered by anybody. What I know is what the Eskimos who accompanied Cook and Peary tell me. They may not be scientists, but they made their observations just the same. For instance, you remember that Peary had four Eskimos with him on the last 180-mile dash to the place where he said, 'Here we are — we go no further.' I've been living with Uutaaq, Iggiannguaq, Sigluk and Ukkujaaq, who were with Peary. They know just how many days passed during the journey. Wouldn't it be interesting to compare their records with Admiral Peary's proofs of his discovery? I've also talked with Ittukusuk and Aapilak, the men who accompanied Dr. Cook on his expedition in 1908."

"All this information is locked up in here," concluded Minik, tapping his forehead. "Tomorrow, after I see a lawyer, I will be ready to receive offers."

But the game was over. The public's interest in the North Pole controversy had in fact been short-lived. It had peaked in late 1909, while newspapers were still touting the merits of the rival claims, but had waned steadily since. Occasionally there was a burst of renewed interest, with a disclosure now and then that there was new information to be had on the subject, but these spates of interest were now forgotten in a day or two by all those save a few who had become aficionados of the controversy. Respectable sums of money had been paid in 1909 for stories of the conquest of the Pole. But now, seven years later, there was no interest. Minik waited in vain for the offers that did not come.

The only interest expressed was that of Ernst C. Rost, a paid lobbyist of Dr. Cook who was promoting the doctor's claims in Washington. Rost misrepresented himself as the secretary to Representative Helgesen and invited Minik to go to Washington to meet with Helgesen to "impart the information he says he obtained from the natives of Greenland regarding the relative merits of the claims of Admiral Peary and Dr. Cook. . . ." Rost intimated that Minik should go to Washington the first week in October. But the trip never took place.

On October 24, by which time he had still not received an official invitation to Washington, Minik wrote the congressman. He received a reply from Helgesen's real secretary, who informed him that the congressman was in his home state and would not be back in the capital until early December. The letter was not encouraging: ". . . I have no doubt whatever but what the Congressman would be interested to a certain extent in meeting you and hearing your story or any statement you might care to make, but at the same time, there is nothing in the circumstances in the case to warrant you in predicating your future conduct on any interest that Mr. Helgesen might have in your particular version of the Peary-Cook controversy, and I want to assure you that so far as this office is concerned you are perfectly free to make any disposition of any information you have as you deem best for your own interests. . . ."

The simple fact was that in 1916 the United States was not interested in the Arctic; it was interested in the war that was being fought in Europe. In fact, in that year, the government of the United States formally renounced any claim it may have had to any part of Greenland at the same time that it paid the Kingdom of Denmark $25,000,000 to acquire the Danish West Indies, since known as the Virgin Islands.

The game was over in another sense, too. The newspapers did not take the same interest in Minik that they had a decade earlier, for he was no longer a wronged child but a grown adult. The trauma he had undergone a decade earlier when he had discovered his father's skeleton in the American Museum of Natural History had been largely forgotten by the public, if not by Minik.

The newspapers treated him briefly as a minor curiosity. The *Tribune* reported that he was "back on Broadway, after spending seven dark years in the igloos of his tribe," and, in fact, he did appear briefly in a vaudeville routine, dressed up in Eskimo garb. The *Times* reported the nonsense that, after checking into the McAlpin Hotel, he "took a bath with a lump of ice in it, donned cool clothing, and inspected Broadway." Minik told the reporter that the memory of "the igloos of Broadway" had made his evenings somewhat dull in the snowhouses of northern Greenland.

Minik was still providing southerners with much of the stereotypical description of northern life that he thought they expected, but there was a more serious and sadder aspect to some of the brief reportage of his seven years in Greenland:

"I had to learn the language again. . . . I lived as they lived; I studied their needs; I tried to find what civilization could do for them. My food consisted of walrus, seal and narwal [*sic*] fat, always boiled over an oil lamp. When I go down to dinner tonight I may ask for cold blubber just by habit.

"Was I satisfied with the crude life there? Yes and no. The climate suited me and my health was better than when here. But the hard, dreary life of the people and the conditions under which they live are very monotonous to one who knows of the high state of civilization here.

"For my own part, I could have been happy there — but for this. In fact there were times, and I still have the impression that it would have been better for me had I never been brought to civilization and educated. It leaves me between two extremes, where it would seem that I can get nowhere.

"It would have been better if I had never been educated. . . . It's like rotting in a cellar to go back there after living in a civilized country."

Minik announced that this trip to New York was only a visit and that he would eventually go back north. He thought he might try to start a trading company there. And, he mused, he might try marriage again. "Of course, I made a hit with the ladies when I first went back," he claimed, "but I found I couldn't settle down and marry. You see, I'd been educated." In thinking that he might try again, he noted that, "You can support a family cheaply there, and at night there is no place to go but home."

For now, though, there was no place to go at all. He was in touch with Beecroft from time to time, and periodically visited William Wallace, who had never managed to win again the lifestyle he had once enjoyed as superintendent of buildings at the American Museum of Natural History. He found his childhood playmate, William Jr., living in Manasquan, New Jersey, with his wife, Matilda, and two young sons. His friend Harry Radford had come to a tragic end. In 1911 he had gone again to northern Canada to collect musk oxen and wood bison specimens for American museums. He and a man named Thomas George Street had pushed far into the central Arctic. Early in 1912 they were in Bathurst Inlet, and it was there that the Eskimos killed both men in July of that year. When the Royal Canadian Mounted Police finally investigated the killings, they laid no charges, concluding that the killings had been done under severe provocation from Radford, who had viciously whipped an Eskimo who had refused to travel because his wife was ill. Radford was well known to the Mounties and surprisingly, in light of his kindly interest in Minik a few years earlier, they noted that it was well known that "he did not get on with natives."

Minik hung about the McAlpin Hotel for much of the fall, awaiting the offers that never came for his story of Cook's and Peary's attempts on the Pole. He received a letter from a gentleman who proposed that he and Minik start a trading company in the Thule District in the interest of "assisting the tribe and protecting them from dishonest traders." Nothing came of the scheme except that for a time the pursuit of the idea provided Minik with free lodging at the home of the proponent. During the winter he considered a publishing company's idea for a book about his life, but that project too came to naught.

210

He was in touch with the museum's president, Henry Fairfield Osborn, not to renew efforts to secure the release of his father's body, but rather to request payment of $50 for work he had done for Elmer Ekblaw at North Star Bay. Museum officials noted that he was entirely friendly to the museum. They sent him the requested payment and Osborn, who felt considerable sympathy for him, wrote a brief memo to a colleague asking, "Can we not find some employment for Minik?"

He applied for American citizenship early in 1917 and registered with the Military Census in June.

He took work for a time in a machine shop, but he once again felt the urge to go back north, although, again, there was no way to get there. He expressed an interest in going to Alaska, where he knew there were Eskimos like himself. In May of 1917, he secured an introduction to the manager of the Alaska Mines Corporation in Nome, but he never made the trip.

He received a letter from a woman who had been his first nurse in America, in the Wallace home so many years before. This was Lizzie, who had taught him to say his prayers each night. In June of 1917, he went to Pennsylvania to pay her a short visit. He was a handsome man in his late twenties. At five feet, six inches, he was average in height, and at 155 pounds a sturdy and employable individual. But he was restless and rootless. Most of the time he drifted, from one odd job to another, from one city to another.

The fears that had been expressed by a reporter, more perceptive than most just before he had returned to the Arctic in 1909 had been realized, and now, "neither fish nor fowl, no longer a simple Eskimo and yet not a complicated Yankee, he was more than ever alone."

His wanderlust took him to Boston in late 1917, and there he sought work through a local employment agency.

23

THE NORTH COUNTRY

THE NORTHWESTERN CORNER of the state of New Hampshire has had a turbulent and somewhat ridiculous history. Its troubles began with the Treaty of Paris in 1783; that treaty drew the border between the new United States of America and Canada along the Connecticut River. The only problem was that, in the absence of surveys, nobody was quite sure where the head of that river was. In 1789, New Hampshire sent Colonel Jeremiah Eames to survey the boundary. Unfortunately, Eames was a scoundrel — he drew the border along a more westerly waterway, Hall's Stream, and then bought all the land between it and the Connecticut River for himself from an Abenaki Indian chief, in return for a promise that the chief and his two wives would be fed and clothed for the rest of their lives. Three years later the governor of Lower Canada refused to recognize Hall's Stream as the border and began to survey Eames's stolen territory, naming it Drayton Township. The Canadian authorities invited settlers in and gave land grants to homesteaders.

Settlers drifted in, along with renegades and fugitives of every stripe. The area was as remote from the authorities in Sherbrooke, Canada, as it was from those in Lancaster, New Hampshire, and for a time it mattered little to the pioneers who were carving homesteads out of the wilderness that two countries claimed the territory. In 1819, Canada offered to settle the dispute by agreeing on a boundary along the Indian Stream, which wanders right through the middle of the territory. The United States refused, however, and the dispute was submitted to the king of the Netherlands for arbitration. In 1831, the Dutch king upheld the Treaty of Paris and decreed that the boundary should follow the Connecticut River, but the United States Senate refused, by a vote of twenty-three to twenty-two, to abide by his decision. In the meantime, the efforts of both countries to tax the disputed area's few inhabitants were becoming intolerable.

There were few enough inhabitants in the territory — the total population was about a hundred. In 1832, they made a dramatic move to settle the dispute themselves — by a vote of fifty-six to three they declared themselves an independent republic under the name of United Inhabitants of Indian Stream. They adopted a constitution and drew up a bill of rights, which established freedom of religion and the right to life, liberty, and property. Every male inhabitant over the age of twenty-one was to be a member of the General Assembly. Taxes were levied and a forty-man reserve army created. Three judges were appointed, as well as a sheriff. Since he had no jail, the sheriff kept his prisoners one at a time in a 700-pound potash kettle turned upside down over a flat rock.

Of course neither Canada nor the United States recognized this upstart republic, but it took three years for either of them to do anything about it. A series of arrests and attempted arrests by both Canadian and American authorities finally resulted in an armed invasion of the Indian Stream Republic by the New Hampshire militia in November of 1835. One key individual was jailed, and others fled to Canada. The president, Luther Parker, quietly packed his wagon and emigrated with his family to Wisconsin. The Indian Stream Republic had been conquered. Or so it seemed. But then the General Assembly of the republic met for one final session. It realized that the New Hampshire militia was firmly in control; the militia force, however small, was half the size of the republic's entire population! There had been no loss of life yet in the affair, and so, instead of resisting, the proud members of the assembly passed a series of resolutions that legislated an end to their four-year-old republic, surely the only country in the world ever to legislate itself out of existence.

The area became Pittsburg Township in the state of New Hampshire. The old-time families there call it and its surroundings simply "the north country."

By the turn of the century, the Connecticut Valley Lumber Company had become the dominant industry in northern New Hampshire. The company too had an unusual beginning: A New York banker had gained the timberland of the Connecticut Lakes region as payment for a debt. From that unexpected start, he built an empire that came to dominate commerce in the region.

Pittsburg, the largest town in this sparsely populated area, was a farming community. But this was a rugged and mountainous part of the state in which to eke a living from the soil. Lumbering was a godsend to the local farmers, for lumbering meant winter work. There was not much to do on the farms in winter anyway; with the crops in and the winter hay stored, the farmers took to the woods, leaving the women at home to attend to the milking and routine chores.

The lumber industry's need for manpower in the harsh winter months was such that local labor could not meet the entire demand. Workers had to be imported from out of state. Many were inexperienced men who had never held an axe before. Connecticut Valley Lumber recruited them through a Boston employment agency.

In the fall of 1917 Minik Wallace stepped off a train in North Stratford, New Hampshire, bound for the lumber town of Pittsburg. The agency had paid for his ticket; its cost would be deducted over the course of the winter from his salary of fifty cents per day. Bill Buck's livery stable in nearby Canaan, Vermont, provided the only transportation to Pittsburg, in an open wagon. Many of the workers arrived so ill-clad and poorly prepared for winter in the mountains that they had to run behind the team much of the distance into Pittsburg just to keep warm. The lumber company maintained a large bunkhouse that was home to these out-of-state recruits. For a time this was Minik's new home.

Life here was different from anything Minik had ever known. The lumbering crews were a mixed bag of French Canadians, Poles, Finns, Swedes, and local Yankees, and among them were a fair sampling of misfits, rejects, and the plain unfortunate. Minik was not a freak here, unless they were all freaks together. No one was going to pander to him. These were tough men, hard workers earning a living here in a hard industry. Those from out of state had all had their share of life's ups and downs, or they wouldn't have ended up here in the first place.

Here in Pittsburg, New Hampshire, Minik determined to make a new start. Here there would be none of the bravado of his earlier days in New York. His fellow lumberjacks were, like him, mostly young, single, and self-reliant. Ironically, he spoke English much better than many of the other migrant workers. He did his best to fit in, and for the first time in his life he succeeded. He is remembered in Pittsburg as a good worker and a genuinely "nice fellow to have around."

The work was hard. In this mountain environment the winters were long and harsh. It wasn't as dark as the sunless winter months of northern Greenland, but it could be just as cold. While the ground was frozen the workers felled the trees and carved slick roads out of the forests to skid the trees to the riverbanks to await the spring runoff and the log drives downriver to the mills.

The novice in the lumber camps started as a swamper, clearing brush from the swamps in preparation for the construction of the slick roads. The next position in the hierarchy of jobs was that of chopper, followed by scaler, a man who had to be expert at estimating the board feet or cords in a log. Minik learned quickly during his winter in Pittsburg, for he reached the position of scaler.

He soon tired of living in the company bunkhouse. It was not that he disliked any of his colleagues; quite the contrary — he liked them and the feeling was mutual. But they were a noisy and rowdy bunch, and Minik had put noisiness and rowdiness behind him in New York before embarking for this new world. He would rather spend his evenings reading and working sporadically on the autobiography he had promised a New York publisher. So he built himself a tiny shack up across from the little cemetery where the unclaimed river drivers were buried. Here he could be alone and keep his books. Nobody minded. As long as he was there when there was work to be done, a man could be excused his eccentricities.

To the taciturn natives of northern New Hampshire, early spring is "mud season." The lumber camps closed down then. Those who were not needed for the river drives were let go, to find whatever work they might back in the cities. But Minik didn't board the train in North Stratford in the spring of 1918 for the long journey back to the prison of an American city; during the winter he had made a strong and lasting friendship with one of the local farmers.

His name was Afton Hall and he was just a few years older than Minik. Quiet and reserved, like Minik he was a loner. He was single and lived with his father and mother in a tidy frame house in rural Clarksville, high on a hill overlooking the Connecticut River and Pittsburg. Afton Hall, like his father Fred, his brother Barney, and all the other farmers of the area, worked for Connecticut Valley Lumber in the winter. Minik had met Afton in the lumber camp. When mud season brought the winter's work to an inglorious end, Afton had invited the Eskimo to come and live with the Hall family. Minik spent the rest of the spring, the summer, and the early fall with them. He helped about the farm, taking his part in the planting and the harvest, as well as the milking and the routine chores. The Halls were poor folk and had nothing to offer him except their hospitality. That was enough for Minik. He was content to work for his room and board.

He loved it here. It was the happiest period of his adulthood and the most peaceful he had experienced since leaving Lawyersville in 1904. Physically, the area reminded him of Lawyersville. Both were mountainous, and both were farming country. But here in Pittsburg, he was no one special. He was not the adopted Eskimo son of a seemingly wealthy local businessman and philanthropist, shown off as a curiosity at the agricultural fair and made to sing his native songs in the local Sunday school. Neither was he the wronged Eskimo boy that he had been a few years later in New York City, suffering the trauma of finding that his father's skeleton was on display in the American Museum of Natural History and being pandered to by

217

the press in search of sensational copy. Here he was virtually anonymous, and he was content to have it that way. He seldom even went into town. He preferred to remain on the farm and spend his free time wandering the hills, valleys, and riverbanks of the surrounding countryside.

He felt a part of the Hall family, and they were content to have him. The independent, old-time families of the north country are a reserved lot and it is difficult — some say impossible — for an outsider to penetrate their shell of reticence. But with the Halls, Minik succeeded. As one long-time resident put it, "It's hard for them to take a stranger into their hearts. If he hadn't been a good worker, he wouldn't have kept a job here long." He told Afton that he never wanted to leave. That was fine with Afton and his parents. They liked Minik. He was welcome to stay.

But like the youthful idyll of life in Lawyersville, it was too good to last. In the fall of 1918, just as the men had returned to lumbering, the Spanish flu swept the camps, as it swept the world. In the close confines of the company bunkhouse, it wrought havoc. The sick from the camps were brought in and laid out on the floor of the bunkhouse, each with his own blanket. A doctor came once a day, earning a dollar per visit to remove the dead and do what he could for the living. The dead were buried immediately; those with no identification were interred in a common grave. But Minik Wallace was not among those.

The flu hit him hard. But Afton Hall would not hear of him suffering his illness in the common bunkhouse. Afton took him to the Hall home, where both his parents were already down with the flu. There Afton nursed him, but to no avail. On October 29, after a short illness, Minik died of bronchial pneumonia.

In December, James Beecroft of New York City received a letter from Afton Hall:

"I am asking a favor of you which I feel sure you will grant. I would like to get into communication with Mr. William Wallace that I might inform him of the death of Minik at my home October 29 of pneumonia following influenza. Although everything possible [was done] that the best physicians could do, the fight seemed against him from the start, and he only lived seven days. The doctors said he must be

218

buried at once, so I had him interned [*sic*] in the cemetery here. He often spoke of you and your brother, and of all the people I heard him speak of, yours was the only address I found among his papers.

"Our home was a regular hospital for six weeks; my father and Minik had pneumonia and my mother and myself were down with the influenza. We had a hospital nurse and a doctor in daily attendance most of the time. My father is just up around the house, and I wish poor Minik was also. Any information you can give me or, better still, if you could have Mr. Wallace communicate with me, I will try and supply any information he will wish to know."

Minik was buried in the little cemetery on the banks of the Indian Stream on October 30. His grave, covered with a small stone placed there by the Hall family, is on a grassy knoll overlooking a bend in this slow-moving, meandering stream. In a remote corner of the state that boasts the motto LIVE FREE OR DIE, the man without a country found his final resting place, here in the no-man's-land of the Indian Stream Republic, the country that could never be.

They still remember Minik in Pittsburg, not for the sadness or excitement with which his short and tragic life was filled, but simply because, in the words of a local historian, "he was a nice guy and everybody liked him."

EPILOGUE

OBERT PEARY DIED IN 1920 at the age of sixty-three, embittered over the vicious controversy surrounding the discovery of the North Pole, a controversy that he felt had robbed him of some of the glory due him. The rival claimant to the Pole, Frederick Cook, died in 1940, at the age of seventy-five. The controversy has never been resolved. Herbert L. Bridgman died in 1924, aged eighty. Active to the very end, he died of a heart attack aboard the New York State School ship, *Newport,* in the mid-Atlantic while returning from a European cruise.

Franz Boas, Alfred Kroeber, and Ales Hrdlicka all went on to distinguished careers in anthropology. Boas was the most influential anthropologist of his time.

Knud Rasmussen succeeded in his long-held dream of a sled trip through the Canadian Arctic and Alaska to the Bering Strait. The trip, known as the Fifth Thule Expedition, was the triumph of his distinguished career. He died in Denmark in 1933. His life-long friend, Peter Freuchen, ran the Thule Station until 1920. He participated in the Fifth Thule Expedition and went on to become a prolific writer and well-known lecturer, usually on Arctic subjects. He died in Alaska in 1957. His body was cremated and his ashes scattered over his beloved Thule Mountain.

Arnannguaq continued to live with Peter Freuchen and Navarana for some time after her separation from Minik. Eventually she married a hunter, Ittullak, with whom she had two children. Her love of sleep made her a poor wife for a hunter and she and Ittullak eventually separated. Later in life, she married another man, Qaerngaaq; she died at Uummannaq in the mid-1940s. Navarana Freuchen, like so many Eskimos, died an early death from influenza in 1921 at Upernavik, Greenland. Her husband buried her himself — the local priest would not consent to her burial in the churchyard, for she was unbaptized.

Pamela Wallace died in East Orange, New Jersey, in March of 1937 and is buried in the Wallace plot in the Cobleskill Rural Cemetery in Cobleskill, New York. William Wallace never recovered from the financial setbacks he suffered at the turn of the century. He drifted from job to job and from one address to another in New York City and East Orange. His disgrace at the American Museum of Natural History dogged him for the rest of his life; in 1940 he was described as being "in bad shape physically and financially" and as having "comingled the funds of the Museum with his personal funds." He died penniless in November of 1941 in Greystone Park, a home for the mentally ill in Parsippany, New Jersey. He was eighty-six years of age and senile. He and his son had not gotten along well for many years, and although William Jr. was living at the time near New York City, as were his two sons, then married and with families of their own, no one claimed the body and he was given a pauper's funeral at the expense of the state. In the spring of the following year, a long-time friend of the family, Florence Padula, had the body disinterred and moved to the family plot in Cobleskill.

William Wallace Jr. had left home while still in his teens. As a young man, he was a race-car driver. Later he became a chauffeur for the Kohler family, of piano manufacturing fame; he and his wife lived in a house on the Kohler estate in Mahway, New Jersey. He died in 1955 in Suffern, New York.

Afton Hall married briefly. He died in 1969 at the age of eighty-three and is buried a few yards from Minik in the Indian Stream Cemetery. After his death, his nephew, Howard Young, purchased a small stone marker bearing Minik's name and had it placed over the grave of Hall's Eskimo friend.

Sechmann Rosbach left Thule in 1916, about a month before Minik did. He moved to Godhavn in Disko Bay, where, a few years later, he met Peter Pedersen, captain of Knud Rasmussen's ship, and learned from him that Minik had returned to America. But he also heard, erroneously, that Minik had collected his $20,000 and had been doing quite well for himself when suddenly he had taken ill and died.

In 1934, Rosbach published a short account of Minik's life in *Avangnaamioq*, a small Greenlandic regional newspaper. Most of the account told of Minik's fictitious adventures in America, which Rosbach had taken as fact. Rosbach's story has been accepted as true for the fifty years since its publication. In 1982, it was reprinted in its entirety in Greenland's national newspaper, *Atuagagdliutit*, to fool a whole new generation of Greenlandic readers. The editor of that paper, Jorgen Fleischer, then used the article as his sole source for a chapter on Minik in a book published in 1983 in Danish and Greenlandic, and that chapter has been translated into English and published in *Arctic Policy Review*, the organ of the Inuit Circumpolar Conference.

At the end of the account Rosbach speculated on what might have become of Minik's money after his death. It had been a large sum and, he suggested, most of it must still be there, somewhere, in America. He ventured a simple and touching suggestion. In those years, he wrote, there was never enough money to build proper houses for the people of the far north, the Polar Eskimos whom he remembered with such fondness. Perhaps, if Minik's money could be found, it could be used to build houses for his people. In that way, could not this unimportant Eskimo, about whom no one had cared very much in life, be of real assistance to this people in the end?

It was a naive hope. There was no money. There never had been. There was only a small stone lying forgotten in a quiet rural cemetery to remind anyone that there had ever been a Minik.

The American Museum of Natural History bore a continuing shame and sense of guilt over its role in the tragic events that surrounded Minik's life in New York. In 1950, a high-school student,

Ruth Sturm, wrote the museum from Cobleskill; she was preparing an essay on the subject of the Eskimos who had once lived in the area and she requested information from the museum's files to help her in the project. The museum's vice director wrote her a kind letter, advising her that the museum's files on the subject were sketchy but suggesting that she might contact George Pindar, retired registrar of the museum, who, by coincidence, lived in Sharon Springs, a town neighboring Cobleskill, and whose recollection of the events would be clear and helpful. On the same day the vice-director wrote to Mr. Pindar as well, suggesting that, if the student approached him, he should not give her any details of the incident but should, instead, try to dissuade her from pressing the inquiry further.

Another inquirer was given similar treatment in 1963; museum staff concluded that the incidents had placed the museum in a bad light at the time of their occurrence and no good could come from bringing them all before the public again. In the interim, however, a member of the museum's own staff, Dr. Robert Cushman Murphy, had published an article on Minik and his father. Called "Skeleton in the Museum Closet," it is by far the most tasteless and offensive article ever to appear on Minik. The article made light of the problems that had been created through the museum's acquisition of Qisuk's skeleton. Wrong in most of its details, it ends with the ludicrous statement that, after a lifetime of attempts to get the release of his father's bones, Minik's own skeleton ended up in the box next to his father's. That the article did not create embarrassment for the museum is probably due only to the fact that it appeared in the *Peruvian Times*.

Many times in the 1970s I visited Qaanaaq, today the main village of the Polar Eskimos, and I often heard the elders of the community reminisce about Minik. To them, his adventurous life had begun to take on the character of legend. When he left the district, World War I was raging. He had told some of the Eskimos that he intended to become a pilot and fight in that war. They didn't doubt but that he would try — he had had so many fascinating adventures already. And so, some said, he had gone back to America, become a skilled pilot, and died a hero's death in a spectacular crash after being shot down by the enemy. For others he had returned to America, collected his baptismal gift — the amount has fluctuated wildly in their recollections and their imaginations — and lived a long and respectable life. He spoke the language of the Americans so well and he had proved, by the way he had become such a skilled hunter in his seven years back home in the Arctic, that he could adapt to almost any circumstances. But to most of the Eskimos, he had simply disappeared. They talked about him from time to time, recalling his adventures and the ultimate sadness of his life, but no one was sure until 1979 what had been his final fate.

In 1977, I married Navarana, a Polar Eskimo who had been named for Peter Freuchen's wife. Two years later, with my mother-in-law, Amaunnalik, who had been named for Minik's maternal aunt, we visited the United States. I had become fascinated by the fragmented details of Minik's life that I had heard recounted in Greenland, and I was in search of Minik. On a warm spring afternoon, we found him in the quietness of the Indian Stream Cemetery.

Amaunnalik had been born in 1907, and as a little girl, she had known Minik and seen him many times on his travels about the district. Uutaaq, with whom Minik lived for some time, was her uncle. She had heard Minik's stories, and after he left the district she listened to the tales her elders told as Minik passed slowly into legend. She had tears in her eyes, as did we all, as we stood beside the inconspicuous grave. The mystery of what had finally become of Minik would be a mystery no more to the Polar Eskimos.

AFTERWORD

FOLLOWING THE FIRST PUBLICATION of this book in 1986, the American Museum of Natural History was embarrassed. They had succeeded for many years in covering up the story of Minik and their treatment of the remains of Qisuk and his fellow Eskimos. Now, almost a century after the events in question, the story had come back to haunt them. But public attention waned, and Qisuk's bones continued to lie in a box in the museum under accession number 99/3610, alongside those of Nuktaq, Atangana, and Aviaq. Minik's desire to have his father's bones released from the museum and properly buried went unrealized. From time to time, representations were made to the museum to have the bones released, but to no avail. And the museum continued to lie, when necessary, to deny its part in the whole sordid affair. At one point following publication, a politician from Greenland, Aqqaluk Lynge, while visiting in New York, contacted the museum about the matter, only to be told that the museum knew nothing about the story.

I had long felt that, if the museum would ever release the remains, the proper place for Qisuk to rest would be beside his son in the peaceful Indian Stream Cemetery. This was the place where Minik had found true happiness with his friend, Afton Hall, and Hall's relatives in the northern mountains of New Hampshire. Members of the Hall family still remembered Minik and still tended his small grave marker. They remembered Afton's stories of Minik with fondness. Were Qisuk to be buried beside Minik, father and son could pass together into eternity, as they had passed together into legend. As for the other Inuit, they should be returned to northern Greenland for burial, if that was the wish of the community there. But the museum would not hear of my suggestion. I was not a relative of the deceased or an official of a government responsible for the deceased. I was merely the author who had embarrassed them. The museum's position was that the bones should remain in the museum.

Then, in 1992, two reporters rediscovered *Give Me My Father's Body*. They were Miro Cernetig of Toronto's *Globe and Mail* and William Claiborne of the *Washington Post*. Both interviewed me and wrote articles that were prominently featured in their newspapers. Once again, ninety-five years after six Eskimos had first been brought to New York, the museum was embarrassed. And once again came the demands for the bones of Qisuk and his countrymen to be released from the museum and properly buried. A request came from as far away as Saudi Arabia, where William Wallace's great-granddaughter, Wendy Wallace, was working. Stating that she was a relative, through adoption, of Minik, she felt she had a legitimate interest in seeing his father buried, and she too requested that he be buried in the Indian Stream Cemetery in Pittsburg, New Hampshire, beside his son. But we both agreed that if the museum refused to consider such a request, it would be appropriate for the remains of all four Eskimos to be transported to Greenland for burial. Better that than that they should continue to languish in the museum.

This time the interest in having the bones removed from the museum for burial remained high. Since 1986, things had changed in the conservative world of American museums. Native Americans had made progress in forcing museums to deal appropriately with the remains of their ancestors.

In 1990 the Native American Grave and Burial Protection Act was passed. Under that legislation, American museums are required to return skeletal remains to native groups that request them. Qisuk and the other Polar Eskimos, however, were not covered by this legislation. They were Greenlanders, not Americans, and the American Museum of Natural History was under no obligation to send their bones to Greenland or anywhere else for burial.

But the museum authorities had had enough. In the summer of 1992, they decided to lay the story to rest once and for all and quietly dispatched their agents to Qaanaaq to meet with the local community council. Jorgen Melgaard, an archaeologist with the Danish National Museum, and Edmund Carpenter, an American anthropologist, brought a simple message to the community: Ask the American Museum of Natural History for the remains to be returned for burial, and the museum will comply with your request. Bureaucracy works no faster in Greenland than it does elsewhere, and it was not until well into 1993 that the request was officially made. It was a request for the remains of all four Eskimos to be returned to Qaanaaq for interment.

I contacted Wendy Wallace to advise her. She was delighted, as I was, that the episode begun so long ago, one in which her great-grandfather had played such a major role, would at last come to an appropriate end.

On July 28, 1993, the bones of four Polar Eskimos were loaded aboard an American military transport aircraft at Maguire Air Force Base in New Jersey and transported to Thule Air Base in northern Greenland. The journey that had taken over a month in 1897 was accomplished in a few short hours. At Thule, the cargo was transferred to a Greenlandair helicopter for the trip to Qaanaaq, less than an hour away.

Officialdom almost had one last surprise for the souls of the four returning Eskimos. The Lutheran church, the state church of Greenland and Denmark, had initially decided that, because the Eskimos were pagans and unbaptized, they could not be buried in a Christian ceremony. That decision, however, was reconsidered, and the bodies were received at the small church in Qaanaaq. Torben Diklev, curator of the community's museum, looked after the logistics of the ceremony. On August 1 the bodies, each in its own small casket, were placed in a common grave in hallowed ground on a hillside with a splendid view of the sea to the west. Rocks were piled on top of the graves in the traditional manner. A brief service was held at the graveside. Three people spoke: the priest, Hans Johan Lennert; the mayor of the community, August Eipe; and Edmund Carpenter, representing the American Museum of Natural History. A number of Polar Eskimos were in attendance, along with Emil Rosing, director of the National Museum of Greenland, and Jorgen Melgaard. A plaque was provided for eventual erection at the gravesite. It began with the terse statement, NUNAMINGNUT UTEQIHUT, which translates simply as "They have come home." This statement is followed by the names of the four Eskimos with details of their births and deaths and the statement 1897 NEW YORK-IMUT, 1993 QAANAAMUT.

Perhaps a Christian burial was not what the Eskimos would have wanted after all. One should remember that Atangana, before her death in New York, had stated that she did not want to be buried under the sand and wanted no coffin. Nor did she want the stones to be placed too closely together, for fear that she might not breathe. Nonetheless, the burial of all four was carried out in the modern Christian manner.

On August 4, 1997, one hundred years after Qisuk, Nuktaq, Atangana, and Aviaq left the Thule district for New York aboard the *Hope*, and four years after the return of their remains to Greenland and their burial in the graveyard at Qaanaq, the memorial plaque was finally placed over their common grave. Queen Margrethe of Denmark and her husband, Prince Henrik, attended its unveiling in a touching ceremony presided over by the mayor, Lars Jeremiassen, who spoke of the community's wish to honor their forefathers who loved their living and grieved their dead.

Among the Polar Eskimos there is a profound sense of relief that the events that began over one hundred years ago are finally at an end. As my research into the story of Minik and his fellow New York Eskimos proceeded in the 1970s and 1980s, many Polar Eskimos followed the story with fascination. Whenever I was in Qaanaaq, people would question me about the story, about the fate of Minik, and about the four unfortunate souls who had succumbed to disease so soon after their arrival in Peary's land. There was tremendous interest when Amaunnalik, Navarana, and I reported our finding of Minik's simple grave marker in the Indian Stream Cemetery, and a feeling grew that Minik's fondest wish should be realized and that Qisuk, along with the other Eskimos, should be properly buried. The

228

American Museum of Natural History has now complied with the
people's request, and with common sense, and the Eskimos have
been given the burial that they so long deserved.

I am often asked, should Minik be disinterred and taken also to
Qaanaaq for reburial? The answer must be an unequivocal no. Minik
lived a tortured and lonely life. Out of place in New York, he felt no
more at home when he returned to northern Greenland. That feeling
of alienation led him back to the United States in 1916, where he told
his old friend, John D. Clark, that the bright lights of Broadway attracted him more than the Northern Lights. In the fall of 1917 he arrived in northern New Hampshire and died there one year later. He
died among friends, the Hall family, perhaps the truest friends he
ever had. At their own expense, they placed a tiny marker over his
grave and tended his final resting place. Minik died among friends.
Let him remain there.

KENN HARPER
August 1999

APPENDIX

NAMES

There are a number of different spellings used in the original sources for most of the Eskimo names of both places and people in this story. Both Peary and MacMillan butchered the spellings of Eskimo names to such an extent that it has sometimes been almost impossible to decipher what is meant by their renditions. Danish and Greenlandic sources generally follow the old Greenlandic orthography (the so-called Kleinschmidt orthography), although there are occasional deviations from this.

In the text, all Eskimo words have been spelled consistently following the current official Greenlandic orthography (a revision of the Kleinschmidt orthography), with some minor provision being made for the peculiarities of the Polar Eskimo dialect that mark it as different from West Greenlandic. This has required changing the spellings of the names of many people who were written about in the past and — more difficult to deal with — of some people still living. In many instances it has also necessitated changing the spellings used in direct quotations. While this has been done throughout the text, the original spellings have of course been retained in the bibliography and in the chapter references. I have allowed two exceptions to the above guideline. The well-known home of so many polar expeditions, Etah (really Iita), has been spelled consistently as Etah for over a hundred years by English, Danish, and Greenlandic writers. It remains Etah in this book as well. Likewise, the well-known place name, Neqe, has retained its traditional spelling in this book.

Most American references to Minik spell his name as Mene. In fact, the only Americans who have ever spelled his name correctly were the scientists Boas and Kroeber. Official references to him in the United States, such as his declaration of intent to become an American citizen, use the name Mene Peary Wallace or Mene Wallace, the name he used himself when in America. All references to him from Danish and Greenlandic sources spell his name correctly as Minik. I have spelled it consistently as Minik throughout the book. When I considered all the injustices of his short and unhappy life, I thought the least I could do was to spell his name correctly.

A list follows of Eskimo words (people and place names as well as other words) found in the text. Beside some of them are given some of the more common variant spellings one will find in the original source material. This will help those who may want to refer to sources in which Eskimo names have been used so inconsistently. For words other than names, English glosses have been given.

PEOPLE

STANDARD SPELLING	VARIANT SPELLINGS
Aapilak	Apilyah
Ajaku	Ajago
Aleqasersuaq	
Aleqasina	
Aleqasinnguaq	Allakasingwah
Aleqatsiaq	Tallakoteah
Amaunnalik	
Angutilluarsuk	Angutidluarssuak, Angutiluajuk
Arnannguaq	Arnanguaq
Arrottarsuaq	Arrotoksuah
Aserpannguaq	Iopungya, I-o-oung-wa

Atangana	Atana, Artona, Ahtungahnak(soah), Ahtungnah
Aviaq	Hawia, Ahweah, Ahweelah
Eqariusaq	Eqariussaq, Ek-kai-a-sha
Equ	Ikwa, Ikwah, Ik-qua
Eri	Ere
Iggiannguaq	Egingwa, Egingwah, Iginwa
Imiina	Ee-meen-ya
Inugaarsuk	
Inukittoq	Inighito, Inukitsoq
Ittukusuk	Etookashoo, Itookuechuk
Ittullak	
Ivik	
Kuuttiikittoq	Kutsikitsoq, Kuutsiikitsoq
Majaq	Myah, Mayark
Mannik	Mane
Meqqusaaq	Merkoshak, Merktoshar
Mequpaluk	
Minik	Mene, Menie, Meenie, Minnie
Navarana	
Nukappiannguaq	Nookapingwa
Nuktaq	Nooktaq, Nuktan, Natooka, Nooktak, Nooktan
Panippak	Panikpak, Panikpa, Panikpah
Piugaattoq	Piuvaitsuq, Pee-a-wah-to
Piuli	Peary
Piulerriaq	Pearyaksoah
Piulersuaq	Pearyaksoah
Qaerngaaq	
Qajuuttaq	Kaiota, Kai-oto, Kyutah
Qillarsuaq	Qitdlarssuaq
Qisuk	Kishu, Kissuk, Kessuh, Kissuh, Kubliknik, Qissuk, Kusshan
Qisunnguaq	Qisunguaq, Ka-shung-wa
Qujaukittoq	Kyogwito, Qujaukitsoq
Qulutana	Koolootoonah, Koolatoonah
Sigluk	Sigdluk, Seegloo, Siglook
Siuleqatuk	
Soqqaq	Sorqaq
Suersaq	Suerssaq
Taliilannguaq	Teddy-ling-wa

Tautsiannguaq	Tau-ching-wa, Tawchingwah
Torngi	Tornge, Tung-we
Uisaakassak	Uisaakavsak, Ujaragapsuck, Wee-shak-up-si, Yaragapsuk, Weakupshi, Ujaragapssuq, Wesharkoupsi
Ukkujaaq	Ookeyah, Ooklya
Ulloriaq	Ooblooya, Ooblooyah
Uutaaq	Odaq, Ootah, Wootah

PLACES

STANDARD SPELLING	VARIANT SPELLINGS
Anoritooq	
Etah	
Itilleq	Ittibloo
Kangerlussuaq	Kangerdluksuaq, Kangalookswa
Natsilivik	Netiulume
Neqe	
Pitoraarfik	Peteravik
Qaanaaq	Qanaq, Kanak
Quinisut	Koinisuni
Savissivik	
Siorapaluk	
Tuttulissuaq	Tugtuligssuaq, Took-too-lik-suah
Upernavik	
Uummannaq	Umanak

WORDS

STANDARD SPELLING	VARIANT SPELLING	MEANING
amerlaqqaat		many
angakkoq	angakoq	shaman
Avangnaamioq		resident of a northern district (also the name of a newspaper published in Godhavn, Greenland)
kalaallit		West Greenlanders
kiisa	kissa	finally

naalagapaluk		the little boss (Polar Eskimo name for Donald MacMillan)
nallinnaq		pitiable, to be pitied
qallunaaq	koblunah	white man
qavangangnisat		residents of a southern district
qulittaq	qulitsaq	parka
sapinngilaq		not incapable
sermeq	sermik	glacier, ice-cap
sermersuaq	sermik-soak	great glacier, ice-cap
tikeqihunga	tikeri-unga	I've arrived
toorngat	toornat	helping spirit
tupiq	tupik	tent
upernaallit		whalers
uppissuaq	opiksoak	snowy owl

NOTES

In the chapter notes that follow, all archival references are summarized as follows:

AMNH refers to the American Museum of Natural History. All file references are to that institution's General Files, unless specified as being from the Department of Anthropology or the Rare Book and Manuscript Collection.

PFC refers to the Peary Family Collection in the U.S. National Archives, Record Group 401 (1).

PAC refers to the records of the Peary Arctic Club in the archives of the Explorers Club.

APS refers to the American Philosophical Society.

NYHS refers to the New York Historical Society.

Rigsarkivet refers to The Royal Archives, Copenhagen, Denmark, Records of the Danish Ministry of Foreign Affairs, File A.S.95/08 of the Royal Danish Consulate, New York.

Other references are abbreviated as follows: Books, manuscripts, magazines, and journals are referred to by author's name, with the year in brackets if more than one source is used from one author. The title is given if more than one item was published in one year. Newspaper references name the paper and date. Complete references are given in the bibliography.

All references are to the page on which each quotation appears.

Introductory Quotation / Notes

vii "To many a good person": Peary, 1898 (vol. 1), pp. 507–8.

vii "Our tales are narratives": Rasmussen, p. 27.

vii "This Minik seems gradually": Holtved, p. 11.

1 / Peary's People

2 "many in Peary's command": Green quoted in Eames, p. 20.

3 "a big boat"and "a whole island of wood": Rasmussen, pp. 1–2.

3 "turned towards the sea": ibid.

3 "If you point to the east": Gilberg, 1974–75, p. 160.

4 "Then it really grew winter": Hans Hendrik, p. 24.

6 "incorrigible scamps": quoted in Oswalt, p. 114.

6 "When they were first allowed": quoted in Green, p. 71.

7 "He learned to drive": Green, pp. 76–78.

8 "I have often been asked": ibid., p. 68.

8 "did not produce": Malaurie, p. 235.

8 "a great leader": Malaurie, p. 233.

8 "their respect for the man": Rasmussen, p. 8.

8 "by threats": Malaurie, p. 235.

9 "my faithful, trusty Eskimo allies": Peary, 1898 (vol. 2), pp. 207–8.

9 "effective instruments": Peary, 1910, p. 47.

9 "these people are much like children": ibid., p. 50.

9 "their feeling for me": ibid., p. 48.

9 "It would be misleading": ibid., pp. 51–52.

9 "People were afraid of him": Malaurie, p. 234.

2 / The Iron Mountain

13 "I scratched a rough 'P'": Peary, 1898 (vol. 2), p. 147.

13 "This means that if the ship comes": Green, p. 125.

13 "I have failed": ibid., p. 140.

13 "I shall never see the North Pole": Freeman, p. 45, quoting *New York Tribune*, 2 October 1895.

14 "The summer's voyage": Peary, 1898 (vol. 1), p. xlix.

14 "the knowledge an explorer has acquired": Weems, 1967, p. 229, quoting a typescript fragment, undated, in the Peary Family Papers.

15 "Never was a man more fortunate": Peary, 1898 (vol. 1), p. lv.

15 "I sent my faithful Eskimos": Peary, 1898 (vol. 2), p. 591.

17 "a man of fine instincts": quoted in Rasky, p. 185.

17 "faithful hunter": Peary, 1898 (vol. 1), p. 508.

17 "the old man is aging": Peary, 1898 (vol. 2), p. 416.

18 "Panippak . . . tells me": ibid., p. 403.

18 "little Minik had meanwhile heard": Peary, 1904, pp. 35–36.

19 "I can remember very well": World, 6 January 1907, p. 3.

19 "he coaxed my father": San Francisco Examiner (Magazine Supplement), 9 May 1909.

19 "They promised us": World, 6 January 1907, p. 3.

19 "He asked with so strong a will": Rasmussen, p. 6.

19 "Our people were afraid": San Francisco Examiner (Magazine Supplement), 9 May 1909.

20 "Uisaakassak wants to go": PFC, Journal of 1897 Expedition, entry for 26 August 1987.

The story of Atangana burning the lodge comes from personal communication with Balika Jensen, Qaanaaq, Greenland.

The story of Arrutarsuaq's prowess as a shaman comes from personal communication with Inuutersuaq Ulloriaq, Siorapaluk, Greenland.

3 / ARRIVAL IN AMERICA

21 "The crowd afterward boarded": New York Times, 3 October 1897.

22 "The children are sick": ibid.

22 "The ship's men brought off the cask": PFC, Journal of 1896 Expedition, p. 134.

24 "You go ahead"and "when she failed": Green, p. 132.

24 "You must understand": Brown, p. 191.

24 "to reach the farthest northern point": Peary, 1907, p. 288.

24 "I understand Peary brought this party": AMNH, File 517; handwritten note by Morris Jesup on bottom of memo from William Wallace to Jesup, 31 March 1898.

25 "I beg to suggest": AMNH, Department of Anthropology, File 1896–38; letter of Franz Boas to Robert Peary, 24 May 1897.

25 "It was believed": New York Tribune, (Illustrated Supplement), 27 March 1898.

26 "it was his idea": Green, p. 158.

26 "We have on board six Eskimos": New York Times, 27 September 1897.

26 "when I leave again": New York Times, 25 September 1897.

26 "A collection of the implements": New York Times, 1 October 1897.

27 "All of the Eskimos": New York Times, 3 October 1897.

27 "It was felt": AMNH, File 517; memo by Dr. Bumpus, April 1909.

27 "Oh, I can remember": *World,* 6 January 1907.

27 "When they took us ashore": ibid.

27 "the several scores of visitors": *New York Times,* 11 October 1897.

28 "The unusual crowd": ibid.

28 "For the first time": ibid.

28 "insisted upon their rights": ibid.

29 "when . . . some ten or fifteen": ibid.

29 "Qisuk's little son": ibid.

30 "the little fellow": ibid.

30 "One of the most amusing forms": ibid.

30 "in the United States": Kroeber, "The Eskimo of Smith Sound," 1899, p. 306.

31 "much attached to the children": *New York Tribune* (Illustrated Supplement), 8 January 1899.

31 "had begun to pick up": *New York Tribune* (Illustrated Supplement), 27 March 1898.
    On the purchase of skeletons from Peary, the records of the AMNH, Department of Anthropology (Accession file 99/105–111) show that in 1896 the museum purchased from Robert Peary three skeletons (a man, a woman, and a child), three crania, and one calvarium.

4 / AN ESKIMO ORPHAN IN NEW YORK

33 "He was dearer to me": *San Francisco Examiner* (Magazine Supplement), 9 May 1909

35 "What do the Eskimos do all day?" and "Oh, we try": *New York Tribune* (Illustrated Supplement), 27 March 1898, p. 7.

36 "an attendant (speaking Eskimo)": Kroeber, "The Eskimo of Smith Sound," 1899, p. 313.

36 "perhaps the customs are somewhat modified": ibid.

36 "When informed that his wife was dying": ibid., pp. 314–16.

38 "When you found they were sick": *New York Tribune* (Illustrated Supplement), 27 March 1898, p. 7.

39 "Deeply regret Eskimo's death": AMNH, Department of Anthropology, File 1900–6; telegram from Robert Peary to Secretary John Winser, 25 February 1898.

40 "I would like very much" and "This matter is left with Wallace": AMNH, File 517; letter of William Wallace to Morris Jesup, 31 March 1898.

40 "very ill of consumption": *Cobleskill Index,* 19 May 1898, p. 8

41 "he had refused to return": ibid.

41 "Only one of the Eskimo": AMNH, File 517; letter of William Wallace to Morris Jesup, 25 May 1898

41 "jumped about the deck": *New York Times,* 3 July 1898, p. 11.

41 "the sun was burning": ibid.

41 "he would always keep it": ibid.

42 "As I sit here writing" and "Fortunately for them": Peary, 1898 (vol. 1), pp. 508–9.

42 "Among the tribe": Peary, 1904, p. 31.

5 / MINIK, THE AMERICAN

44 "lived in mortal fear": *San Francisco Examiner* (Magazine Supplement), 9 May 1909.

44 "Minik's father is gone": ibid.

44 "give Minik a name": AMNH, File 517; letter of Wallace to Jesup, 21 January 1907.

44 "Taming a Little Savage": *World,* 27 January 1899, p. 9.

45 "If there is one small boy": *New York Tribune* (Illustrated Supplement), 8 January 1899, pp. 1–2.

45 "Born in a land": *World,* 27 January 1899, p. 9.

45 "he is an American now": ibid.

45 "his expression has gained wonderfully": *New York Tribune* (Illustrated Supplement), 8 January 1899, pp. 1–2.

45 "the care and comforts of civilization": *Brooklyn Daily Eagle,* 7 April 1899, p. 13, col. 4.

45 "No boy in all the city": ibid.

45 "We hope that this little ward": Sheldon, p. 527.

45 "an experiment, and a promising one": *New York Tribune* (Illustrated Supplement), 8 January 1899, pp. 1–2.

45 "one of the ordinary duties of life": *New York Tribune* (Illustrated Supplement), 18 November 1900, p. 1.

45 "Rather guarded and conservative": *World,* 27 January 1899, p. 9.

45 "Once my father had a very good dog": Sheldon, p. 526.

46 "My father let me drive his dogs": ibid., pp. 526–27.

46 "We play hide-and-seek": ibid., p. 527.

46 "never better pleased": *New York Tribune* (Illustrated Supplement), 8 January 1899, pp. 1–2.

46 "I learned to read and write": *World,* 6 January 1907, p. 3.

46 "uncommonly sturdy": *New York Tribune* (Illustrated Supplement), 18 November 1900, p. 1.

47 "He doesn't like to be too warm": Sheldon, p. 527.

47 "handshakes, smiles and familiar pats": *New York Tribune* (Illustrated Supplement), 18 November 1900, p. 1.

47 "he can impart": *World*, 17 January 1899, p. 9.

48 "seated on a bench": *New York Tribune* (Illustrated Supplement), 18 November 1900, p. 1.

48 "I am going back north": Von Linden, p. 20.

48 "if Minik still retains his native tongue": AMNH, File 517; letter of Herbert Bridgman, Peary Arctic Club, to John Winser, 15 June 1899.

48 "with a view to preparing him": *San Francisco Examiner* (Magazine Supplement), 9 May 1909.

48 "being educated by Mr. and Mrs. Wallace": *Cobleskill Index*, 7 July 1898, p. 4.

49 "with such foster parents": *World*, 27 January 1899, p. 9.

49 "I want to stay here": *World*, 6 January 1907, p. 3.

49 "Mr. Wallace has more orders": *Cobleskill Index*, 4 November 1897, p. 8.

50 "Mr. Wallace is the children's friend": *Cobleskill Index*, 7 July 1898, p. 4.

50 "Mr. Wallace believes": *Cobleskill Index*, 8 June 1899, p. 1.

51 "Resolved. That it is contrary": *Cobleskill Index*, 22 June 1899, p. 1.

52 "Well, Minik": *New York Tribune* (Illustrated Supplement), 8 January 1899, pp. 1–2.

52 "when he started for bed": ibid.

52 "Tired to-night": ibid.

52 "sang in his native language": *Cobleskill Index*, 7 July 1898, p. 4.

52 "introduced the Eskimo": *Cobleskill Index*, 22 September 1898, p. 1.

6 / THE WALLACE AFFAIR

56 "somewhat anxious": AMNH, File 517; Statement of Albert S. Bickmore, 8 December 1900.

56 "he feared that": ibid.

56 "there was usually a long delay": ibid.

57 "our friend Mr. Wallace": ibid.

57 "engaged extensively in the milk business": AMNH, File 517; letter of J. C. Cady to Jesup, 26 November 1900.

57 "I have just seen your report": AMNH, File 517; letter of Jesup to William Wallace, undated.

57 "on the pretext": *New York Tribune*, 20 March 1901, p. 1.

57 "old friends": ibid.

58 "I can say nothing": ibid.

58 "never contemplated": ibid.

58 "did not do a particle": AMNH, File 517; letter of Assistant to the President to Robert M. Fox, 26 April 1901.

59 "macerating plant" and "bone-bleaching plant": AMNH, File 517; both terms are used in official letters of the museum.

59 "macerated over time" and "turned in as regular work": AMNH, File 517; letter of Assistant to the President to Robert M. Fox, 26 April 1901.

60 "would not indicate any obligations": ibid.

60 "merely superintendent of the Museum": AMNH, File 682; Form for Insertion in Minutes of Meeting of Executive Committee held on 18 April 1901.

60 "a great institution": AMNH, File 517; letter of Jesup to Professors Henry F. Osborn and H. C. Bumpus, 24 July 1901.

60 "the City has paid": ibid.

60 "appropriated by the City"; ibid.

60 "everything that went into the building": ibid.

61 "given him for the express purpose": ibid.

61 "laid down the law": ibid.

61 "fabulous prices": ibid.

61 "those who have resorted": ibid.

61 "he paid for the orders": ibid.

62 "I am called on": AMNH, File 517; letter of Wallace to Jesup, 9 June 1899.

62 "not what he should be": AMNH, File 517; letter of Mrs. David Minckler to Jesup, 8 April 1899.

62 "from some woman"; ibid.

63 "We try to make an honest living": AMNH, File 517; letter of Mrs. David Minckler to Jesup, 8 April 1899.

63 "I investigated these": AMNH, File 517; letter of Jesup to Professors Henry F. Osborn and H. C. Bumpus, 24 July 1901.

63 "Wallace, a trusted servant": ibid.

63 "was done by proper method": ibid.

64 "examined by the municipal authorities": AMNH, File 517; letter of Assistant to the President to Jesup, 5 February 1902.

64 "The only mistake I have made": AMNH, File 517; letter of Jesup to Professors Henry F. Osborn and H. C. Bumpus, 24 July 1901.

64 "I am not strong": ibid.

66 "most of the time": Osbon, "Cook and Peary," September 1910, p. 210.

67 "I send the president": PAC, File 1.2.11; letter of Peary to Peary Arctic Club, Cape York, 25 July 1898.

67 "two or three bundles": PAC, File 1.2.22.

67 "The sportsmen know": Rudolph Franke quoted in Osbon, "Cook and Peary," October 1910, p. 309.

68 "a consignment of goods": Freeman, p. 115, quoting *Brooklyn Daily Eagle,* 16 November 1908.

68 "We shall be very glad": PAC, File 1.2.22; letter of Hermon C. Bumpus, American Museum of Natural History, to Herbert Bridgman, Peary Arctic Club, 26 October 1908.

68 "Among the material sent up": PFC, File 1907, Letters Sent; letter of Peary to Bumpus, 1 April 1907.

68 "He feels that in everything received": PAC, File 1.2.21; letter of Morris Jesup's secretary to Herbert Bridgman, 5 June 1907.

69 "From that dazzling May morning": Peary, 1898 (vol. 2), p. 614.

69 "peerless and unique": ibid., p. 618.

70 "I have offered the three meteorites": PFC, File 1907, Letters Received; letter of Jesup to Peary, 29 April 1907.

70 "the Museum of Natural History": ibid.

70 "enable a person like myself": APS, Franz Boas Papers; letter of Jesup to Boas, 28 April 1905.

70 "P.S. You must remember": ibid.

71 "I think it only fair": AMNH, File 124; letter of Josephine Peary to Henry F. Osborn, 15 March 1908, p. 3.

71 "at present Wallace seems": AMNH, File 682; letter of Edward M. Shepard to Jesup, 14 February 1901.

72 "I shall have to say": NYHS, Osborn Papers, Box XX, File: Bumpus Affair, Item III — The Recent Administration of the Museum Statement of Edward M. Shepard, 7 October 1910.

<hr>

8 / "Destined to a Life of Tears"

75 "Bills paid by the museum": AMNH, File 517.

75 "which we understood": AMNH, File 517; letter of A. Raymond and Company, Clothiers and Outfitters, to Jesup, 15 February 1900.

76 "give Minik a name": AMNH, File 517; letter of Wallace to Jesup, 21 January 1907.

76 "You probably know something": AMNH, File 517; letter of Jesup to Winser, 3 April 1902.

77 "never heard you speak": AMNH, File 517; letter of Winser to Jesup, 8 April 1902.

77 "you had requested him": ibid.

77 "Hush, Minik," "poor little fellow," and "beckoned her family": San Francisco Examiner (Magazine Supplement), 9 May 1909.

79 "a woman of kind heart": *Cobleskill Index*, 31 March 1904.

79 "besides her bereaved husband": ibid.

79 "heart failure": ibid.

81 "made a reputation for grit": "Esquimau Mimi [*sic*] Now Selling Lots," unidentified newspaper article, 9 October 1904; AMNH, File 517.

81 "thrash the first one": ibid.

81 "promptly got a whipping": ibid.

81 "given up his idea": ibid.

81 "like a prison": *San Francisco Examiner* (Magazine Supplement), 9 May 1909.

81 "We had planned much for him": *Evening Mail*, 21 April 1909, p. 4.

9 / "GIVE ME MY FATHER'S BODY"

83 "Minik, the Esquimau boy": *World*, 6 January 1907, p. 3.

85 "I hardly believe": AMNH, Department of Anthropology, File 1900–6; memo, Robert W. Daley, Bellevue Hospital to Franz Boas, 17 February 1898.

85 "The disposition of the body": *New York Daily Tribune*, 19 February 1898, p. 10.

86 "visit the (supposed) grave": Kroeber, "The Eskimo of Smith Sound," 1899, p. 316.

86 "It is an Eskimo custom": *Evening Mail*, 21 April 1909, p. 1 and 4.

87 "when a woman dies": Kroeber, "The Eskimo of Smith Sound," 1899, p. 301.

87 "when Qisuk died": ibid., p. 316.

87 "On the death of a man": ibid., p. 312.

87 "When a person is dying": ibid., p. 311.

87 "That night some of us gathered": *Evening Mail*, 21 April 1909, p. 4.

88 "to appease the boy": *Evening Mail*, 24 April 1909, p. 4.

88 "nothing particularly deserving severe criticism": ibid.

88 "Oh, that was perfectly legitimate": ibid.

89 "Wallace made effort": AMNH, File 517; unsigned penciled notation

on the first page of a typescript of a letter from William Wallace to Secretary Loeb, 14 January 1907.

89 "Superintendent Wallace contends": *Brooklyn Daily Eagle*, 18 February 1898, p. 3.

89 "Superintendent Wallace . . . in whose care": *New York Daily Tribune*, 19 February 1898, p. 10.

90 "Dr. Boas requested me": AMNH, File 517; letter of William Wallace to Morris Jesup, 16 May 1898.

90 "We were only acting": *Evening Mail*, 21 April 1909, p. 4.

10 / IN THE INTEREST OF SCIENCE

92 "These six individuals": Hrdlicka, 1910, p. 223.

92 "The brain in question": ibid.

93 "gaunt and dedicated decapitator": Sagan, p. 13.

93 "It is a little unfair": ibid., p. 12.

94 "Many things heretofore unknown": *New York Tribune* (Illustrated Supplement), 27 March 1898, p. 7.

95 "as a specimen of the race": *New York Tribune*, 15 June 1899, p. 16.

95 "It would be interesting": *New York Tribune*, 14 June 1899.

95 "We think the body of the girl": *New York Tribune*, 17 June 1899, p. 16.

96 "Little Eskimo girl died": *amnh*, File 517; letter, Franz Boas to Dr. Bern Gallaudet, June 1899.

96 "Before Captain Bruce went away": *New York Tribune*, 17 June 1899, p. 16.

96 "I am sorry to see": AMNH, File 517; letter, Franz Boas to Dr. Bern Gallaudet, June 1899.

96 "The newspapers had found out": *Evening Mail*, 21 April 1909, p. 4.

97 "Unexpectedly one day": *San Francisco Examiner* (Magazine Supplement), 9 May 1909.

Both the inspiration and information for many of my comments on the early development of the science of anthropology come from Carl Sagan's brilliant essay, "Broca's Brain," in his book of the same name (London: Hodder and Stoughton, 1980).

The Eskimos at the World's Columbian Exhibition in Chicago in 1893 were from Labrador and had been brought to Chicago by a promoter who subsequently abandoned them. Dr. Frederick A. Cook, "out of the goodness of his heart, was taking care of them and seeing that they were returned to their home in Labrador." Cook planned to return them to Labrador in 1894 when he went north with the *Miranda* expedition, a popular excursion that he was organizing to the Arctic for fare-paying passengers; in the meantime he was exhibiting them and some "arctic paraphernalia" to raise interest in the trip. The quotations and the information are from *The Arctic Diary of Russell Williams Porter*, edited by Herman Friis (Charlottesville: University Press of Virginia, 1976, p. 6). In 1894 these Eskimos lived for a time in Cook's backyard in New York; see "Cook Gave a Show in a Dime Museum," in the *New York Times*, 10 September 1909, p. 2.

Regarding the boost to the careers of Boas, Kroeber, and Hrdlicka by the publication of their researches on the Smith Sound Eskimos, their publications on this subject are as follows: Kroeber: (1) "The Eskimo of Smith Sound," *Bulletin of the American Museum of Natural History*, vol. 12, 1899, pp. 265–327; (2) "Tales of the Smith Sound Eskimo," *Journal of American Folk-Lore*, vol. XII, no. 46, July–September 1899, pp. 166–182; (3) "Animal Tales of the Eskimo," *Journal of American Folk-Lore*, vol. XII, no. 44, January–March 1899, pp. 17–23. Hrdlicka: (1) Contribution to the Anthropology of Central and Smith Sound Eskimo, *Anthropological Papers of the American Museum of Natural History*, vol. v, 1910, pp. 175–280; (2) "An Eskimo Brain," *American Anthropologist*, vol 3, 1901, pp. 454–500. Boas did not publish directly on the Smith Sound Eskimos but oversaw the work of Kroeber.

11 / "THE VERY PITIFUL CASE OF MINIK"

99 "Esquimaux matter was fully settled": AMNH, File 517; letter of Wallace to Jesup, 10 January 1907.

99 "simply carrying out your unkindly feelings": ibid.

99 "a gentleman of your standing": ibid.

99 "it requires more means": ibid.

100 ". . . you too well know": ibid.

100 "I beg to call your attention": AMNH, File 517; statement of Chester Beecroft, 12 January 1907.

100 "a National guest," "his condition," and "the most abused": ibid.

100 "only interest in Minik": Sun, 16 April 1909.

100 "particular and peculiar interest": ibid.

100 "meagerly clad" and "improperly cared for": AMNH, File 517; statement of Chester Beecroft, 12 January 1907.

101 "still forming": ibid.

101 "the matter has not been brought": ibid.

101 "an officer of the United States": ibid.

101 "gentle, kind and hospitable" and "received Peary warmly": ibid.

101 "It would be reasonable": ibid.

102 "What private griefs": ibid.

102 ". . . might not the directors": ibid.

102 "right shall at last be done": ibid.

103 "I would thank you": AMNH, File 517; letter of Wallace to Loeb, 14 January 1907.

103 "No better": quoted in Eames, p. 69.

104 "afterward we learned": *Evening Mail*, 13 April 1909, p. 3.

105 "urgent request": AMNH, File 517; notation in Bumpus's handwriting at end of typescript of article in the *Washington Post*, 12 January 1907.

105 "absolutely declined": ibid.

105 "to do nothing whatever": ibid.

105 "insisting that I lay the matter": AMNH, File 517; letter of Wallace to Jesup, 21 January 1907.

106 "the President should be informed": AMNH, File 517; letter of Strong to Bumpus, 22 January 1907.

107 "you are not adapted": AMNH, File 561; letter of Bumpus to Jenness Richardson Jr., 15 February 1907.

12 / "A Hopeless Condition of Exile"

109 "I am unwilling": *San Francisco Examiner* (Magazine Supplement), 9 May 1909.

109 "As far as Peary is concerned": ibid.

110 "ascertain how far": ibid.

110 "I can't be a burden": ibid. (This interview was not published until 9 May 1909, but must have been given in 1907, for in the article both Minik and Wallace refer to Jesup, who had died on 22 January 1908.)

112 "exceptional charm": *The National Cyclopedia of American Biography*, vol. XXXII, p. 331.

112 "temperamentally unfit": NYHS, Osborn Papers, Box XX, File: Bumpus Affair, Item III — The Recent Administration of the Museum, Statement of Dr. Dean, page 50 of file.

113 "pleading for a Christian burial": *World* (Magazine Supplement), 6 January 1907, p. 3.

113 "out of gratitude": ibid.

113 "If all these things happened": ibid.

114 "the skeleton of which": *World,* 13 April 1909, p. 1.

114 "thoroughly mystified" and "As for his father's body": *Sun,* 16 April 1909.

114 "Dr. Bumpus . . . has had some hesitancy": *Evening Mail,* 26 April 1909, p. 4.

115 "he seemed inclined": *Evening Mail,* 13 April 1909, p. 3.

115 "I asked Dr. Bumpus": *Evening Mail,* 26 May 1909, p. 1 and 13.

117 "I attempted to do this": AMNH, File 517; "Notes on Mene. . . ." memo by Bumpus, April 1909.

117 "Minik is very anxious": PFC, File 1908, Letters Received; letter of Wallace to Peary, 23 June 1908.

117 "I have your letter": PFC, File 1908, Letters Sent; letter of Peary to Wallace, 26 June 1908.

117 "If you expect": *Sun,* 16 April 1909.

117 "The plight of this poor Esquimau": "Peary Dooms Esquimau Boy to Sorrowful Exile" (unidentified), 30 June 1908, copy in PFC.

118 "under one or another pretense": Rigsarkivet, no. 227, 10 September 1908.

118 "made room for the Eskimos": Rigsarkivet, no. 295, 9 November 1908.

119 "the boy would never have known": ibid.

119 "systematic campaign": ibid.

119 "He has heard so much": ibid.

119 "at least for the time being": ibid.

119 "down here, he will hardly become": ibid.

13 / THE POLAR PLAN

122 "Our . . . object": *Evening Mail,* 21 April 1909, p. 1 and 4.

122 "The explorers who are trying": *Sun,* 22 January 1909.

122 "They fit out nice comfortable ships": *The Evening Telegram,* 22 January 1909.

123 "The North Pole will never be discovered": *Sun,* 22 January 1909.

123 "The record of recent Arctic exploration": *New York Times,* 30 October 1876, p. 4.

125 "I would like to return": *The Tribune,* 22 January 1909.

126 "I have known Minik": ibid.

14 / RUNAWAY

127 "I cannot bear": *San Francisco Examiner* (Magazine Supplement), 9 May 1909.

127 "more or less a freak": ibid.

129 "When this reaches you": *World*, 13 April 1909, p. 1.

130 "If Minik is making for Newfoundland": *Sun*, 16 April 1909.

130 "I want Minik to return": *Evening Mail*, 13 April 1909, p. 3.

132 "The treatment which has been accorded": *Evening Mail*, 21 April 1909, p. 1 and 4.

132 "Everywhere Minik looked": *Sun*, 16 April 1909.

132 "When I woke up": *Evening Mail*, 26 May 1909, p. 1, 13.

133 "This is probably": *World*, 23 May 1909, p. 2.

134 "Think of the injuistice [*sic*]": *San Francisco Examiner* (Magazine Supplement), 9 May 1909.

135 "I went to a boarding house": *Evening Mail*, 26 May 1909, p. 1, 13.

135 "I left New York": *World*, 26 May 1909, p. 2.

136 "Yes, I had a hard time": *Evening Mail*, 26 May 1909, p. 1, 13.

Dr. Roswell O. Stebbins, chairman of the Arctic Club of America's committee on the relief of Cook, stated incorrectly in early June of 1909 that Peary had never refused to take the boy back but "had simply made it a condition of giving him passage that the Esquimo should agree to remain in Greenland. The boy refused, desiring to be brought back here and permitted to join a circus." Dr. Stebbins added that "the Arctic Club of America would send the Esquimo north if he would agree to remain at Etah" ("Peary Relief Ship Will Seek Dr. Cook," *New York American*, 10 June 1909).

15 / "AN IRON-CLAD AGREEMENT"

137 "I would shoot Mr. Peary," "I can never forgive Peary," and "And if he does meet Peary": *San Francisco Examiner* (Magazine Supplement), 9 May 1909.

138 "hopping mad": AMNH, File 517; quoted in letter from Bridgman to Bumpus, May 1909.

138 "our policy": AMNH, File 517; American Museum of Natural History to Bridgman, 14 May 1909.

138 "Peary suspected": *World*, 27 May 1909, p. 6.

138 "Minik is you know": *New York Times*, 14 April 1909, p. 5:2.

142 "the conversation counted": PFC, letter of Bridgman to Mrs. Peary, 3 July 1909.

142 "we are under no obligation": ibid.

142 "an iron-clad agreement": PFC, letter of Bridgman to Mrs. Peary, 8 July 1909.

143   "Minik and his friends": PFC, agreement dated 9 July 1909.

143   "Thirteen years ago": ibid.

143   "Minik's feelings": PFC, letter of Bridgman to Mrs. Peary, 14 July 1909.

143   "to avail himself": ibid.

144   "I will endeavour": PFC, letter of Bridgman to Samuel Bartlett, 10 July 1909.

144   "Minik Wallace still has no contract": PFC, letter of Bridgman to Mrs. Peary, 13 July 1909.

144   "he had become my devoted slave": Matilda Alice Powles De Frece, p. 201.

145   "They say they are not": *Evening Mail*, 9 July 1909.

145   "You're a race of scientific criminals": ibid.

145   "bequeath his brain"; *New York Times*, 12 July 1909, editorial, p. 6:3.

145   ". . . to Minik, the polite request": ibid.

145   "I sail north tomorrow": *Evening Mail*, 9 July 1909.

145   "You Americans": ibid.

146   "It is this fact": *Evening Mail*, 10 July 1909, p. 1.

147   "But even if he gets there": *San Francisco Examiner* (Magazine Supplement), 9 May 1909.

148   "I bade Minik good-bye": PFC, letter of Bridgman to William Wallace, 10 July 1909.

16 / RETURN TO GREENLAND

149   "too many Eskimos" and "smoke cigarettes": *Herald* (New York), undated, 1909, clipping in PFC.

149   "Shortly after my arrival": Fleming, p. 38.

150   "My surprise and delight": ibid., pp. 38–39.

150   "discontented and even bitter": ibid., p. 39.

150   "just waiting for him to die": ibid.

151   "My heart went out": ibid.

151   "a fine assortment": *Herald* (New York), undated, 1909, in PFC.

152   "Minik was now a 'qallunaaq,'": *Herald*, 20 September 1909.

152   "he soon fraternized": ibid.

153   "Commander Peary has given": ibid.

153   "made his peace": *New York Times*, 13 September 1909.

153   "of special interest" and ". . . besides the obvious advantage": PFC, letter of Bridgman to Mrs. Peary, 15 July 1909.

153   "I hereby acknowledge"; PFC, document, dated 23 August 1909.

155   "On this day": Gustav Olsen, p. 17.

17 / An Eskimo Again

157 "MINE . . .": quoted in Eames, p. 92.

157 "as subject to my will": ibid., p. 89.

157 " . . . although they were not qualified": quoted from Robert Peary, *The Secrets of Polar Travel* (originally in "Peary and the Eskimos," *Christian Science Monitor,* undated 1918); copy in PFC, File: Newsclippings, 1918–20.

158 "I had come to regard": Peary, 1910, p. 333.

158 "I have used the Eskimos": ibid.

158 ". . . can anyone think": Rasmussen, p. 7.

158 "The Eskimos here": quoted from Robert Peary, *The Secrets of Polar Travel* (originally in "Peary and the Eskimos," *Christian Science Monitor,* undated 1918); copy in PFC, File: Newsclippings, 1918–20.

161 "An orphan who has a hard time": Freuchen, 1961, p. 60.

163 "The life I have led": Rosbach, no. 12, p. 98.

165 "I am still alive": Appendix to the Congressional Record, 25 January 1916, pp. 323–24.

18 / The Thule Station

169 "Minik was a great nuisance": Freuchen, 1935, p. 79.

169 "In a whisk": ibid., pp. 119–20.

170 "We must realize": ibid., p. 161.

170 "Up in our country": ibid., p. 263.

170 "Don't you think": ibid., p. 161.

170 "probably a good enough fellow": ibid., p. 162.

170 "I saw Minik": ibid.

171 "he did not want to make appointments": Freuchen, 1961, p. 104.

171 "To circumvent": Freuchen, 1935, p. 163.

172 "none too enthusiastic": ibid., p. 168.

172 "Some of the women": Rosbach, no. 12, p. 98.

19 / Uisaakassak: The Big Liar

173 "The ships sailed in": quotation from Knud Rasmussen in Gilberg, 1969–70, p. 85.

174 "the streetcars": ibid., p. 86.

174 "distance shrinker": ibid.

174 "Uisaakassak, go tell your big lies": ibid.

174 "can tell a lot": quotation from Mylius-Erichsen in ibid.

174 ". . . a biting wind": PAC, File 1.2.11; report by Robert Peary dated 28
   August 1899.

175 "The following natives": PAC, File 1.2.10; instructions by Robert Peary,
   written 31 March 1900

175 "the belle of the tribe": PFC, Arctic Expeditions, 1896, Journal, p. 74.

175 "who has a bad habit": quotation from Mylius-Erichsen in Gilberg,
   1969–70, p. 86.

175 "not the kind of person": ibid., p. 88.

175 "Yes, Uisaakassak": quotation from Knud Rasmussen in ibid., p. 89.
   Uisaakassak's wife, who later became the wife of Sigluk, was
   named Aleqasinnguaq. Similarity between her name and that of Piugaattoq's wife has given rise to confusion in some ethnological investigations. Piugaattoq's wife, whom he sometimes exchanged with
   Uisaakassak and regularly shared with Peary, was named Aleqasina.
   To make the matter more confusing, Peary, in his written references
   to her, always called her Aleqasinnguaq (although he spelled it in an
   irregular manner), the suffix "-nnguaq" being a suffix of endear-
   ment. To further muddy the matter, there was another woman at
   the time, somewhat older, with the name Aleqasina, whom the Eskimos usually called Aleqaherruaq; she was the wife of Soqqaq's son,
   Eri.

---

20 / WANTED: DEAD OR ALIVE

180 "There are many large ships": Rosbach, no. 11, p. 86

180 "If I hadn't had": ibid.

180 "It was so hot": ibid.

180 "Unlike Jesup": ibid., p. 87.

181 "What are you doing here": ibid.

181 "I have never met": ibid.

182 "There were many display rooms": Rosbach, no. 12, p. 91.

183 "He lived in a large, fine house": ibid., p. 92.

184 "If Christian people"; ibid., p. 95.

186 "I was the only one": ibid., p. 95.

187 "She was smiling"; ibid., p. 96.

189 "In America"; Freuchen, 1935, p. 79.

189 "He believed that the world": ibid., pp. 79–80.

190 "When you go" and "Poor woman!": ibid., p. 236.
   Rosbach, who recorded an account of Minik's life, misunderstood

Jesup's name and wrote it as "Josofi" and "Josoe" throughout the account. He also misdated the trip to America and the death of Qisuk by one year, as 1896 and 1897 respectively.

The American spelling of Minik's name was usually "Mene." Official documents give his name as "Mene Peary Wallace" and the headstone at his grave reads MENE WALLACE.

The Wallaces were members of Park Presbyterian Church (now West Park Presbyterian Church) at 165 West 86th Street, New York, from 1886, the year of their marriage. Their son, William Jr., born in 1887, was baptized there the following year. The Register of Baptisms shows no baptism of Minik.

21 / THE CROCKER LAND EXPEDITION

191 "reach, map the coast-line": MacMillan, introduction.

192 "Our home was overcrowded": ibid., p. 33.

192 "Mac feels": AMNH, Rare Book and Manuscripts Collection, Fitzhugh Green, Journal on the Crocker Land Expedition, 1 December 1913.

192 "Minik Wallace, the English-speaking Eskimo": AMNH, Rare Book and Manuscripts Collection, Jerome Lee Allen, Journal on the Crocker Land Expedition, 1 December 1913.

193 "He seems to be": Hunt and Thompson, pp. 39–40.

193 "Last month": AMNH, Crocker Land File, Extract from letter of Dr. Harrison Hunt to Mrs. Hunt, 9 January 1914.

194 "Can't discover new land without tobacco": AMNH, Rare Book and Manuscripts Collection, Donald B. MacMillan, Field Note Book no. 22, Crocker Land Expedition, 13 February 1914.

194 "an almost vertical wall of ice": MacMillan, p. 56.

194 "who simply loved hard work"; ibid., p. 57.

195 "when gossip and tobacco smoke": ibid.

195 "Tautsiannguaq had": ibid.

195 "Young Eskimos": ibid., p. 54.

196 "I shot once": AMNH, Rare Book and Manuscripts Collection, Fitzhugh Green, Journal on the Crocker Land Expedition, 1 May 1914.

196 "not only a man": AMNH, File 1016; translation of letter from Knud Rasmussen to Right Reverend Dean C. Schultz-Lorentzen, 6 January 1921.

197 "We cooked up some beans": AMNH, Rare Book and Manuscripts Collection, Jerome Lee Allen, Journal on the Crocker Land Expedition, 3 April 1914.

197 "Our supplies were gone": Ekblaw, "The Summer at North Star Bay," in MacMillan, p. 327.

198 "very repentant": MacMillan, pp. 143–44.

198 "At length": ibid., pp. 151–52.

199 "Th.. .. .... begun : ibid., p. 152.

199 "We hardly knew": ibid., pp. 220–21.

200 "absolutely unfit": ibid., p. 193.

201 ". . . He asked me what crime": Freuchen, 1935, p. 303.

201 "a mild little man": ibid., p. 300.

201 "a tactless, impolite person": ibid., p. 306.

201 "whined and expostulated": ibid., p. 304.

201 "called the Eskimos"; Hunt and Thompson, p. 76.

201 "He showed me the gifts": Freuchen, 1935, p. 301.

201 "Evidently he had believed": ibid., pp. 301–2.

202 "I would have sat": Malaurie, p. 237.

202 "Not just a mannequin": ibid.

202 "We could all be rich": ibid.

202 "Now I am only waiting": Rosbach, no. 12, p. 99.

22 / BACK ON BROADWAY

205 "various alleged Arctic explorations," "Robert E. Peary's claims," and "for services": Appendix to the Congressional Record, 21 July 1916, p. 1626.

206 "not a defender": ibid., 4 September 1916, p. 42.

206 ". . . Is it possible": ibid., p. 70.

207 "I've got a big story": New York Tribune, 22 September 1916, p. 9.

207 "No, I don't know"; ibid.

208 "impart the information": New York Times, 29 September 1916, p. 8.

208 ". . . I have no doubt"; letter, Secretary for Congressman Helgesen to Mene Wallace, 26 October 1916, Minik Wallace personal papers, private collection.

209 "back on Broadway"; New York Tribune, 22 September 1916, p. 9.

209 "took a bath": New York Times, 22 September 1916, p. 7.

209 "the igloos of Broadway": ibid.

209 "I had to learn": New York Tribune, 22 September 1916, p. 9.

209 "Was I satisfied": New York Times, 22 September 1916, p. 7.

209 "It would have been better": New York Tribune, 22 September 1916, p. 9.

210 "Of course, I made a hit": ibid.

210 "You can support": *New York Times,* 22 September 1916, p. 7.

210 "he did not get on with natives": Steele, p. 169.

210 "assisting the tribe": letter, Edwin S. Brooke Jr. to Mene Wallace, 24 September 1916, Minik Wallace personal papers, private collection.

211 "Can we not find": AMNH, Department of Anthropology, File 1900–6; memo of Osborn to Sherwood, 13 January 1917.

211 "neither fish nor fowl"; Bunnell, p. 60.

23 / The North Country

216 "nice fellow to have around": Bunnell, p. 61.

218 "It's hard for them": Ellsworth Bunnell, personal communication.

218 "I am asking a favor": "Eskimo Guide Who Helped Peary Find North Pole Dies in New Hampshire," *The Evening Telegram,* undated (December 1918), p. 2.

219 "he was a nice guy": Bunnell, p. 27.

Epilogue

221 "in bad shape" and "co-mingled the funds": Notes in a file on the estate of Willis Sharpe Kilmer, in the office of Colin T. Naylor III (lawyer), Binghamton, N.Y., p. 12.

Afterword

The 1992 newspaper articles that spurred new interest in Minik and in the bones held in the American Museum of Natural History were "Bones of history buried in a bureaucratic Limbo," by Miro Cernetig in *The Globe and Mail* (Toronto), 10 April 1992, page A1 and A5, and "The Skeleton in the Museum's Closet," by William Claiborne in the *Washington Post,* 5 April 1992, page F1 and F6. These two newspapers were also the first to break the news of the impending return of the bodies to Qaanaaq for burial, three weeks before the event happened. Those stories were "Minik's saga will finally be laid to rest," by Miro Cernetig in *The Globe and Mail* (Toronto), 6 July 1993, page A1 and A2, and "The Eskimos Finally Go Home," by Charles Truehart in the *Washington Post,* 6 July 1993, p. C1 and C3.

BIBLIOGRAPHY

ARCHIVES AND LIBRARIES

American Museum of Natural History (New York, N.Y.), Administrative Archives, Department of Anthropology Archives, and Rare Book and Manuscript Collection.

American Philosophical Society (Philadelphia, Penn.), Franz Boas Papers.

Cobleskill Town Library (Cobleskill, N.Y.).

Explorers Club Archives (New York, N.Y.), Peary Arctic Club records.

National Archives (Washington, D.C.), Record Group 401 (1), Peary Family Collection.

New York Historical Society (New York, N.Y.), Osborn Papers.

Manhattan College (Riverdale, N.Y.), Newspaper clippings in a scrapbook.

Rigsarkivet (The Royal Archives, Copenhagen, Denmark), Records of the Danish Ministry of Foreign Affairs, File A.S.95/08 of the Royal Danish Consulate, New York.

NEWSPAPERS

New York Times
"The Arctic Mystery," 30 October 1876: 4.
"Peary's Vessel Returns," 21 September 1897: 7.
"Peary Goes to Washington," 24 September 1897: 5.

"Peary to Stake His Life," 25 September 1897: 5.

"Returned From the Arctic," 27 September 1897: 8.

"Back From the Far North," 1 October 1897: 12.

"The Big Meteorite Landed," 3 October 1897: 24.

"Too Warm for Eskimos," 11 October 1897: 12.

"Off For the North Pole," 3 July 1898: 11.

"Judgments," 20 November 1900: 15:2.

"Eskimo Mene in College," 2 February 1909: 2:3.

"Mene Gone To Balk Peary?" 14 April 1909: 5:2.

"Latest Bulletin From Mene. New Letter Says Eskimo Boy is Thinking of
    Suicide," 23 May 1909: 4:3.

"Euipping for Arctic Trip," 4 July 1909: 5.

"Mene Wallace Going Home," 9 July 1909, 10:1.

"Eskimo Mene Off For Home," 11 July 1909: 2:4.

"Mene's Opinion of Us," (editorial) 12 July 1909: 6:3.

"Cook Gave a Show in a Dime Museum," 10 September 1909: 4:1.

"Cook Did Not Claim the Pole to Whitney," 13 September 1909: 2:1.

"Calls Peary a Falsifier," 14 September 1909: 2:5.

"Peary Denies Mene Letter Charge," 14 February 1911: 3.

"Says He Has Secret of Pole's Discovery," 22 September 1916: 7:1.

"Eskimo Going to Capital," 29 September 1916: 8:6.

"Peary's Eskimo Dead," 13 December 1918: 6:2.

World

"Mene, The American, Late of Smith's Sound," 27 January 1899: 9.

"Give Me My Father's Body" (Magazine Supplement), 6 January 1907: 3.

"Land of Snow Beckons Meenie, Esquimau Boy," 30 June 1908: 1, 3.

"Missing Esquimau Boy Mene Writes He's Going North," 13 April 1909: 1.

"Esquimau Boy Mene Threatens to End His Life," 23 May 1909: 2.

"Goes North to Save Eskimo from Suicide," 24 May 1909: 16.

"Esquimau Boy Mene Back in New York," 26 May 1909: 2.

"Peary Fears Him, Says Mene, the Esquimau," 27 May 1909: 6.

"Plans for Relief of Dr. Cook are Complete," 10 June 1909: 4.

The Evening Mail

"Angry Over Skeleton of Eskimo," 13 April 1909: 3.

"Why Mene, Young Eskimo Boy, Ran Away From His Home," 21 April 1909:
    1, 4.

"Mene Reaches Ottawa on Way Home," 22 April 1909: 8.

"Prof. Boas Defends the Fake Funeral," 24 April 1909: 4.
"Eskimo Boy Tells of His Wrongs," 26 May 1909: 1, 13.
"Eskimo Boy to Go Home at Last," 8 July 1909.
"Mene Calls Us Race of Cannibals," 9 July 1909.
"Mene Cnan, Agrees Not to Return Here," 10 July 1909: 1.
"Morris K. Jesup Left $12,814,894," 22 July 1909.

New York Tribune
"Going Home to Greenland" (Illustrated Supplement), 27 March 1898: 7.
"An Attractive Esquimau" (Illustrated Supplement), 10 July 1898: 5.
"Mene in His New Home" (Illustrated Supplement), 8 January 1899: 1, 2.
"A Question Under the Burial Law," 14 June 1899.
"Esquimau Girl Dead," 15 June 1899: 10:4.
"It Has Not Been Dissected," 17 June 1899: 16:3.
"Esquimau Children" (Illustrated Supplement), 18 November 1900: 1.
"Work Halted For Inquiry," 20 March 1901: 1.
"Esquimau Hunts Pole," 22 January 1909.
"Mene Wallace, Eskimo, Back with North Pole 'Secret,'" 22 September 1916: 9.

New York Daily Tribune
"Trouble Over the Dead Esquimo," 19 February 1898: 10:6.
"The Windward Sets Sail," 3 July 1898: 12:1.
"William Wallace Resigns," 14 January 1901: 4:3.
"Last of Peary's Esquimaus Ill," 9 May 1903: 16:2.

New York Herald
"Ready for Rescue of Dr. F. A. Cook," 4 June 1909.
"Mission of the Relief Ship Jeanie Ends," 20 September 1909.
"'My Word!' Says Briton of Mene Wallace," undated clipping, 1909.
"Holds Data at 'Million,'" 16 September 1916: 4:7.

Brooklyn Daily Eagle
"The Esquimau's Body," 18 February 1898: 3:1.
7 April 1899: 13:4.

Sun
"Eskimo to Hunt the Pole," 22 January 1909.
"Wallace to Seek Dr. Cook," 23 January 1909.
"Last Peary Eskimo Dies of Pneumonia," undated clipping, 1918.
"Queer Case of the Lost Eskimo," 16 April 1909.

Cobleskill Index

4 November 1897: 8.

18 November 1897: 6.

28 April 1898: 5.

28 April 1898: 8.

19 May 1898: 1.

"The Esquimaux," 19 May 1898: 8.

16 June 1898: 5.

23 June 1898: 5.

30 June 1898: 8.

"The Esquimaux," 7 July 1898: 1.

7 July 1898: 4.

1 September 1898.

22 September 1898: 1.

20 October 1898.

2 February 1899.

"Wallace Prize," 8 June 1899: 1.

"The Wallace Prize," 22 June 1899: 1.

"Mene, the Esquimaux," 29 June 1899: 1.

6 July 1899: 2.

20 July 1899: 1.

27 July 1899: 2.

3 August 1899: 5.

19 July 1900: 5.

31 July 1902: 5.

21 August 1902: 5.

"Obituary," 31 March 1904.

"Mrs. William Wallace," 18 March 1937: 8.

25 March 1937: 5.

Dansk-Amerikaneren

"Den forladte Eskimodreng!" 8 July 1908.

"Den Danske Regering Retter Forespørgsel om en Eskimodreng in New York," 23 September 1908.

"Eskimodrengen Meenie," 21 October 1908.

"Eskimoen Meenie funden i syg og hjælpløs Tilstand," 25 November 1908.

"Eskimodrengen Meenie, vil være Civilingeniør," 27 January 1909.

"Eskimodrengen Meenie," 3 February 1909.

"Eskimodrengen Meenie," 7 April 1908.

"Menee," 28 April 1909.
"Mene er gaaet hjem!" 14 July 1909.
"Mene Wallace," 4 August 1909.

Other

"Esquimau Mimi Now Selling Lots," unidentified clipping, 9 October 1904.
"To Train Young Eskimo," *Washington Post*, 12 January 1907: 11.
"Peary Dooms Esquimau Boy to Sorrowful Exile," unidentified clipping,
    1908.
"Dr. Cook's Wife Plans Arctic Relief Trip," *New York Evening Journal*, 8 Janu-
    ary 1909.
"Eskimau Boy, First to Take College Course, Will Seek North Pole," *The
    Evening Telegram*, 22 January 1909.
"Why Arctic Explorer Peary's Neglected Eskimo Boy Wants to Shoot Him,"
    San Francisco Examiner (Magazine Supplement), 9 May 1909.
"Peary Relief Ship Will Seek Dr. Cook," *New York American*, 10 June 1909.
"Off to Etah to Relieve Peary," *Commercial* (Bangor, Maine), 4 August 1909.
"Peary Relief Ship," *United Sun* (Lockport, N.Y.), 17 August 1909.
"Peary Accused of Reading Mail Sent Out By Cook," unidentified clipping,
    1909.
Untitled, *Clubfellow* (undated clipping), 1909.
"The Tender Eskimo," *Journal* (Chicago, Ill.), 17 December 1918.
"Eskimo Guide Who Helped Peary Find North Pole Dies in New Hamp-
    shire," *The Evening Telegram*, (undated clipping), December 1918: 2.
"Peary and the Eskimos," *Christian Science Monitor* (undated clipping),
    1918.
"Confederate Money Held by East Orange Resident," undated clipping,
    1938.
"Eskimo Introduced at 1898 Cobleskill Fair" (by Norman Olsen), *Times-
    Journal* (Cobleskill, N.Y.), 30 June 1976.
"Minik fra Thule—gangster i USA," *Jyllands-Posten* (Denmark), 9 October
    1983, 5:1.

BOOKS, MANUSCRIPTS, MAGAZINES, AND JOURNALS

Appendix to the Congressional Record. Analysis of "Evidence" Presented
    by Robert E. Peary to Committee on Naval Affairs, 1910–11. 25 January
    1916: 323–24.
———. Extension of Remarks of Hon. Henry T. Helgesen. 25 January 1916:
    268–327.

———. Extension of Remarks of Hon. Henry T. Helgesen. 21 July 1916: 1626–46.

———. Extension of Remarks of Hon. Henry T. Helgesen. 4 September 1916: 42–70.

Aylmer, Kevin, and Roger Bowen. "The Lost Republic." *Yankee,* March 1968: 60–67, and 101–3.

Borup, George. *A Tenderfoot with Peary.* New York: Frederick A. Stokes Company, 1911.

Brown, William Adams. *Morris Ketchum Jesup.* New York: Charles Scribner's Sons, 1910.

Bunnell, Ellsworth H. "Mene." *New Hampshire Profiles,* January 1969: 26–61.

De Frece, (Lady) Matilda Alice Powles. *Recollections of Vesta Tilley.* London: Hutchinson and Co. (Publishers) Ltd., 1934.

Eames, Hugh. *Winner Lose All.* Boston: Little, Brown and Co., 1973.

Epps, Bernard. "The Republic of Indian Stream." *Canadian Frontier,* 1978: 72–74.

Fleischer, Jørgen. *Udsteder.* Copenhagen: Gyldendal, 1983.

Fleming, Archibald Lang. *Archibald the Arctic.* New York: Appleton-Century-Crofts, 1956.

Fogg, Katherine A. "Pittsburg, New Hampshire—The Last Frontier." *Outlook,* Winter 1977: 12–15.

Freeman, Andrew. *The Case for Doctor Cook.* New York: Coward-McCann, Inc., 1961.

Freuchen, Peter. *Arctic Adventure.* New York: Farrar and Rinehart, 1935.

———. *Book of the Eskimos.* New York: The World Publishing Company, 1961.

Friis, Herman, ed. *The Arctic Diary of Russell Williams Porter.* Charlottesville: University Press of Virginia, 1976.

Gilbers, Rolf. "Changes in the Life of the Polar Eskimos Resulting from a Canadian Immigration into the Thule District, North Greenland, in the 1860s." *Folk,* vol. 16–17 (1974–75): 159–70.

———. "Missionen Iblandt Inuhuit." Den Grønlandske Kirkesag, no. 120 (January 1984): 18–27.

———. "Uisaakavsak, 'The Big Liar.'" *Folk,* vol. 11–12 (1969–70): 83–95.

Green, Fitzhugh. *Peary, The Man Who Refused to Fail.* New York: G. P. Putnam's Sons, 1926.

Hendrik, Hans. *Memoirs of Hans Hendrik, the Arctic Traveller.* Ed. Dr. Henry Rink. London: Trubner and Co., 1878.

Holtved, Erik. "Contributions to Polar Eskimo Ethnography." Meddelelser om Grønland, vol. 182, no. 2, Copenhagen: C. A. Reitzels Forlag, 1967.

Hrdlicka, Ales. "Contribution to the Anthropology of Central and Smith Sound Eskimo." *Anthropological Papers of the American Museum of Natural History*, vol. 5 (1910): 175–280.

———. "An Eskimo Brain." *American Anthropologist*, vol. 3 (1901): 454–500.

Hunt, Harrison J., and Ruth Hunt Thompson. *North to the Horizon*. Camden, Maine: Down East Books, 1980.

Kroeber, A. L. "Animal Tales of the Eskimo." *Journal of American Folk-Lore*, vol. XII, no. 44 (January–March 1899): 17–23.

———. "The Eskimo of Smith Sound." *Bulletin of the American Museum of Natural History*, vol. XII (1899): 265–327.

MacMillan, Donald B. *Four Years in the White North*. New York: Harper, 1918.

Malaurie, Jean. *The Last Kings of Thule*. New York: E. P. Dutton, 1982.

Murphy, Robert Cushman. "Skeleton in the Museum Closet." *Peruvian Times*, 20 November 1959: 13.

The National Cyclopedia of American Biography, vol. XXXII. New York: James T. White and Company, 1945.

Olsen, Gustav. *Palsip Ajoqersuiartortitap Gustav Olsen Ivnaanganermiititdlune Uvdlorsiutaisa Ilait*. Nuuk, 1923.

Olsen, Knud. *Avanerssuarmiune Ajoqersuiartortitaq*. Nuuk: Det Grønlandske Forlag, 1980.

Osbon, Captain B. S. "Cook and Peary." *Tourist* (1) vol. 6, no. 3 (September 1911): 208–16; (2) vol. 6, no. 4 (October 1911): 309–18; (3) vol. 6, no. 5 (November 1911): 443–50.

———. "A Little City in the Farthest North," in "Department of Exploration." *Tourist*, vol. 6, no. 5 (November 1911): 451–52.

Oswalt, Wendell H. *Eskimos and Explorers*. Novato, California: Chandler and Sharp, 1979.

Peary, Robert. *Nearest the Pole*. New York: Doubleday, Page and Co., 1907.

———. *The North Pole*. New York: Frederick A. Stokes Company, 1910.

———. *Northward Over the Great Ice* (2 volumes). New York: Frederick A. Stokes Company, 1898.

———. *Snowland Folk*. New York: Frederick A. Stokes Company, 1904.

Rasky, Frank. *The North Pole or Bust*. Toronto: McGraw-Hill Ryerson Limited, 1977.

Rasmussen, Knud. *Greenland by the Polar Sea*. New York: Frederick A. Stokes Company, n.d.

Rosbach, Sechmann. "Inuup Kalaatdlip Minik-mik Atigdlup Inuunera." *Avangnaamioq*, no. 11 (1934): 84–88; no. 12 (1934): 91–99 (manuscript translation by Kenn and Navarana Harper).

Sagan, Carl. *Broca's Brain*. London: Hodder and Stoughton, 1980.

Sheldon, Mary B. "The Only Eskimo in the United States." St. Nicholas, vol. 28 (April 1901): 525–27.

Smith, Gordon W. *The Historical and Legal Background of Canada's Arctic Claims*. Ph.D. Thesis, Columbia University, 1952 (unpublished).

Steele, Harwood. *Policing the Arctic*. Toronto: Ryerson, 1935.

Sturm, Ruth. *When the Eskimos Came to Lawyersville*. 1950 (unpublished high-school essay).

Tarrant, Isabel. *Dam it All*. Privately published, 1973.

Von Linden, Hal. "Cold Enough for an Eskimo? Old Schoharie Winters Weren't." *Schoharie County Historical Review*, Fall–Winter 1977: 20–21 (reprinted from *Knickerbocker News*, February 1961).

Weems, John Edward. *Peary, the Explorer and the Man*. London: Eyre and Spottiswoode, 1967.

———. *Race for the North Pole*. London: Heinemann, 1961.

Who Was Who in the Theatre: 1912–1976. Detroit: Gale Research Company, n.d.

ACKNOWLEDGMENTS

The author wishes to acknowledge the assistance of the following:

Polar Eskimos
Inuutersuaq Ulloriaq, the historian of the tribe;
Qaarqutsiaq, the grandson of the shaman, Soqqaq;
Qisuk, who bears the name of Minik's father;
Amaunnalik, my mother-in-law, named for Minik's mother's sister;
and Navarana, my former wife.

Greenlanders
Ulrik Lennert, former chief of the Royal Greenland Trade Department in Qaanaaq, who had a deep and compassionate interest in the life of Minik;
and H. C. Petersen, scholar, for directing me to Sechmann Rosbach's account of Minik's life in an old copy of *Avangnaamioq*.

In Schoharie County, New York
Jared Van Wagenen III, Lawyersville, who provided me with an excellent photograph of Minik, and whose father knew the Eskimo boy;
Norman Olsen, Town Historian, Cobleskill, who gave generously of his time and advice;
Jim Poole, Editor, *Times-Journal*, Cobleskill, for running an article of mine soliciting information on the Wallace family;

Tom Johnson, Lawyersville, who lives at William Wallace's former Cold Stream Farm;

Ruth Sturm Graulich, Sharon Springs, who sent me a copy of a high-school social studies essay she had written on the Eskimos in Lawyersville thirty years earlier;

Reverend Jeffrey van der Wiel, of the Reformed Church of Lawyersville, who accompanied me on a visit to many of the eldest members of his church;

Bill McGovern, Mereness Funeral Home, Cobleskill;

Timothy Holmes, Librarian, Cobleskill;

Mrs. Wanda Van Tassel, Town Clerk, Cobleskill;

Morris Karker, Central Bridge;

Mrs. John Dow, Cobleskill;

Loraine Foster, Afton;

Edith Osterhout, Cobleskill;

Luanna Strouse, Cobleskill;

Frank Andrew, Cobleskill;

and Margaret N. Bliss, Middleburgh, New York;

In New Hampshire

Alice Young, niece of Afton Hall, Pittsburg;

Howard Young, nephew of Afton Hall, Littleton;

Fay Chappell, Pittsburg, who lives at the old Hall farm;

Joanne Carlson, Town Clerk, Pittsburg;

Ruth Dwinell, Pittsburg;

Ellsworth Bunnell, Colebrook;

and Isabel Tarrant, Manchester.

Institutions

Lee Houchins, Smithsonian Institution, Washington, D.C.;

Alison Wilson of the Scientific, Economic and Natural Resources Branch, U.S. National Archives, Washington, D.C.;

Beth Carroll, Assistant Manuscript Librarian, American Philosophical Society in Philadelphia;

George Michanowsky, Chairman of the Archives Committee, and Janet Baldwin, Librarian, of the Explorers' Club in New York;

Mary Genett, Assistant Librarian for Reference Services of the American Museum of Natural History in New York;

J. R. Starkey of East Orange Public Library, East Orange, New Jersey;

the staff of the New York Public Library, Newspaper Division;

Frank J. Carroll, Head, Newspaper Section, Library of Congress;

Rolf Gilberg, Museum Inspector, Ethnographic Department, National Museum, Copenhagen;

James H. Hutson, Chief, Manuscript Division, Library of Congress;

Edward P. Cambio, Reference Specialist (International Political Scientist), Library of Congress;

Lee Birch, Executive Director, National Taxidermists Association, Cleveland, Ohio;

Annegret Ogden, Reference Librarian, University of California, Berkeley;

William Asadorian, Long Island Division, Queen's Borough Public Library;

Brother Philip Braniff, Admissions Office, Manhattan College, New York;

the late Dr. Junius Bird, Department of Anthropology, American Museum of Natural History;

Paul Woehrmann, Milwaukee Public Library;

Hans Sode-Madsen, Archivist, Second Department, Rigsarkivet, Copenhagen, Denmark;

Harriet Culver, Culver Pictures Inc., New York;

William Finley Dalley, Curator of the Theodore Roosevelt Collection, Harvard College Library, Cambridge, Massachusetts;

Richard A. Baker, Historian, United States Senate, Washington, D.C.;

Stuart W. Campbell, Archivist, Robert Hutchings Goddard Library, Clark University, Worcester, Massachusetts;

Jeanette McBride, West Park Presbyterian Church, New York City;

and Rolf Gilberg, National Museum, Copenhagen, Denmark, for information on sources.

Others

Hans Engelund Kristensen, Editor, *Hainang*, the local newspaper of Qaanaaq, Greenland;

Janet Vetter, Tequesta, Florida, granddaughter of Dr. Frederick Cook;

Lars Toft Rasmussen, Copenhagen, Denmark, journalist, formerly Information Officer, Inuit Circumpolar Conference, Nuuk, Greenland;

Ruth Hunt Thompson, Hancock, Maine;

Dangler Funeral Home, Morristown, New Jersey;

Greystone Park Psychiatric Hospital, Parsippany, New Jersey;

Gloria Ann McCausland, Great Neck, New York;

Mrs. Lauraine Horbak, Fallsburg, New York;

Mrs. Stanley Smith, Cooks Falls, New York;

R. A. Mickler, Montgomery, Alabama;

Kathleen Minckler Dolan, Spring Lake Heights, New Jersey;

Willis Kling, Lima, New York;

Mrs. Tricia Becknell, Franklin Lakes, New Jersey;

Mrs. Joyce Clark, Staten Island, New York;

Mrs. Louis Zeh, Binghamton, New York;

Colin T. Naylor III, Binghamton, New York;

John and Carolyn MacDonald, Igloolik, N.W.T., for the constant encouragement and critical comments;

Prof. Iain Prattis, Carleton University, Ottawa, Ontario, for encouragement and insight;

Dr. Trevor Lloyd, Ottawa, Ontario, for critical comment and inspiration;

Hon. Dennis Patterson, former Minister of Education, Northwest Territories, for support and encouragement;

and Roberta, Steven, and Michael Roberts of Nortext, for the design and layout of the original version of this book, and for their good advice and friendship.

The author acknowledges permission to quote from archival material from the following institutions: New York Historical Society; American Philosophical Society; Explorers Club Archives; National Archives, Washington, D.C. (and Mr. Edward Stafford for the Peary Family Collection); The Royal Archives, Copenhagen, Denmark; and the American Museum of Natural History.

The author acknowledges the following permissions to quote from published material: (1) E. P. Dutton, Inc., for selections from Jean Malaurie, *The Last Kings of Thule;* (2) Elsevier-Dutton Publishing Co., Inc., for selections from Archibald Lang Fleming, *Archibald the Arctic;* (3) Harold Matson Company, Inc., for selections from Peter Freuchen, *Arctic Adventure* and *Book of the Eskimos.*

PHOTOGRAPHIC CREDITS

1 Photo: Robert E. Peary. Courtesy Edward P. Stafford and the National Geographic Society.
2 in Kroeber. "The Eskimo of Smith Sound." *Bulletin of the American Museum of Natural History,* vol. XII (1899), following p. 326.
3 in Hrdlicka. "Contributions to the Anthropology of Central and Smith Sound Eskimo." *Anthropological Papers of the American Museum of Natural History,* vol. 5 (1910), following p. 233.
4 Courtesy Peabody Museum of Archaeology and Ethnology, Harvard University.
5 in Hrdlicka. op. cit.
6 in Hrdlicka. op. cit.
7 in Kroeber. op. cit.
8 in Green. *Peary, The Man Who Refused to Fail.* New York: G. Putnam's Sons, 1926, facing title page.
9 Library of Congress: 12244 US262 8234.
10 Library of Congress: 12244 USZ62 30426.
11 Photo of Matthew Henson, Library of Congress: 12244 USZ62 42993.
12 Dartmouth College, Rauner Special Collections Library, Stefansson Collection, Manuscript Collection 198, item 5:84.
13 in "The Snow Baby and Her Mother" (Marie and Josephine Peary). *Children of the Arctic.* New York: Frederick A. Stokes Company, 1903, p. 73.
14 *St. Nicholas Magazine,* vol. 28 (April 1901), p. 526.

15 in Hrdlicka, op. cit.
16 *New York Tribune* (Illustrated Supplement), 08 January 1899.
17 Photo: Kenn Harper.
18 *New York Tribune* (Illustrated Supplement), 18 November 1900.
19 Neg. No. 220545, Courtesy Department Library Services, American Museum of Natural History.
20 Courtesy: Jared van Wagenen III.
21 Photo: Kenn Harper.
22 Photo: Kenn Harper.
23 *The Evening Mail* (Night Edition), 21 April 1909, p. 1.
24 Courtesy: Cobleskill Public Library, Cobleskill, New York.
25 Neg. No. 46326. Courtesy Department of Library Services, American Museum of Natural History.
26 Neg. No. 2A 5161. Courtesy Department Library Services. American Museum of Natural History.
27 Library of Congress: 12244 USZ62 16216.
28 Neg. No. 319950. Courtesy Department Library Services, American Museum of Natural History.
29 in *The White World.* New York: Lewis, Scribner and Co., 1902, p. 192.
30 in *The White World.* op. cit., p. 360.
31 *The World* (Magazine Supplement), 6 January 1907.
32 *San Francisco Examiner* (Magazine Supplement), 9 May 1909.
33 in De Frece. *Recollections of Vesta Tilley.* London: Hutchinson and Co. (Publishers) Ltd., 1934, facing p. 198.
34 Library of Congress: 12243 B2–881-7.
35 Photo: Thomas N. Krabbe. Neg. L 199. Danish National Museum, Ethnographic Department.
36 Photo: Thomas N. Krabbe. Neg. L 214. Danish National Museum, Ethnographic Department.
37 Photo: Thomas N. Krabbe. Neg. L 202. Danish National Museum, Ethnographic Department.
38 Photo: Thomas N. Krabbe. Neg. L 205. Danish National Museum, Ethnographic Department.
39 Photo: Thomas N. Krabbe. Neg. L 209. Danish National Museum, Ethnographic Department.
40 Neg. No. 234232. Courtesy Department of Library Services, American Museum of Natural History.
41 Photo: Thomas N. Krabbe. Neg. L 210. Danish National Museum, Ethnographic Department.

42   in Peary, *Northward Over the Great Ice,* vol. I, op. cit., p. 478.
43   Photo: Thomas N. Krabbe. Neg. L 212. Danish National Museum, Ethnographic Department.
44   Photo: Thomas N. Krabbe. Neg. L 207. Danish National Museum, Ethnographic Department.
45   Photo: Thomas N. Krabbe. Neg. L 211. Danish National Museum, Ethnographic Department.
46   Photo: Unknown. Neg. L 186a. Danish National Museum, Ethnographic Department.
47   No. 161889. Royal Library, Copenhagen, Denmark.
48   Photo: probably Peter Freuchen. Neg. L 1066. Danish National Museum, Ethnographic Department.
49   Photo: Peter Freuchen. Danish National Museum, Ethnographic Department.
50   Neg. No. 230128. Courtesy Department Library Services, American Museum of Natural History.
51   Photo: W. Elmer Ekblaw. Neg. No. 233668. Courtesy Department Library Services, American Museum of Natural History.
52   Photo: W. Elmer Ekblaw. Neg. No. 233666. Courtesy Department Library Services, American Museum of Natural History.
53   in MacMillan. *Four Years in the White North.* Harper, 1918, facing p. 33.
54   Photo: W. Elmer Ekblaw. Neg. No. 233667. Courtesy Department Library Services, American Museum of Natural History.
55   Photo: E. O. Hovey. Neg. No. 234193. Courtesy Department Library Services, American Museum of Natural History.
56   Neg. No. 36573. Courtesy Department Library Services, American Museum of Natural History.
57   Photo: D. B. MacMillan. Neg. No. 231238. Courtesy Department Library Services, American Museum of Natural History.
58   Courtesy: Alice Young.
59   Courtesy: Alice Young.
60   Courtesy: Alice Young.
61   Courtesy: Alice Young.
62   Photo: Kenn Harper.